1·12·78

The Dark Angel

THE DARK ANGEL

Aspects of Victorian Sexuality

FRASER HARRISON

UNIVERSE BOOKS

NEW YORK

Published in the United States of America in 1977
by Universe Books
381 Park Avenue South, New York, N.Y. 10016

Library of Congress Catalog Card Number: 76–58096

ISBN 0–87663–229–0

Printed in Great Britain

To Sal, with love

Dark Angel, with thine aching lust
To rid the world of penitence:
Malicious Angel, who still dost
My soul such subtle violence!

From 'The Dark Angel' by Lionel Johnson, 1895

Contents

List of Illustrations

MIDDLE-CLASS
SEXUALITY

I

Mid-Victorian Marriage

To study Victorian sexuality is, in effect, to trace the evolution of Victorian marriage.

Marriage enjoyed a *belle époque* in Britain during the mid-Victorian era. The bourgeoisie was then at the height of its commercial vigour and enterprise and in its eyes marriage had assumed a new and magnified importance. A well-born wife represented the means by which a man might add the lustre of social prestige to his recently acquired fortune, just as the daughter of a rich man afforded the gentlemanly but impecunious suitor a unique opportunity of refurbishing the dignity of his family name. (The nicety with which money could be balanced against breeding in order to compound an equable match was a theme much favoured by novelists of the period; it was perhaps most compulsively explored by Trollope who made such calculations with an accountant's precision.) For the enormous numbers of affluent middle-class men living in towns who could not utilize more old-fashioned, rural tokens of prestige, a capacious family house, located in some fashionable district, lavishly furnished and staffed, excelled as an advertisement of its owner's social standing. The procreation of numerous children had also come to serve as a sign, admittedly an often empty one, of the illustriousness of the paterfamilias. And at a time when it was possible for unprecedented numbers of people to accumulate personal wealth on an unprecedented scale, marriage attained a profound significance through its ability to guarantee the provision of legitimate offspring to whom a husband could leave his property and wealth.

Since the general acceptance of Christian monogamy, all Western socieities have required their members to respect the sexual code of behaviour which taboos all sexual intercourse except in marriage. The significance of marriage as a licence to copulate legitimately has varied according to the laxity or severity with which each society has enforced obedience to this basic law. The sexual conventions and social mores employed to safeguard marriage have directly reflected the economic ambitions of the class or community responsible for their creation. By the same token, the outlawing and suppression of those forms of sexual activity likely to endanger the security of marriage have been essential to the protection of the economic interests vested in the marriage contract.

None of these considerations is peculiar to Victorian marriage – they obtain today to some extent and have formed a fundamental part of marriage in most societies – but they exercised a particularly powerful influence over those generations of middle-class men who contributed to and benefited from the protracted phase of affluence and expansion that stretched, despite occasional recessions from the eighteen-fifties to the eighteen-seventies.

With so much at stake, to say nothing of religious and other social considerations, it is not surprising that middle-class Victorians revered the institution of marriage and imposed the traditional sexual code upon themselves with exceptional severity. It is true that, in practice, men were able to abuse the code and go unpunished, providing they restricted their activities to women outside their own class, but this did not mean that they achieved any degree of freedom from the basic discipline governing relations between the sexes; they remained completely subject to the psychological authority of the code, and never drew the deadly sting of guilt from illicit sexuality. Such sexual pleasure as was derived from dealings with prostitutes, or liaisons with servants, was rarely accompanied by emotional fulfilment. Only the rich could afford to support mistresses in alternative households and develop any kind of sustained, reciprocal affection, but even they were obliged to keep their affairs absolutely isolated from the rest of their lives. All forms of extra-marital sexuality, from the meanest to the most opulent, had to be paid for and indulged in secretly. Thus, the sexual privileges reserved for married couples were maintained intact, and continued to be valuable to those who possessed them and highly desirable to those who did not.

During the course of the last three decades of Victoria's reign attitudes to sexuality underwent a series of radical changes. Male supremacy, the fundamental principle on which mid-Victorian sexual conventions were founded, was vigorously challenged; the fraudulence of the moral double standard was exposed; submissiveness ceased to be the universally accepted hall-mark of

femininity; the increasing use of contraceptive techniques decisively reduced the middle-class birth rate and the size of the
average family; the awe in which fathers had previously been held
was diminished and wives were released from the hitherto inescapable round of pregnancy and childbirth. But, for all the controversy they provoked and the fears they unleashed, these changes
did nothing to endanger the primacy of marriage. It was preserved
unscathed as the ideal way of life to which both sexes aspired – the
summit of male ambition, and the target of female expectation.
Nor, by the same token, was the power of the traditional sexual
code even minimally impaired, for it prevailed, and has done almost
to our own day, as the standard of moral rectitude by which the
wickedness of all other forms of sexual behaviour might be
measured.

Although its position was not undermined, the character of
marriage did, however, suffer a distinct transformation. Since it
stood at the very centre of middle-class life, it was bound to furnish
a cockpit for the many bloody battles that were fought between the
sexes during this period. As the social values on which the established, patriarchal concept of marriage had depended came under
harsh scrutiny, and as the vigour of the economy that had sponsored
those values began to ail and decline, so the note of expansive
confidence that had characterized mid-Victorian marriage gave
way to a new, deeply disturbing sense of anxiety. The domestic
harmony of earlier years was replaced by discontent and, occasionally, by open warfare.

The origins of that war, its various phases and, in particular, the
propaganda employed by either side to vindicate its cause, are the
subject of the first section of this book.

Marriage: The Crassest Prostitution
Writing in 1884, after more than forty years' residence in England,
Frederick Engels offered the following account of monogamy and its
inception in his book *The Origin of the Family, Private Property and
the State*: 'Monogamy arose from the concentration of considerable
wealth in the hands of a single individual – a man – and from the
need to bequeath this wealth to the children of that man and of no
other. For this purpose, the monogamy of the woman was required,
not that of the man, so this monogamy did not in any way interfere

with open or concealed polygamy on the part of the man.' It was, he contended, the first form of family to be based not on natural but on economic conditions. Far from being the reconciliation of man and woman, and farther still from being the highest state of such a reconciliation, it was in fact the subjugation of one sex by another. Marx himself had declared that 'The first division of labour is that between man and woman for the propagation of children', and Engels likened the relationship between husband and wife in the family to that between the bourgeois and the proletarian in society. At worst the wife was reduced to the status of a slave, at best she was permitted to hold the rank of head servant.

The picture he painted of monogamous marriage, as conducted by the bourgeoisie of modern Europe, made it out to be a bleak, cold-blooded enterprise. In his opinion, the very nature of the institution precluded the development of 'individual sex love', for matrimony was essentially a matter of convenience negotiated by the parents of the couple in question. In Catholic countries, the parents simply procured a suitable wife for their son, with the result that the contradiction inherent in monogamy fully revealed itself – the husband abandoned himself to hetaerism (promiscuity) and the wife to adultery. In Protestant countries, on the other hand, a measure of freedom of choice was extended to the son, as long as he understood that his selection had to be strictly limited to girls of his own class, and this made room for the possibility of love in the marriage; indeed, he asserted that, in accordance with Protestant hypocrisy, the presence of love was always assumed for decency's sake. In the case of Protestant monogamy, 'the husband's hetaerism is a more sleepy kind of business, and adultery by the wife is less the rule. But . . . all that [this] achieves, taking the average of the best cases, is a conjugal partnership of leaden boredom, known as "domestic bliss".'

He pointed out that, even in those countries where parental consent to marriage was not legally required, parents still retained a powerful hold over their children because they were at liberty to disinherit them whenever they wished; the freedom to marry, among those who stood to inherit, was not in reality increased by the absence of obligatory consent. The making of a match was inevitably conditioned by class priorities, and to that extent all marriages were arrangements of convenience. 'This marriage of convenience', Engels wrote, 'turns often enough into the crassest prostitution – sometimes of both partners, but far more commonly of the woman, who only differs from the ordinary courtesan in that she does not let out her body on piece-work as a wage worker, but she sells it once and for all into slavery.'

The justice of Engels' analysis of monogamy may be tested by examining the body of laws, as they stood in 1850 or thereabouts, which defined the legal identity of a wife and her position in relation to her husband. When John Stuart Mill reviewed these laws in *The Subjection of Women* (1869) he concluded that 'the wife is the actual bond-servant of her husband, no less so, as far as legal obligation goes, than slaves commonly so called.'

Once married, a woman ceased to possess a legal existence; in common with minors and idiots, she had no responsibility under the law. Unless she committed murder or treason, her husband was liable for her crimes. She could not sign a contract, make a will or cast a vote. Prior to 1884, she could be imprisoned for refusing her husband his so-called conjugal rights. 'However brutal a tyrant', Mill commented, 'she may unfortunately be chained to . . . he can claim from her and enforce the lowest degradation of a human being, that of being the instrument of an animal function contrary to her inclinations.' Until 1891, she could be legally detained against her wishes by her husband in his house. She could not obtain a divorce, except by special Act of Parliament, a procedure sufficiently expensive to impede all but the wealthiest.

The true nature of the wife's slavery was, however, enshrined in those laws relating to her property. During the engagement period, her manacles were tried on for size in that she was forbidden to dispose of any of her possessions without her fiancé's permission. When she married, the fetters were firmly clamped on. All her property, including inheritances and earnings, passed automatically into the ownership of her husband, and he was legally free to do with it whatever he wished – if he chose, he could disinherit her. Only by setting up a trust on behalf of his daughter, always a tricky and expensive procedure, could a father keep his money out of his son-in-law's pocket. But, as Mill observed, even the rich could not contrive to place a wife's inherited property under her own control; 'the most they can do', he wrote, 'only prevents the husband from squandering it, at the same time debarring the rightful owner from its use.' Nor could a wife lay claim to her own children, for they too belonged in law to her husband, and he alone had any rights over them. Even after her husband's death, she did not automatically become their legal guardian – a special provision to that effect had to be incorporated in his will.

In 1855, a spirited assault was made upon this process of legalized embezzlement. Barbara Leigh Smith, daughter of a radical MP and cousin to Florence Nightingale, took up cudgels and published an inflammatory pamphlet, *A Brief Summary in Plain Language of the Most Important Laws Concerning Women*, in which she bitterly denounced the iniquity of the wife's legal status. Armed with this document, she campaigned strenuously, withstood the scorn and enmity of those who saw in her criticisms intimations of society's downfall, acquired 26,000 signatures of support and persuaded the Law Amendment Society to introduce a bill designed, among other things, to grant wives the right to make wills and to own property.

The resultant Married Women's Property Bill of 1857 passed its second reading, but, in the event, failed to graduate further; for it was neatly sabotaged by a tendentious interpretation of another piece of legislation which, it was believed, presaged upheavals on an even greater scale of calamity – The Matrimonial Causes Act 1857. Ferociously opposed, chiefly by Gladstone, this Act established a secular divorce court to replace the old ecclesiastical court; it defined new conditions under which divorces might be obtained and restored to the divorced or separated wife certain rights over her property. It is significant that no provision was made for the restitution of property owned before, or inherited, or earned during the marriage. Having passed this, for its day, revolutionary Act, Parliament was able to dismiss the Married Women's Property Bill by arguing that the new laws protected the interests of the deserted or neglected woman, and provided for her maintenance, thus rendering redundant any proposed legislation on behalf of the happily married woman, who was of course presumed to rejoice in the tutelage of her husband. On the strength of this sophistry, the husband's right to expropriate his wife's every penny and possession was given the benefit of a Westminster blessing.

In 1870, the first Property Act was finally passed, but the sacrifice husbands were called upon to make amounted to no more than allowing their wives to retain personal earnings in employment carried on separately from their husbands, or earnings obtained by the exercise of literary, artistic or scientific skill. Although other

Acts followed, it was not until the twentieth century that wives succeeded in wresting complete control of their property from their husbands.

The feminists who campaigned for the Property Acts were determined to wring from husbands a symbolic gesture of acknowledgement of their right to a measure of autonomy within marriage; the extraction of this gesture was just one in a series of humiliations and shocks that compelled men to revise and depreciate their opinion of their own sexual prestige. But the women who inflicted these defeats should not be thought of as freedom fighters. With the possible exception of the Malthusian League's crusade to disseminate birth-control information, which measurably improved the condition of working women's lives, none of the feminist campaigns that took place during the second half of the nineteenth century was remotely revolutionary in ambition; indeed, some were positively reactionary – for example, Mrs Butler's twenty years' war against the Contagious Diseases Acts. On the whole, the feminists were animated not so much by a desire to subvert the *status quo*, but by an eagerness to acquire their own opportunity, alongside their male counterparts, of benefiting from the largesse created by a thriving economy. The slaves did not want to overthrow their masters; they longed to join them.

The cause of emancipation was not advanced by the introduction of the Matrimonial Causes Act which, if anything, further consolidated the husband's inequitable position. The new Act provided that the husband could petition for divorce on the grounds that his wife had been guilty of adultery. The wife, by contrast, could only petition on the grounds that 'her husband has been guilty of incestuous adultery, or of bigamy with adultery, or of rape, or of sodomy or bestiality, or of adultery coupled with such cruelty as without adultery would have entitled her to a divorce *a mensa et toro*, or of adultery coupled with desertion, without reasonable excuse, for two years and upwards . . .' (Section 27) In other words, providing a husband could summon up sufficient self-control to resist the temptation to copulate with his sister, his other wife or his cow, and providing he could restrain the urge to rape, sodomize and torture the wife in question, the law decreed that he was free to fornicate at his pleasure. Furthermore, a certain piquancy was added to his philandering by the knowledge that, if his wife soiled her connubial purity but once, he could dispense with her immediately, and would be under no obligation to return the property she had brought to him as a bride.

For those who thought they detected a whiff of injustice rising from these laws, Lord Cranworth, the then Lord Chancellor and sponsor of the Bill, was at hand to correct such misapprehensions. A wife, he assured the House, might, without loss of caste, and bearing in mind the interest of her children and even of her husband, feel inclined to condone an act of adultery in her husband, but no one would venture to suggest that a husband could possibly do so. 'The adultery of the wife', he explained, 'might be the means of palming spurious offspring upon the husband, while the adultery of the husband could have no such effect with regard to the wife.'

The assumptions upon which this candid exposition was founded illuminate the seamier side of respectable monogamy. It was evidently not necessary to remind the honourable members that gentlemen, that is to say men to whom the making of a will was a momentous business, did not indulge in adultery with members of their own class. Since property was seldom at stake, the paternity of the children of servants, seamstresses and the like could hardly be considered important, and it must be inferred that those workers who did have something to leave were beneath the consideration of the legislature.

Lord Cranworth clearly placed great reliance on the class loyalty of gentlemen, and none on that of ladies; for implicit in his argument is the conviction that, while gentlemen could be trusted to refrain from cuckolding their peers, no such faith could be put in their wives. The fear, expressed here so graphically, of being the victim of a paternity con-trick was fundamental to the sexual make-up of the middle classes, and it was no coincidence that it provided the principle on which all nineteenth-century divorce law was based. The fact that half the blood flowing through the veins of this 'spurious' child could be classified as legitimate, in as much as it had been generated by the testator's wife, was presumed, no doubt correctly, by Lord Cranworth to be irrelevant to the way the average man felt about bastardy. So too was the fact that the child who had been 'palmed' on the unwitting father had been brought up and treated by him and his family as his own. The origin of the fear lay not in the adulterous abuse of his wife, although this was an intolerable injury, but in the breaking of the monopoly of inheritance, of which the wife was the steward. The accretion and preservation of family capital could only be successfully attained through the channels of heredity; if these channels failed to function efficiently, the entire purpose of bourgeois life was made futile and destroyed. Suffice it to say that, although the divorce laws were considerably modified during the nineteenth century in respect of the financial support and security guaranteed to the divorced or separated wife, this vital distinction between the grounds on which the two sexes could petition was preserved untouched until as late as 1923.

In her book *Love, Morals and the Feminists* (1970) Constance Rover drew attention to the energy with which the law leapt to the assistance of the cuckolded husband and the cruel indifference it showed to the plight of the unmarried mother. Exceptional courage and determination were required of the woman who proposed to prove the paternity of her child in the courts. A streak of optimistic folly was also called for because, in the unlikely event of her winning her case, she would not be awarded maintenance of more than half-a-crown a week, and one-and-sixpence was the more customary sum. Nor did the procurement of this generous award signal the end of her troubles, for the law exhibited a marked reluctance to pursue the husband who was tardy with his payments, or who simply failed to pay. 'The idiocy of a code of law', wrote Constance Rover, 'which considered women so weak and irresponsible that they should not take part in public affairs and could not handle property but at the same time placed on the allegedly weaker sex the onus of resisting the advance of the stronger and the responsibility of bringing up illegitimate children practically unaided, seems well nigh incredible.'

Such a code only sheds its idiotic aspect when it is seen as an expression, in legal terms, of the major social code which dictated the relationship between marriage and property. The degree of protection a wife received from society at large, and by the same token from the law, was in direct proportion to her significance as her husband's servant and the guardian of his property, the very property which she herself bestowed on him in the first place. Both the unmarried mother and the adulteress forfeited all rights to society's protection, and provoked the law's hostility, by proving themselves a positive threat to the sacred task to which wives had been appointed. To borrow Lord Cranworth's phrase, no husband who was married to a woman of such proclivities could ever be certain that his offspring had not been 'palmed'. The hysteria aroused by even the faintest suspicion of sexual unreliability is only fully explicable in this context, as is the Victorian obsession with virginity. In order to qualify as a wife, a woman had to be able to demonstrate, above all other capabilities, her absolute trustworthiness as a medium of legitimate heirs.

The High Price of Marriage

When a man contemplated marriage, he was as a matter of course obliged to take stock of his eligibility, a quality, he rapidly discovered, which resided largely in his breeding and his bank, and preferably in both. Inevitably, he was also prompted to meditate on such notions as he cherished of love and beauty and the ideal form they might take in the woman he hoped to marry, but the world soon taught him that he had no choice but to place these romantic aspirations at the humble service of more mundane priorities. When he actually came to grapple with the practicalities of seeking and securing a mate, his perception of women and their sexuality was unavoidably influenced, if not completely determined, by his estimation of their material value, and by his assessment of their capacity to fulfil the crucial wifely duties outlined above. By the same token, he was made all too aware of the uncomfortable fact that his own attractiveness as a potential husband, and therefore his sexuality, was being measured against correspondingly harsh standards.

Consistent at all points with society's eagerness to foster the interests of property, convention ordained that, before a suitor wooed the daughter, he first sought the permission of her father. Coventry Patmore, author of perhaps the most popular nineteenth-century celebration of conjugal love, *The Angel in the House*, narrated in detail the conversation that took place between his hero, Felix Vaughan, and the father of his heart's desire, to whom, as yet, he had not disclosed his feelings. It should be noted that Vaughan's love for Honor, subsequently his wife, was conceived on the loftiest moral plane.

> He hoped the business was not bad
>   I came about: then the wine pass'd,
> A full glass prefaced my reply:
>   I loved his daughter, Honor; I told
> My estates and prospects; might I try

> To win her? At my words so bold
> My sick heart sank. Then he: He gave
> His glad consent, if I could get
> Her love. A dear, good Girl! she'd have
> Only three thousand as yet;
> More bye and bye.
>
> (Canto VI)

The girl's father, who had not one but three daughters to dispose of, knew a bargain when he saw one. Though modest, Vaughan's attributes marked him out as a suitable match: he was indisputably a gentleman, his rented land yielded a far from contemptible £600 a year (the precise figure is given), he lived in a Tudor house standing in its own park and he had recently graduated with honours from Cambridge. Vaughan, for his part, can hardly have been insensible to that gratifying conjunction of virtues discovered in his fiancée-to-be: a good girl *and* three thousand a year. Naturally, these vulgar calculations went unremarked by the author, although he did not neglect to supply the necessary statistics. The key to the scene lies, however, in the plush, board-room atmosphere so deftly invoked by Patmore. The masculine conclave, the passing of the wine and the civilized after-dinner chat about assets and growth-prospects momentarily lull the reader into thinking that a merger, rather than a marriage, is under discussion, and it is with something of a jolt that he then reads of Vaughan rushing, not to a telephone to inform anxious colleagues of the successful outcome of his negotiations, but into the garden in search of 'chaste and noble' Honor.

And yet, many a young man must have read those lines with cynical envy; for the impecunious suitor with nothing to offer but his ambition and willingness to work had to be prepared, in the happy event of his not being positively rebuffed, to consign himself to the tedium of a long engagement. An arrangement of this kind was generally terminable as and when the fiancé's income was deemed sufficient to support his wife in a manner commensurate with her social standing; often the terms were fixed by the young man himself and not by the girl's parents. The relationship supposedly sustained by couples who had dedicated themselves to engagements of indefinite length was held to be particularly admirable. Joined only by a bond of mutual self-sacrifice, and unrelieved by any reward save the far-distant prospect of marital

joy, these couples represented the embodiment of an ideal highly
prized by the Victorians – that of chaste devotion.

Chastity was, of course, expected of all men, whether engaged or
unattached, although in reality a double code operated which
permitted the latter a measure of covert laxity. Patmore, however,
sternly repudiated this distinction, and placed the significance of
the single man's self-restraint firmly within the context of marriage,
interpreting it as a kind of prospective fidelity to the wife he had
yet to meet.

> They safely walk in darkest way
>   Whose youth is lighted from above,
> Where, through the senses' silvery haze,
>   Dawns the veil'd moon of nuptial love.
> Who is the happy husband? He
>   Who, scanning his unwedded life,
> Thanks Heaven, with a conscience free,
>   'Twas faithful to his future wife.
>
> (Canto V)

It is often suggested that the burden of celibacy was borne by the
women, while the men were able to escape its cruellest rigours
because of the favourable partiality of the unwritten moral code.
Certainly Engels maintained this point of view. 'What for women is
a crime', he wrote, 'entailing grave legal and social consequences, is
considered honourable in a man or, at worst, a slight moral blemish
which he cheerfully bears.' He emphasized the disastrous effect of
this arrangement: '. . . it demoralizes men far more than women.
Among women prostitution degrades only the unfortunate ones
who become its victims . . . But it degrades the character of the
whole male world.' He was particularly contemptuous of the long
engagement which, he asserted, was in nine cases out of ten a
'regular preparatory school' for conjugal infidelity.

On 7 May 1857 readers of *The Times* were given an opportunity
of forming their own opinions on this contentious topic when a long
letter, headed 'The Other Side of the Picture', appeared in the
correspondence columns above the signature of 'Theophrastus'.
According to the pseudonymous correspondent, the real cause of
'our social corruption' (prostitution) was the unnecessarily high
price of marriage. The world decreed that a son could not marry
until he was able to maintain an establishment on the same footing

as his father's. Should he attempt to defy the world by marrying and making do with the mere essentials of life, his family would lose caste, and he and his bride would be quietly dropped from the circle in which they had hitherto moved. The most society would permit was an engagement, and then 'we have the sad but familiar sight of two young lovers wearing out their best years with hearts sickened with hope long deferred.'

He assured his readers that he had no intention of advocating improvident marriage, but he begged them to study the consequences of enforced celibacy. Prior to marriage, 'thousands' of thirty-five-year-old bridegrooms had lived in sin and, although 'wretched under the convictions of their conscience', they had not dared to lose their social position by making what the world would call an imprudent marriage.

In the face of the powerful tyranny of social law, he found it difficult to suggest any remedy for this evil, but since the mischief was on the increase owing to 'our increasing worship of money', he felt obliged to appeal to public opinion. To his mind, the solution was for men to claim the position in society to which they were qualified, not by money, but by education and character. Many a girl 'now doomed to joyless celibacy' would then be transformed into a happy wife and mother. The character of our young men would be improved through the healthful exercise of the 'home affections', and frivolity and effeminacy would be driven out before the realities of steady work which early marriage would oblige them to face. Our streets would be purified, and many a bitter pang of conscience would be checked and many a soul saved.

In an editorial *The Times* pronounced with approval on this letter: 'love in a cottage' was not to be recommended, but there was no doubt that 'this undue, artificial and unnatural postponement of marriage ends in a great blot on our social system.' Modern caution, it declared, had indeed outstepped all reasonable limits.

It will be instructive at this point to look at a specific example of a young man in precisely the difficulties alluded to by Theophrastus in order to discover with what equanimity, or lack of it, and with what strength of will, he squared up to the privations of a celibate engagement.

George Du Maurier: *A Thoroughly Bad Man*

Born in 1834, Du Maurier served his apprenticeship as an artist in

Paris and Antwerp, and it was on those Bohemian years, as he liked to think of them, that he based his celebrated novel *Trilby* (1894). In 1860, he came to England and made his living as an illustrator of novels and magazine stories and serializations; in 1864 he joined *Punch*, and for the next thirty years he was its most characteristic and prolific cartoonist. He did not take up novel writing until late in life: his first book, *Peter Ibbetson*, was published in 1892. *Trilby*, his second, sold in enormous quantities, making him rich for the first time in his life, and his third and last, *The Martian*, was serialized in 1896, the year of his death.

In 1860, at the age of twenty-six, Du Maurier fell in love with Emma Wightwick who, by virtue of her sound middle-class background, was deemed a suitable choice. Their relationship prospered, he was made welcome by her parents and he got into the habit of calling two or three times a week. But in October 1860, the Wightwick family business suffered a partial collapse. Du Maurier immediately stopped seeing Emma. His mother wrote urging him to give her up. For once, he was a move ahead of her: 'You are mistaken', he replied, 'when you think I want to flirt with Emma – it would be absurd now.'

His mother bluntly exhorted him to marry an heiress, a proposition by no means repugnant to the struggling young illustrator. He was attracted and a little terrified by a Greek beauty – the reputed possessor of £80,000 – whose smouldering melancholy has been portrayed by Rossetti and Burne-Jones, but his hopes were scuppered when she married, for love, an impoverished doctor, with whom, incidentally, she then led a very unhappy life. Mrs Du Maurier extolled the suitability of numerous other candidates, but Emma continued to dominate her son's affections. 'Well, I adore Emma,' he wrote to his sister, '. . . but what's the use, you know, *pas le sou, hein*? and then her relations – what?! I wonder how she likes me, the dear prude.' He began to see her again. In May 1861 love triumphed over grosser considerations and he asked her to marry him. She accepted, but her parents insisted that he should first establish himself financially; Du Maurier proposed that they should marry when his bank account stood at one thousand pounds. The engagement was announced, and both parental factions had to satisfy themselves with the hope that the monetary hurdle would prove too high for Du Maurier.

He, in his turn, adopted an emotional posture towards his

fiancée which, though virtually *de rigueur*, afforded him a deep sense of reassurance. 'Her influence on me is wholesome; good in every way; had it not been for her I should have yielded to the seduction of society and other seductions very much more dangerous (in Society) – perfect ruin to an artist like me.' He wished to take his place among the ranks of the respectable and was willing to earn the privilege, but he was nearly crippled by the price demanded of him. The contradiction inherent in his position soon became insupportable. 'I live the quietest and most wholesome life,' he wrote, '... In spite of my great anxiety, and little pecuniary deficiencies, I am happy as I have never been before, so full of hope and conscious of the power of fulfilling it in the end.' In fact, his 'little pecuniary difficulties' were all but overwhelming him, for although his skill as an artist was steadily developing along lucrative lines, and his illustrations were in demand, his earnings continued to fall hopelessly short of that critical thousand pounds. He had freely entered a trap from which he could not extricate himself: he had accepted the principle that marriage was a prize accessible only to those willing to work for it, and he had gladly dispensed with his former 'bohemianism' in favour of a virtuous and improving passion, but he had not bargained for his inability to meet the harsh terms he himself had imposed. He feared that they would never get married, and terrified himself with the thought of falling back into his old way of life; in a letter to Emma, he addressed her as 'Miss Salvation' and begged her not to desert him.

His debts piled up, his health began to deteriorate and he grew so nervous he was unable to concentrate on his work. Mrs Du Maurier, whose application of the Victorian moral code was never less than pragmatic, recommended his resorting to the therapy of a temporary mistress; in this she misunderstood her son, for whom the horrors of illicit sexuality were, by now, even less acceptable than the exactions of frustration. 'Your advice Madam' he wrote to her, 'won't do, I simply can't follow it. It is in the nature and constitution of your firstborn to be passionate and exclusive, and every woman but one is a gorilla.' In September 1861 he was afflicted by a bout of violent stomach upsets, and in February 1862 he became seriously ill; by March, he was in the throes of a nervous breakdown.

The residual effect of the illness upon the hero of his novel *Trilby* was the loss of his capacity to love: 'for some mysterious cause his power of loving had not come back with his wandering wits', but

Du Maurier's own letters written during that winter express more precisely the condition of his mind: 'I awoke early to the same fearful state, feeling myself utterly lost for ever and ever, dead to all natural affection, and resolving hard to lead henceforth a life of martyrdom to duty.' He refused Emma's loving attention, remaining 'as hard to her and as insensible as a flint'. Inevitably, it was to his mother that he was able to explain himself fully:

> It suddenly came across me that I was a thoroughly bad man who had by a marvel been sustained by good example until now, and that the original badness of my nature was just going to break out at last like a regular conflagration, and that the last year's virtue had been the crowning point of my goodness on earth – a temptation suddenly to break loose and indulge in every riotous excess, drink, opium, and the most shameless intrigues, for I felt that come over me (*as it seemed* you know) that no woman in the world could resist – and that when I felt downright madness reach me, as it would inevitably have done according to my theory at the time, I would kill myself and escape the asylum.[1]

The idea of one's mind splitting into its component parts, good and bad, with the originally sinful part threatening to overpower and destroy the virtuous part, formed the basis of an obsession that consistently recurred throughout the nineteenth century, and found its most hallucinatory expression in Stevenson's story *The Strange Case of Dr Jekyll and Mr Hyde*.

'Theophrastus' had used the phrase 'wretched under the convictions of their conscience' to describe the state of guilt suffered by those who turned for relief to prostitution. Du Maurier had committed no such sin, indeed he had positively rejected his mother's incitement to do so; but, innocent though he was, he nevertheless felt intensely 'wretched'. The deluge of guilt which submerged him had been released by his failure to 'earn' his wife, and the prospect of being refused admittance to the temple of licensed sexuality filled him with profound despair. He characterized his inability to sustain 'his last year's virtue' as a submission to the 'original badness' of his nature. Salvation had been extended to him in the form of Emma's 'good example', but to no avail, for in the end he had fallen victim to the impending 'conflagration'.

His guilt located itself around his belief in his own fundamental sinfulness. The sins themselves, which scarcely bore the stamp of reality, lay in the future, but he was convinced of his capacity to commit them on the grounds that he was a 'thoroughly bad man'. His vision of the depravity which he was just about to 'break out' and 'indulge in', and of which he had such a dread, consisted more of fantasy than of actual, lived experience. As we have seen, although his little transgressions of the past provoked dire consequences, they were in themselves innocuous. 'Riotous excess', 'opium', 'the most shameless intrigues' were incantations borrowed from the vocabulary employed by novelists when they wished to portray debauchery at its most ineffable; similar references to scarlet sins and hideous opium dens pullulate in the more lurid pages of *The Picture of Dorian Gray*, for example. The anxiety torturing Du Maurier was, however, none the less painful for being articulated in the language of fantasy.

He had persuaded himself that a direct connection lay between his inadequacy as a 'worker' and his imminent slide into madness, with its ghastly prelude of degradation. He saw his mind as a battleground on which the forces of good grappled for his sanity with those of evil, inspired and commanded by his insurgent sexuality, '[which] no woman in the world could resist'. It was only logical that he should translate his inability to accumulate Emma's purchase price into an inability to love, and that he should denounce sexuality as the enemy of marriage.

There was but one possible escape from this headlong tumble into hysteria, and it was speedily supplied by the Wightwicks: the price of Emma's hand was devalued to two hundred pounds. Du Maurier recovered, took up his career again and produced some of his best drawings – his illustrations for *The Notting Hill Mystery* which appeared in *Once A Week* between November 1862 and January 1863.

On 3 January 1863 Du Maurier and Emma were finally married. The wedding breakfast was, he reported, very merry. Unfortunately, Bill Henley, one of his oldest friends, was unable to contribute to the celebrations, having recently forfeited his place in polite society by marrying his mistress. Du Maurier's response to this folly defined his attitude to marriage: 'you will be very much shocked', he wrote to another friend, 'to hear that he has married this woman – the same he lived with in London years ago . . . [he] married this woman to "*do her proper justice before the world*",

"*feeling that he owed her no less*"[2] as if he didn't owe 50 times
as much to his father and mother. I think his conduct has been as
heartless as it is stupid, that such a nice fellow should be pumper-
nickled away from us all in this fashion!' In Du Maurier's eyes
marriage was essentially an act of conformity, and he could not
sustain a friendship with one whose choice of wife amounted to a
deliberate act of dissociation from society.

The Du Mauriers evidently enjoyed their honeymoon which, in
its turn, proved to be the prelude to a happy marriage. 'Once
married I am safe', Du Maurier is supposed to have said shortly
before the event, and very little occurred during their marriage to
discredit this prophecy.

Although they were arguing from very different premises, both
Engels and 'Theophrastus' underestimated the willingness of
young men to submit to the scarcely supportable middle-class
code of sexual behaviour. Du Maurier had not broken down under
the yoke of celibacy, nor had he resented or even questioned the
convention which required him to postpone his wedding until his
bank account stood at an acceptable figure. On the contrary, he
had wholeheartedly subscribed to the code and had only collapsed
when he found himself unable to attain its standards.

The state of torpid cynicism in which, according to Engels, the
young bourgeois wallowed can hardly have been the norm; for the
courtship ritual of that period contained too corrosive a streak of
anxiety to permit its adherents peace of mind, however shallow.
Admittedly, the regiments of prostitutes parading the streets of
every large town by day and night attested to the futility of enforcing
a sexual code that demanded rigid abstinence of all but married
couples. But, although the enormous number of prostitutes did
indicate the extremes of poverty endured by the working-class
inhabitants of these towns, the statistics in themselves did nothing
to prove that the code possessed no power to terrify. The point which
neither writer underlined was that emotional satisfaction could
only be found within the confines of legitimate matrimony. In an
age when the majority of the population no longer enjoyed the
companionship and sense of belonging which small, rural communities had offered their members, but was struggling to come to
terms with the alienation and isolation inflicted on the inhabitants
of large, industrialized towns, the value of marriage was dramatically

inflated. Far from holding the legendary attractions of forbidden fruit, illicit sexuality was fraught with terror; for to indulge in extra-marital pleasure was to demonstrate one's unfitness for marriage. It was not the fear of being caught and exposed that deterred the middle-class young man – the inhospitable urban environment guaranteed anonymity, if nothing else – it was the fear of revealing to himself that he was morally unqualified for marriage. As long as celibacy was held to be a prerequisite of marriage, men were prepared to embrace it with a fervour commensurate with the intensity of their longing for the privileges, both sexual and material, that marriage alone was able to confer.

The affecting vision, conjured up by 'Theophrastus', of the flower of Britain's youth wistfully knocking on the hymeneal gate, only to be repulsed by snobbish parents, who thereby condemned them to seek forlorn consolation in the arms of prostitutes, lacks credibility. It suggests that these disappointed suitors apprehended a scale of values less worldly than their elders' 'increasing worship of money', and this was not the case. Parents and their would-be sons-in-law shared a common belief in marriage as a prize to be striven for. They believed that, like wealth, it was only to be acquired through the strenuous exercise of self-control, through devotion to duty (Du Maurier spoke of 'martyrdom to duty') and unremitting industry. The man who was determined to gain possession of a wife could no more afford to be extravagant, idle or self-indulgent than he who dedicated himself to the accumulation of riches.

'Thrift', wrote Samuel Smiles, the famous author of *Self-Help* (1859), 'produces capital; and capital is the conserved result of labour. The capitalist is merely a man who does not spend all that is earned by work. He is a man prepared to forgo present satisfaction for the hope of future reward . . . The principal industrial excellence of the English people lies in their capacity of present exertion for a distant object.' 'Future reward' and 'distant object' exactly characterized the far-off prospect of marriage as it loomed in the minds of young men who diligently laboured to amass the substance required of eligible suitors. The concepts of saving themselves for marriage and of saving their money became inextricably interwoven. Celibate and capitalist alike resolutely fought off the desire to spend.

Nor was marriage, when finally achieved, to be thought of as a licence for unbridled sexual expenditure. Dr William Acton, venereologist, author and acknowledged expert on sexual matters, took considerable pains to warn married men of the dangers attending sexual intemperance: 'It is a common notion among the public, and even among professional men, that the word *excess* chiefly applies to *illicit* sexual connection . . . [but] the married man who thinks that, because he is a married man, he can commit no excess, however often the act of sexual congress is repeated, will suffer as certainly and as seriously as the unmarried debauchee who acts on the same principle in his indulgences.'[3] It was his opinion that hard-working, intellectual men should not 'indulge in connection' more frequently than once in seven or, to be on the safe side, ten days. This rough guide was, however, applicable only to strong men in the best of health. The man who was foolish enough to indulge in nightly intercourse could expect nothing less than 'simple ruin', or, as Steven Marcus interpreted this phrase in his study of Acton, *The Other Victorians*, 'he goes bankrupt and is sold up'.

The penetration of sexuality by money was the factor which determined the character of relationships between middle-class men and women. The sexual appeal of women had become indistinguishably associated with their material worth and, similarly, male virility was inseparably identified with monetary power. It is by this basic scale of bourgeois values that mid-Victorian marriage must be assessed, if it is to be understood.

Gentle Submission

The structure of bourgeois marriage described in the last chapter depended for its perpetuation on a vigorously expanding economy, a phenomenon that generations of Victorians learnt to take for granted, and one that breathed life into so many cultural institutions which, in the volatile economic atmosphere of today, tend to appear unnatural.

The interdependent relationship that exists between a society's economy and its culture may be clearly discerned in the similarity of attitudes adopted by middle-class Victorians towards their financial and spiritual investments; the former could be relied on, at least until the eighteen-seventies, to produce handsome dividends, while the latter were expected to prove correspondingly profitable. The economic conditions which sustained men in their belief that the steady application of thrift and industry would inevitably pay off in direct proportion to the degree of their self-abnegation, also encouraged them to submit willingly to a highly disciplined code of sexual behaviour that promised the paradise of marriage as a reward for enduring the purgatory of abstinence.

The crucial equation which each individual must make, if he is to establish any sense of harmony with his social environment, between himself – the vulnerable disengaged single unit – and the seemingly inhospitable mass of society at large, became increasingly difficult to achieve for the inhabitants of large, industrialized towns. The old cultural props on which members of smaller, rural communities had relied in order to ascertain and confirm their social roles were rendered inadequate or meaningless in the context of huge, mobile agglomerations of disconnected people. Under these conditions, an officious moral regime proved profoundly attractive. By obeying a common code and by satisfying its exacting demands, men felt themselves to be in unison with their fellows.

Women, on the other hand, were placed in a quite different relationship with both the economy and the sexual code; they were not required, indeed were positively forbidden, to work or play any part, save a purely aquiescent one, in the economic system. They too were educated to believe in marriage as a reward, in their case the only reward, for virtuous behaviour, but the virtues they were called upon to exercise were, by contrast, of a strictly passive nature. The myth of marriage as a prize to be won only by those men who had demonstrated their material eligibility through spiritual self-denial depended on the readiness of women to play out their part of complaisant victim. The mid-Victorian marriage had no place for female initiative.

Just as the legal status of wives was akin to slavery, so the social status of women in general differed little from that of a subjugated race. Engels did not mince his words when he came to describe their situation. After the establishment of the exclusive supremacy of man in primitive societies, woman 'was degraded and reduced to servitude; she became the slave of his lust and a mere instrument for the production of children. This degraded position of the woman . . . has gradually been palliated and glossed over, and sometimes clothed in a milder form; in no sense has it been abolished.'

This chapter examines some of the methods employed by society to ensure the preservation of that state of servitude.

Queen Victoria produced a great many children – her first seven were born within a space of ten years – and she found the process of pregnancy and childbirth humiliating and repugnant, 'so very animal and unecstatic'. When her eldest daughter, the Princess Royal, suffered a severe attack of post-natal depression following the birth of her first child, Victoria dispatched an embittered letter on the subject of male rapacity – 'That despising of our poor degraded sex (for what else is it, as we poor creatures are born for Man's pleasure and amusement) . . . is a little in all clever men's natures; dear Papa even is not quite exempt though he would not admit it.'

She can, however, hardly be described as having been the slave of Albert's lust; nor can he be said to have kept her in servitude. As Queen she was automatically accorded many of the privileges normally reserved for men and, having an extremely strong-willed and obstinate character, she rapidly appropriated the remainder. It is true that on certain topics, particularly matters connected with the arts, she deferred to what she regarded as his superior taste and knowledge, but she never permitted him to forget that she was monarch of both her country and her household. His position was made unmistakably plain from the very first. Replying to his proposal that their honeymoon at Windsor should last longer than two or three days, she wrote, with sweet steeliness, 'You forget, my dearest Love, that I am the Sovereign and that business can stop and wait for nothing.' As he glumly put it, in a letter to one of his German friends, he was 'the husband, not the master of the house'.

Engels did not, of course, have the Queen, or any other individual, in mind when he denounced the enslavement of women; nevertheless, it is worth studying Victoria's relationship with Albert to see how eager even this exceptional and far from dominated woman was to pay obeisance to the conventional concept of wifeliness.

On the few occasions when she felt she could afford to behave towards Albert in a purely wifely capacity, she displayed a surprising submissiveness, quite at odds with her usually despotic manner. She was, for example, uncompromising in her determination to keep the word *obey* in their marriage service. In her letters she persistently addressed him as her lord and master, her father, guide and protector. Her passionate devotion to him, if anything, intensified as they grew older – he remained the most beautiful being on earth in her eyes, even when towards the end of his life took to wearing a wig before breakfast to keep out the cold – and it was the filial, reverential side of her love which she transmuted into a positive cult after his death.

Most revealing of this dimension of their relationship, however, were their favourite portraits of each other, which were painted soon after they were married, during their period of greatest happiness. For his twenty-fourth birthday she gave him a head and shoulders of herself by Winterhalter. She is seen reclining against a velvet cushion, her hair is loose, one lock falls over her shoulder and her eyes are demurely lowered. Elizabeth Longford has described it as 'a portrait of "Fräuchen" in a mood of gentle submission'.[1] Albert in his turn presented her with a picture of himself clad in a suit of shining armour. Both portraits are classic examples of paintings which sought to lend credence to the conventional identities of the ideal man and woman. In itself, Victoria's portrait was unremarkable: it could have had for its subject any society

woman, or indeed simply a model. To have oneself depicted as a
knight was, however, a gesture not available to most ordinary men
who considered themselves worthy of portraiture, but the concept
of the chivalrous gentleman was fondly nurtured and commoners
no less than princes were earnestly exhorted to model their characters along chivalric lines. These pictures are of special interest
solely on account of their being their subjects' favourite portraits of
each other. Since they were favoured above dozens of others, they
presumably represented that image of the other which each most
treasured; and since they were gifts, they presumably also represented that image of him or herself which each wished to present
to the other.

The Queen's portrait may be compared with a picture now in the
Victoria and Albert Museum – 'The Sisters' by Charles Baxter,
painted in 1845. It is designed within a circular frame, and shows
the head and shoulders of the two girls. The one of the left looks
directly at the spectator, a diffident expression on her face, she wears
a scarf round her head and a ribbon round her neck, her dress is low
but modest, and her left arm embraces her sister's waist. It is,
however, her sister who dominates our attention. Her dress has
fallen away from her shoulder to expose the top of her arm and the
curve of her bosom, the light falls upon her, bringing out the bloom
of her flesh, and she casts a faint shadow over the other girl. The
voluptuousness of her shoulder and throat is further emphasized
by the conventional lock of loose hair which trails gracefully from
the back of her head across her neck to direct the spectator's eye
towards her breast. She clasps her hands together in front of her and
seems to be preventing her dress slipping further. Her expression is
coquettish around the lips, where a slight smile plays, yet melting
in the eyes which are large, soft and dark.

These two sisters stand for the two aspects of woman which, to
the Victorian mind, combined to embody a version of feminine
perfection. The sense of their representing two faces of the same
image is reinforced by our knowing that they are sisters, and by the
physical unity of their pose. The girl on the left offers the ideal
demeanour for a woman to present to the world; hers is the acceptable public face. Her sister on the right offers the antithesis, the
hoped-for private face – sensual, playful, but unimpeachably
submissive. The total image coalesces in the spectator's mind.

Drapery slipping off a woman's body is a promise of nakedness, of erotic pleasure to come; it is, at the same time, a promise made independently of the woman's volition, for her body by its very existence and presence is an object of provocation. When an artist paints a woman whose clothes are about to slip off her, he paints a contradiction that only resolves itself in the eye of the spectator. In reality, if a woman is in the presence of a man, the moment when her clothes are half-on, half-off is invariably part of a process leading either to greater exposure or concealment, depending on her willingness or reluctance to commit herself to active erotic involvement with the man in question. If an artist selects this particular moment to paint and petrify, he is deliberately depriving the woman of her sexual autonomy, for he is forcing her to endure the perpetuation of a state of vulnerability which, in reality, she would not tolerate. If the artist wishes to intensify the sense of vulnerability, he emphasizes the tremulous hold the drapery has on her body and he paints the last split second prior to nakedness. Far from being frustrating, images depicting women in states of imminent nakedness are found to be deeply satisfying; indeed, one such image has become perhaps the best known work of art in the world – the Venus de Milo.

In Baxter's painting the contradiction can be clearly seen. The sister whose dress has fallen off her shoulder to reveal her bosom would, under real Victorian conditions, have immediately 'made herself decent'. Although the picture looks innocuous enough, in the sense that the girl has not bared much more of herself than she might at a dinner party. Baxter had nevertheless gone about as far as he could without being accused of lubricity. It cannot be argued that the sisters are alone and merely careless of their appearance. They do not act as if they are alone, they smile and look out of the picture at a point immediately in front of it, their expressions are communicative. In short, they are responding to the spectator whom they imagine to be looking at them. They are, in the words of John Berger, offering up their femininity to be displayed.[2]

By preserving the woman in a state of improper – by contemporary standards – dishabille the painter has deprived her of the capacity to take the initiative; she can only accede to the wishes of others. More precisely, she can only surrender to the invading gaze of the male spectator; she is defenceless. She is, however, seen to be gladly surrendering: she happily, though modestly, accepts his inspection and she willingly aquiesces to being exposed for his gratification.

Female defencelessness is precious to the male's sense of sexual vanity; his belief in his own potency is enhanced by the sight of a woman who has been denied the means of resistance. The artist who implies that there is an alliance between the woman's body and the desire of the male onlooker which the woman herself is powerless to restrain is furnishing a deeply reassuring image. In a society where the powerlessness of women is generally taken for granted, the artist tends to stress the frailty and tenderness of his model, for the need to reaffirm the inherent readiness of women to be possessed will be less urgent. This was the context in which Charles Baxter was working. His picture is a study of 'gentle submission' – the girl's flesh is soft and inviting, her expression and manner are quite innocent of challenge. Although Victoria's portrait, unlike 'The Sisters', has no explicitly erotic content, it was designed to excite the same emotion – pleasure in the face of acquiescent feminine submission – in the onlooker, who in that instance was one specific man.

Pictures painted in the Baxter vein were immensely popular at the time; they embodied an attitude towards women and the way they were expected to present themselves to the world in general and men in particular which Victoria, along with her middle-class subjects, found highly acceptable. The relationship the two sisters strike up with their (male) spectators dates them as surely as their clothes and hair-styles. During the course of the reign, there was no slackening of determination on the part of painters in their efforts to depict women in attitudes of submission, but the blithe assurance of Baxter's treatment was to prove inaccessible to most artists working after 1870. Nineteenth-century artists were obsessed by the theme of feminine submissiveness, but as the emancipation movement gathered strength and the economic foundations of male authority began to crumble, artists had to resort to more and more elaborate methods of realizing what was steadily ceasing to be a reality.

Languid, Listless and Inert Young Ladies

It was often argued by men, and not a few women, that the essential natures of the two sexes predetermined their social functions and relative positions. It was claimed that men were *naturally* more courageous, pugnacious, energetic and inventive (the adjectives are Darwin's[3]), whereas the gentler sex was naturally more domesticated, passive, imitative and emotional. These fundamental characteristics, which had been inherited from our remotest ancestors, were said to be irremovably embedded in every member of even the most civilized races. Thus, Baxter's portrait of the two sisters was taken to be no more than a faithful representation of those qualities which all truly feminine women possessed in common.

John Stuart Mill, however, fiercely contested this notion. What was known as the nature of woman was, he asserted, an eminently artificial thing, the result of forced suppression in some directions and unnatural stimulation in others. 'No other class of dependants', he wrote, 'have had their character so entirely distorted from its natural proportions by their relation with their masters.' Certain capabilities, those from which their masters derived benefits and pleasure, had been fostered and encouraged with 'hot-house and stove cultivation', others had been left out in the cold 'with ice purposely heaped all round them' and had achieved only a stunted growth, while others still had simply been burnt off and killed. 'Men', he concluded, 'indolently believe that the tree grows of itself in the way they have made it grow.'[4]

In the life of the average middle-class girl this process of distortion no doubt began with the first doll to be thrust into her infant arms, but as she grew older it tended to take the form of prohibitions rather than impositions. The selection of occupations considered suitable for a young lady was severely restricted. She was permitted to pass her time only with those activities likely to enhance her chances of attracting a husband. 'The sum and substance of female education', according to Harriet Martineau, 'is training women to consider marriage as the sole object in life, and to pretend that they do not think so.' Sketching, playing the piano and singing ballads were thought to be amusements in which a young lady might display herself to her best advantage. The construction of shell boxes, seaweed albums and wax flowers were considered fitting tasks for delicate fingers. Decorative needlework was thought charming in a girl; darning and mending, however, were not. Familiarity with literature, say the romantic poets, classical authors and certain lady novelists, was also thought charming, providing no dangerous avant-garde or blue-stocking tendencies obtruded. A girl was expected to love flowers and animals, but to know nothing of biology, particularly its darker side. She was expected to feel

sorry for the poor, to distribute Christmas boxes and behave
decently to the servants, but politics and economics were deemed
to be above her pretty head, and anyway none of her business.
Needless to say, elaborate steps were taken to ensure that sex and
all related matters remained a sealed book to her. In short, she was
required to devote her energies to advertising the fact that her
upbringing consisted only of perfecting a set of dainty aptitudes
which bore no taint of practical utility.

Mrs Sarah Ellis, authoress of books on etiquette published in the
eighteen-thirties and 'forties, among them *Women of England*,
wrote, 'I do not know how it may affect others, but the numbers of
languid, listless, and inert young ladies who now recline upon our
sofas murmuring and repining at every claim upon their personal
exertions, is to me a truly melancholy spectacle.' The contradiction
inherent in the upbringing of these girls may be detected in the
source of Mrs Ellis's melancholy: although the girls were not
allowed to do anything, they were nevertheless supposed to go
about it cheerfully. Writing with the bitterness of personal experience, another woman described the average middle-class girl's
existence as 'that useless, blank, slow-trailing thing'. For an
energetic and intelligent girl, the constraints imposed by continual
imprisonment within the drawing-room were cruel indeed and
barely supportable. 'Women are supposed to be very calm generally,'
wrote Charlotte Brontë in *Jane Eyre* (1847), 'but women feel just
as men feel; they need exercise for their faculties and a field for their
efforts as much as their brothers do. They suffer from too rigid a
restraint, too absolute a stagnation precisely as men would suffer;
and it is narrow-minded of their more privileged fellow-creatures to
say that they ought to confine themselves to making puddings and
knitting stockings.'

At first sight, it is perhaps difficult to see what attraction young
men, potential husbands, found in these paragons of impracticality,
these lethargic young women in whom the virtues of decorous
idleness and pretty ignorance had been so assiduously inculcated.
One of the motives governing men's taste in girls of this type was
exposed during the discussion of the divorce laws in the last
chapter. It was feared that girls who had enjoyed a taste of liberty,
and in whom a spirit of initiative had been implanted, would make
less tractable wives than those who had been closely tethered in the
domestic pen. The ideal wife was she who was amenable to her

husband in every respect. It was assumed, reasonably enough, that a daughter who had been trained since childhood to submit to her father's authority, to content herself with drawing-room amusements and to confine her ambitions to the household sphere, would prove a dutiful and manageable wife. In order to ensure her eligibility, however, a girl had to be able to display a capacity for one form of obedience above all others – fidelity. As we saw, promiscuity in a woman was by no means a simple matter of immorality, for it carried with it the dreadful threat of duping her husband into leaving his property to a bastard. If a woman could not convincingly present herself as a reliable vehicle of legitimacy, she stood no chance of receiving a proposal. By the same token, a parent who failed to instil this capacity in his daughter could depend on having her on his hands for life. The safest and most conventional way for a girl to demonstrate to a would-be suitor her readiness to obey him in all things, and particularly in this, was for her to show absolute fealty to her father who, being a husband himself, would be inclined to think it right and proper that she should subject herself to a regimen of puddings and stockings.

This consideration, though of the greatest importance, does not entirely explain the rigid prohibition of all but impractical and purely decorative pastimes which characterized the upbringing of the average middle-class girl. It may therefore be profitable to turn for help to a social scientist whose best known work was devoted to this very subject.

Thorstein Veblen was born in 1857 to Norwegian immigrant parents in Wisconsin; when he was nine his parents moved to a farm in Minnesota and it was here he returned to live after he had graduated from Yale but failed to find a job. He married and in 1891 took up his first academic post as an instructor in economics at the University of Chicago. His marriage was evidently something of a movable feast for his wife came and went and he was consoled, during her absences, by a variety of other women; the authorities disapproved, however, and he was asked to resign. Temporarily reunited with his wife, he found a new job at Stanton, but the Chicago pattern more or less repeated itself. Next he taught at the University of Missouri; here, separated from his wife, he lived in the cellar of a friend's house and wrote some of his best work, including the most famous of his books, *The Theory of the Leisure Class* (1899). After the First World War he went to New York to write for a little magazine and to lecture, but neither venture was successful. He then went to Stanford and lived in a shack in the neighbouring woods where he died in 1929.

Although Veblen had in mind the American *nouveaux riches* of his day – the Vanderbilts, Goulds, and Harrimans – when he formulated his theory of the leisure class, his observations are nevertheless directly applicable to the wealthier ranks of the middle classes in Victorian England and, by extension, to all ranks, since the wealthy were objects of envy and emulation to those below them.

The emergence of the leisure class, as Veblen conceived it, coincided with that moment in human development when individual ownership became an all-important factor. As soon as the possession of wealth and property are thought to confer honour and reputability (Veblen's word) on their owner, then abstention from labour – leisure – also acquires a unique significance. Leisure is translated into evidence of wealth, it becomes the conventional symbol of triumphant accumulation, and soon enough it becomes the conventional mark of social standing. As men's belief in the capacity of wealth to bestow honour increases, so their insistence upon leisure grows more strenuous, and thus abstention from labour presently comes to be a requisite of respectability. Labour, by contrast, is rendered disreputable, dishonourable and ignominious; it ceases to be morally acceptable to the noble, freeborn man, and is considered incompatible with a worthy life.

All civilized peoples, Veblen says, are familiar with the pervading sense of indignity and shamefulness that attends the slightest manual labour. Indeed, so powerful is this sense in people of delicate sensibility who have long been habituated to 'gentle manners' that it often ousts even the instinct for self-preservation. He cites an example: 'a certain king of France . . . is said to have lost his life through an excess of moral stamina in the observance of good form. In the absence of the functionary whose office it was to shift his master's seat, the king sat uncomplainingly before the fire and suffered his royal person to be toasted beyond recovery. But in so doing he saved his Most Christian Majesty from menial contamination.'

By leisure Veblen means not indolence but the non-productive consumption of time. The leisure class energetically devotes itself to consuming time non-productively partly out of a sense of the unworthiness of productive labour, and partly to indicate its pecuniary ability to afford a life of idleness. One of the difficulties attached to maintaining a life of undefiled leisure is that the gentleman concerned cannot pass all his time under the gaze of those whom he wishes to impress; he must therefore devise ways of demonstrating that his private hours are no less leisurely than those he spends in public. For this purpose, members of his family and retinue are encouraged or employed to take part in various forms of vicarious leisure; on his behalf they indulge in conspicuously leisurely activities and thus sustain his reputable standing in the community. If he is sufficiently wealthy, he employs a corps of personal servants whose exclusive function is to advertise the fact that they have no other function save serving their master's needs; their actual duties in respect of their master may extend no further than wearing his livery.

'Conspicuous consumption of valuable goods is a means of reputability to the gentleman of leisure', but as his wealth accumulates on his hands he finds himself unable by his own unaided efforts to display his opulence. Under these circumstances, that part of the servant class whose chief occupation is vicarious leisure undertakes another set of duties – the vicarious consumption of goods. At its most obvious and prevalent this manifests itself in the consumption of food, clothing, accommodation and furniture by the lady of the house (chief servant) and the rest of the domestic establishment.

Lower down the social scale, among the poorer middle-class families, these relationships undergo a curious inversion: in a household where the husband is required to earn his livelihood, the responsibility for vicarious leisure and consumption devolves upon the wife and her daughters alone. 'It is by no means an uncommon spectacle to find a man applying himself to work with the utmost assiduity, in order that his wife may in due form render for him that degree of vicarious leisure which the common sense of the time demands.' And thus, the wife who was at the outset of her evolution man's drudge and chattel – the producer of goods for him to consume – becomes the ceremonial consumer of goods which he produces. But, Veblen says, in reality she remains his chattel, for the habitual rendering of vicarious leisure and consumption is the abiding mark of the unfree servant.

The leisure performed by the wife in these cases is not of course simple idleness – it is generally disguised under some form of household duty which, on close inspection, proves to serve no ulterior end beyond showing that she does not occupy herself with anything gainful or useful. If in the process beauty or comfort are achieved, and it is more or less fortuitous if they are, they must be seen to exemplify what Veblen calls the great economic law of wasted effort. In wealthier households the employment of servants is justified on the grounds that the wives and daughters of the family are too busy with their 'social duties' to attend to domestic ones, and that the work required by a large house is too severe and too great to be accomplished without help. These social duties, however, turn out to be no more than exercises in conspicuous leisure, consisting of morning calls, drives, visits to clubs and sewing circles, attendance at sports events and charity occasions and similar social functions, many of which call for special kinds of costume (conspicuous consumption). The exigencies of conspicuous consumption run riot within the homes of the better-off where the apparatus of living – rituals surrounding meals, conglomerations of huge pieces of furniture, collections of ornaments, bric-à-brac, and *objets d'art* requiring constant dusting and specialized attention, rituals attending the treatment of guests and so on – grow so elaborate and cumbersome that the family can make no progress without the assistance of innumerable servants. 'Personal contact with the hired persons whose aid is called in to fulfil the routine of decency is commonly distasteful to the occupants of the house, but their presence is endured and paid for, in order to delegate to them a share in this onerous consumption of household goods.'

Veblen is careful to point out that, although he believes the regulating norm of consumption is largely the 'requirement of conspicuous waste', he does not believe that the average consumer, or his vicarious agents, are consciously motivated by this principle in its bald, unsophisticated form. On the whole, they merely wish to conform to established usage, to avoid unfavourable comment and to live up to the accepted canons of decency.

The canons of pecuniary reputability, to use Veblen's own phrase, not only colour men's taste in consumable goods – they tend to prefer hand-wrought silver spoons to their equally serviceable aluminium equivalents – but also colour their taste in personal beauty. When the leisure class valued women for the services they provided, the ideal of female beauty was a robust, large-limbed woman, but when women are only expected to indulge in vicarious leisure, the ideal emphasizes their estrangement from all aspects of vulgarly productive labour, and concentrates its attention upon the delicacy of the face, the minuteness and fragility of the hands and feet, and especially the slenderness of the waist whose perfect proportions imply extreme debility.

In this connection it is worth studying for a moment H. K. Browne's illustration 'Our Housekeeping' from *David Copperfield*. (see illustration facing page 87). His drawing depicts Copperfield manfully struggling to carve a joint of uncooked lamb while the guilty Dora, his pretty wife, looks helplessly on. In the middle of the overloaded, chaotic table sits Jip, Dora's little dog, who is so closely identified with his mistress throughout the book as to die when she dies. John Harvey,[5] the critic, has pointed to the resemblance Browne has established in his drawing between Dora and her dog: their hair shares the same blackness and sheen, they face in the same direction and both look with horror at Copperfield's butchery and she rests her arm on the table in the same way as Jip rests his paw. The artist has contrasted the limp delicacy of the paw and her hand with Copperfield's straining fist, and in the process has inadvertently provided an excellent illustration of Veblen's thesis: her hand is quite unsuited for any practical function – it can no more carve the joint than can her lap-dog's paw – but it is admirable for its extreme slightness and frailty.

In his chapter 'Dress as an Expression of Pecuniary Culture', Veblen explains that the clothes adopted by the leisure class are generally designed to express the fact that they have dissociated themselves from productive labour. 'Much of the charm that invests the patent-leather shoe, the stainless linen, the lustrous cylindrical hat, and the walking stick, which so greatly enhance the native dignity of a gentleman, comes of their pointedly suggesting that the wearer cannot when so attired bear a hand in any employment that is directly and immediately of any human use.' Women's clothes state this fact even more pointedly: the baroque bonnet, high-heeled shoe and voluminous skirt all testify to the absolute impossibility of their owner performing any useful task. The corset represented this tendency at its most extreme, for it mutilated the women who wore it, endangered their health and reduced their vitality to a sluggish minimum. Women's clothes also provide an opportunity of displaying conspicuous waste on a grand scale: the crinoline, for example, not only hampered movement and prevented

the wearer from exerting herself, but also required enormous quantities of material – during its English heyday, in the years immediately
following the Great Exhibition, it was often used to support as
many as twenty yards of silk.

Veblen argues that women's clothes serve yet another purpose,
one that distinguishes them completely from those of men. The
high heel, the skirt, the bonnet, crinoline and corset, combined
with the general disregard for comfort which is a consistent feature
of all civilized women's apparel, all go to prove that woman is still
economically dependent on man, and that she is still his chattel.
The homely explanation behind all this conspicuous leisure and
attire on the part of women lies in the fact that they are really only
servants who have been given the job of advertising their master's
ability to pay.

We cannot leave Veblen without allowing him to state, in his
own inimitable words, the theme that underlies every idea contained in his *Theory of the Leisure Class*: 'Throughout the entire
evolution of conspicuous expenditure, whether of goods or of
services or human life, runs the obvious implication that in order to
effectually mend the consumer's good fame it must be an expenditure
of superfluities. In order to be reputable it must be wasteful.'

The phenomenon of the listless young ladies of whom Mrs Ellis
despaired is easier to understand when examined in the light of
Veblen's theories. The aim and purpose of a daughter's existence
was marriage, and it was the mission of every conscientious parent
to bring up his daughter and educate her, if the enforcement of
ignorance may be dignified by that term, in such a way as to render
her eligible, and to maintain that eligibility in a high state of polish
during the fraught years of her spinsterhood. Veblen's thesis may be
employed to show that a girl could best recommend herself to a
would-be suitor by impressing him with her complete inability to do
anything useful or profitable. This faculty could be forcefully
advertised by bringing to perfection her proficiency in those skills
which were notable for their lack of practical or industrial application and for the enormous quantity of wasteful effort required in
their execution. The irresistible girl was she who clearly expressed
her aptitude for a life of conspicuous consumption and her inadequacy for any other. The woman who could only pass her time
in extravagant wastefulness, who was manifestly incapable of

adapting to any environment outside the boudoir and drawing-room and whose deficient physique and precarious vitality bore testimony to her incapacity for all but the lightest exertion of energy, represented an exhilarating prospect to the man in search of a wife; for such a woman could be relied on to flatter and bear witness to his pecuniary prowess.

As Veblen stressed, people did not organize their behaviour or discipline their taste in direct response to the motives set out above, they simply followed conventions and fashions with more or less slavishness, according to their intellectual and material resources. Nor did men choose girls with, say, petite waists out of a conscious desire to possess wives whose dependence on their husbands' pecuniary power could be immediately inferred from their acute physical frailty. Tiny feet, white hands, a porcelain complexion, long hair elaborately dressed and all the other characteristics prized by Victorian young ladies registered in the male mind as no more than manifestations of beauty and sexiness. It was, however, no coincidence that the delicate, doll-like ideal of the 'forties and 'fifties steadily gave way to a more and more robust ideal as the century wore on and men's dominance over women grew increasingly tentative. A comparison between Browne's portrayal of Dora Spenlow and Du Maurier's own illustrations of his heroine Trilby, a veritable giantess who towers majestically over her exquisite lover shows up the dramatic change in concepts of sexiness which had taken place during the forty-five years which separate the two novels.

The state of extreme physical debilitation and diminution which mid-Victorians revered as the highest pitch of femininity, the grossly overloaded and constricting costumes with which high fashion burdened the respectable woman and the miscellany of accessories – bonnets, jewellery, reticules, gloves, shawls, ribbons, parasols, muffs and so on, each a badge of serfdom – which a woman was required to carry about if she wished to appear decently attired, provide evidence of the acute sense of insecurity experienced by those generations of men and women who had but lately and suddenly been thrust into an affluent, middle-class environment. So many families had achieved wealth and had improved their social standing so rapidly, without having had time to accustom themselves to their new surroundings, or to acquire confidence in their new position, or to banish fears of sliding into the ever-present abyss of poverty, that the need to make plain their pecuniary strength to neighbours, inferiors and the world at large was felt with unusual desperation.

The Enchanting Ignoramus

One of the inevitable dangers attached to bringing up a daughter in the conventionally approved manner was that the girl ran an odds-on chance of being turned into a fascinating little moron. Ill-educated, inexperienced and over-protected, the average daughter of middle-class parents was, in effect, maintained in a state of suspended infantilism; she was never allowed to grow up. Her upbringing had been designed to render her attractive to would-be husbands, but in the process it had left her cruelly ill-equipped to deal with such obtrusions of reality as married life, or for that matter spinsterhood, might inflict upon her. Admittedly, husbands tended to treat their wives in much the same way as fathers treated their daughters, and to that extent the transition from the parental to the marital drawing-room was relatively painless, but nevertheless women were singularly vulnerable and helpless.

They were also, by male standards, stupid, or at least so ill-informed and intellectually circumscribed as to be reduced to a condition equivalent to stupidity. Intelligence will of course make its mark, no matter how unfavourable the circumstances, but in so far as it is possible to compare the average man with the average woman, it is safe to say that the intellectual advantages held by the former over the latter were immeasurable. Thus the perfectly brought-up young lady of unexceptional mental capacity represented something of a dilemma to her, let us say, equally unexceptional suitor. On the one hand, she conformed to his idea of femininity and seemed to be provided with the attributes and talents he sought in a wife; on the other, he found himself more than occasionally wearying of her conversation. Considerations of this kind seldom carry much weight with those enjoying the first, careless raptures of love, and yet the depressing discovery that his wife was dull and incapable of taking any interest in his affairs must have been made by many a husband, and must have contributed in no small way to the 'leaden boredom' of many a marriage.

Dickens explored the ramifications of this dilemma, which we may assume to have been a common one, in his portrayal of the relationship between David Copperfield and Dora Spenlow. She is a classic example of the enchanting ignoramus, and she would have given Mrs Ellis no cause whatsoever for melancholy. She is of course extremely pretty, and we can be sure that Dickens had no quarrel with Browne's depiction of her appearance. The word 'little' frequently recurs in Copperfield's first description of her: she has the most delightful little voice, the gayest little laugh and the pleasantest little ways; indeed, as he says himself, 'she was rather diminutive altogether'. She is also described as a fairy, and, by another character, as 'a thing of light, and airiness, and joy'. She fills her days with pastimes and pleasures sanctified by convention – she picks flowers in her garden, amuses Jip, her dog, paints flower pictures and sings touchingly to the guitar. Copperfield is bewitched by her looks, her vivacity and her whimsical merriment; he is infatuated with her, and believes himself to love her as no man has ever loved before.

They become secretly engaged, but he is prevented from proceeding further by the sudden loss of his fortune. He comes to tell her that he is now a beggar; she hardly understands the term. He explains that they will be very poor and will only be able to survive by dint of great perseverance and strength of character, but he finds it almost impossible to communicate with her. 'Please don't be practical,' she begs him, 'it frightens me so.' He asks her if she will promise to read a little cookery book he proposes to send to her. There are obstacles to be tackled, he says, and they must meet and crush them. The wretched Dora is so terrified by his bleak picture of the future that she faints. Later she revives, and after tea sings a song about 'the impossibility of ever on any account leaving off dancing', which makes him feel like a monster that has gone berserk in a fairy bower.

This incident has no effect upon his love for her, but he is disturbed by the fact that everyone looks on her as a pretty toy: 'they all seemed to treat Dora, in her degree, much as Dora treated Jip in his.' He tries to discuss it with her, but she bursts into tears, saying if he doesn't like her why did he ever get engaged to her. Next, he gives her the cookery book, together with a housekeeping book, a set of tablets and a pretty pencil case, and attempts to introduce her to the mysteries of household accounting. However, these domestic rehearsals come to nothing: recipes make her head ache, figures make her cry and so the books are given to Jip to play with.

Once married, Dora, who asks that she should be called his child-wife, knuckles down to her responsibilities, but to no avail. She cannot keep her records or square her bills with her account books, she cannot concentrate, she cannot add up and the whole business of running a house makes her very unhappy. Although deeply in love, they find themselves unable to bring order and efficiency to their marriage. Their servants steal from them, the tradesmen cheat them and their meals are inedible. Copperfield decides that if chaos is to be ousted Dora's mind will have to be 'formed'. He therefore sets about educating her. He reads Shakespeare aloud and feeds her little scraps of useful information, but only succeeds in fatiguing and depressing her. Finally he abandons his scheme, and by way of showing his affection he buys a collar for Jip and a pair of ear-rings for Dora.

'It's better for me to be stupid than uncomfortable, isn't it?' she asks, and he agrees. At the same time he reflects that, although he loves his wife and is happy, the happiness he had vaguely antici-pated is not the happiness he now enjoys; something is missing. He acknowledges that 'it would have been better for me if my wife could have helped me more, and shared the many thoughts in which I had no partner; and that this might have been; I knew.'

Dickens resolves the dilemma in this particular relationship by dispatching Dora to a youthful grave, leaving Copperfield free to marry the capable and intelligent Agnes, but for real married couples the problems encountered by David and Dora were not only virtually insoluble but were positively magnified by the inevitable appearance of children. It is hardly surprising that the average middle-class household relied entirely for its organization and day-to-day running on the skill and industry of servants.

Copperfield's desire to improve his wife by instructing her in accountancy further demonstrates the proximity in the Victorian mind of sexuality to monetary considerations. By marrying her, Copperfield has of course appropriated her property and her money, but he still expects her to fulfil the function of steward to his domestic economy. Her inability to handle money competently is a deeper source of disappointment to him than her failure to appreciate Shakespeare, and in his eyes her femininity and wifeliness are rendered incomplete by this deficiency. Dora's form of submissive-ness is unacceptable to him. He is dissatisfied with her eagerness to adopt him as a substitute parent, although he thinks her juvenile high spirits and naivety intensely attractive. He requires a more active, productive and companionable style of submissiveness, and he finds it in the saintly Agnes who is both impeccably self-effacing and thoroughly efficient. Dora's ear-rings are replaced by Agnes' key-ring which hangs from her waist, symbol of her domestic proficiency. Both women place themselves in attitudes of inferiority, and he not unnaturally prefers the subtle to the simple, the adult to the child.

3

The Enslaved Angel

The Unselfish Love of Woman
Of all the modes of confinement imposed upon women during the
nineteenth century, the most deceptive and pernicious was embodied in the widely-accepted notion of woman as the moral
saviour of her baser mate. In an age when the power of established
religion was unusually vigorous, the idea of woman as an angel
whose halo cast a feeble but priceless ray of light upon a black and
evil world of man's making possessed a deeply persuasive appeal.
It was held that by her very existence she offered a moral ideal to
which men could aspire through the agency of love – to worship her
was to renounce one's sinfulness and ascend to a purer way of life.
Thus the role of wife was transfigured, for upon her was bestowed
the mystical identity of a priestess through whose selfless ministra-
tions the altar of domesticity was supposed to be kept spotless; at
the same time, the virtue of self-sacrifice was venerated as the
quintessence of femininity. The impossibility of her deserting her
post was absolutely ensured by investing it with all the majesty of a
divine appointment.

It cannot be doubted that this myth obtained a powerful hold
over the imaginations of women themselves. In her study of
Victorian women's magazines, *Heroines in Love*, Mirabel Cecil noted
that the angel-woman who sacrificed her all for the sake of her loved
ones was a theme consistently favoured by the authors, most of them
women, of the fiction published for a specifically female audience.

When a woman paid her twopence – later sixpence, to the editor's
regret – for Samuel Beeton's *Englishwoman's Domestic Magazine*
(1852–79, circulation 60,000) she was buying not just a magazine
but a cornucopia of reading material designed to enhance her home
and invigorate her intellect. The contents of this hugely successful
publishing venture comprised articles offering advice on the care of
goldfish, etiquette, the cleaning of cane-bottomed chairs and the
manufacture of cowslip vinegar, together with exchange columns in

which Royal Family photographs could be swapped for portraits of noted clergymen, or two dozen yards of tatting for a copy of Tenny-son's *Princess*, entry forms for competitions in which prizes could be won by writing essays on such inflammatory topics as 'The Unselfish Love of Woman Contrasted with the Exacting Selfishness of Man', and a correspondence page entitled 'Cupid's Letter Bag'. The magazine also published an unprecedented wealth of stories and serialized novels which reflected the preoccupations and fantasies of its readers no less than its other features.

Apart from possessing a bottomless capacity for self-denial and emotions of the loftiest character – 'Full of intellect, with feelings so profound, so earnest, they would have been passionate had they not been pure, she seemed never to entertain a thought which angels might not have cherished' – the heroines of these stories exuded an unmistakable aroma of saintly martyrdom. Mirabel Cecil remarked on the frequency with which the adjective 'spiritual' was employed to describe them. One girl had 'soft, spiritual-looking hair of palest brown', while another parted her pale brown hair Madonna-style 'upon her serene and somewhat heavy brow, from beneath which her large, patient eyes beamed with a look of touching sadness.'

The sacrifices these paragons were called upon to make, though lugubriously romanticized, provide a poignant insight into the real penalties demanded of women in a world where male requirements invariably took precedence. Some heroines surrendered their lovers to their sisters, feeling that they had more right to the love of a good man; others dedicated themselves to providing money for their brothers' education and others gave up their suitors in order to look after aged parents. Greatest heights of pathos were scaled by those who nursed ailing or, better still, dying children; grief, a common enough ordeal for the magazine's readers, was interpreted as a state of purifying exaltation. The heroines preserved a never-failing faith in God, and they never wavered in their belief that 'all things are ordered for the best by One who cannot err'.

In *David Copperfield* Dickens contrasts the sexy but infantile Dora with the responsible but ethereal Agnes Wickfield. The latter's nobility of soul and readiness to sacrifice herself are heavily emphasized throughout the novel by her devotion to her father who, but for her solicitous attention, would have collapsed into drunken-ness and professional ruin. Copperfield invests her with religious significance: 'I cannot call to mind where or when, in my childhood, I had seen a stained glass window in a church. Nor do I recollect its subject. But I know that when I saw her turn round, in the grave light of the old stair-case, and wait for us, above, I thought of that window; and I associated something of its tranquil brightness with Agnes Wickfield ever afterwards.' Agnes represents a classic embodiment of the angel-woman concept; Copperfield conceives her influence on him to be morally uplifting: 'Ever pointing upwards, Agnes; ever leading me to something better; ever directing me to higher things.'

David Copperfield was published in 1849–50; the idea of the adored woman acting as a moral elevator upon her reprobate man was, however, still going strong in 1893 when Grant Allen came to write his best-selling novel, *The Woman Who Did*, in which the hero credits the heroine, his heart's desire, with the power to 'raise him to moral heights he has hardly yet dreamt of'. It is interesting to note that the men in question are usually depicted on the brink of salvation – they are seldom actually seen in the condition of spiritual regeneration with which their authors claim they will be blessed. Such a state of affairs would have accorded the triumphant women far too powerful a whip-hand over their newly cleansed husbands; angels were permitted passive functions only.

The myth of woman as man's spiritual superior underwent a series of reinterpretations throughout the course of the century, and one of its most enduring forms was to be found in the popular fantasy of a Utopian society founded on chivalric ideals. Albert, we recall, elected to have himself painted in the guise of a knight in armour and presented the result to Victoria who chose it as her favourite portrait of the Consort. His choice of costume was by no means the indulgence of a vain whim. The mid-Victorians looked back with nostalgic yearning on the mythical age of chivalry; medieval legends were exploited by poets and painters, notably Tennyson and the Pre-Raphaelites, as sources of moral inspiration, and the chivalric code held great appeal as the repository of true virtue. Arthurian England was envisaged as an idyllic garden, blissfully free of the squalor, ugliness and greed with which their own industrialized land had been so hideously polluted. The inhabitants of this innocent dreamland – knights and ladies all – were held up as models of romantic behaviour. By serving his lady with what Tennyson called 'sublime repression of himself', the

latter-day knight might hope to attain that state of redemption
which was inherent in all Victorian idealizations of sexual love. The
characterization of the lady in these legends bore all the distinctive
features of the angel-wife: she was extravagantly worshipped only
to be safely confined.

John Ruskin, writing at the age of forty-five and in the throes of
an infatuation with the fifteen-year-old Rose La Touche, appointed
himself arch-prophet of neo-medievalism, and in a series of lectures,
published under the title *Sesame and Lilies* (1865), he explained
how the 'kings' and 'queens' of modern Camelot should conduct
themselves.

He declared that in all Christian ages which have been remarkable
for their purity and progress, there has been 'absolute yielding of
obedient devotion by the lover to his mistress'. He then took a
step or two on thinnest ice by suggesting that the lover should
receive from his lady the *direction* (his italics) of his toil. 'Chivalry',
he wrote, 'in its very first conception of honourable life, assumes the
subjection of the young knight to the command – should it even be
the command in caprice – of his lady.' Needless to say he did not
allow this outrageous proposal to stand, but casuistically qualified it
by adding that 'it ought to be impossible for every noble youth – it *is*
impossible for every one rightly trained – to love any one whose
gentle counsel he cannot trust, or whose prayerful command he can
hesitate to obey.' For the benefit of those male readers still reeling
from the shock of his original pronouncement, he asseverated an
'eternal truth' which made plain the kind of direction he had in
mind, namely that the soul's armour is never well set to the heart
unless a woman's hand has braced it.

Two pages later, however, he was still fretting over the conundrum he had, it seems, inadvertently posed himself: how can the idea
of the guiding function of women be reconciled with 'true wifely
subjection'? The answer was, of course, that it could not be done,
but he contrived to hit on a solution which, though acceptable at the
time, revealed the essentially repressive purpose behind all such
apparently adulatory treatments of women's social role. The key
to the riddle, he assured his readers, lay in putting aside foolish and
misleading assumptions concerning the superiority of one sex to the
other, and in acknowledging that 'each has what the other has not;
each completes the other, and is completed by the other.' Man, he
asserted, was active, progressive and warlike, while woman's

talents were not for invention or creation, but for 'sweet ordering'
and arrangement. 'Her great function', he wrote, 'is Praise; she
enters no contest, but infallibly adjudges the crown of contest.'
The woman's true place and power were to be found in that sacred
hearth, that vestal temple, that place of peace – the home. 'The
stars only may be over her head; the glowworm in the night-cold
grass may be the only fire at her foot; but home is yet wherever she
is; and for a noble woman it stretches far round her, better than
ceiled with cedar, or painted with vermilion, shedding its quiet
light far, for those who else were homeless.'

Ruskin's escapist vision of life must have proved gratifying both
to the ordinary, bread-winning husband whose dull, nine-to-five
job was colourfully transformed into a perilous and heroic adventure,
and to his bored, house-bound wife who discovered herself to be the
mistress not of a three-bedroomed villa but of a 'rock in a weary
land' and a light of Pharos in the stormy sea. The queenly status of
the wife was not, however, without its responsibilities. In order to
justify her accession to the domestic throne, she was required to
develop a set of daunting virtues – she had to make herself incapable
of error, incorruptibly good and infallibly wise. Nor was she to
imagine that by assuming this state of saintliness she acquired the
right to set herself above her husband; on the contrary, 'she must
be . . . wise, not for self-development, but for self-renunciation.' In
short, the point of her perfection was to render perfect service to her
husband.

'Of Queens' Gardens', Ruskin's lecture dealing with the role of
women, cannot be taken too seriously. It was a piece of sentimental
whimsy composed by a man of doubtful sanity who had the greatest
difficulty forming relationships with members of the opposite sex.
It does, on the other hand, provide an eloquent exposition of the
sado-masochism central to the Victorian use of the angel myth.
With the benefit of hindsight, it is possible to recognize Ruskin's
version of chivalry as a blatant confidence trick: he assigned to
women a seemingly glorified status, that of ladies who commanded
the obedient devotion of their knights, while in fact confirming
them in their position of relative inferiority – 'wifely subjection'.
But on those of his female audience who were deceived by his myth-
making, and it must be remembered that in his day he was a greatly
respected figure, he can only have had a damaging influence. By
taking up a grovelling posture of worship before the shrine of his

morally-improving queen, he was in effect perpetrating an act of oppression, for he was recommending to women an idealized concept of themselves which they could not possibly attain. He was exhorting them to adopt an attitude towards themselves which could only foster a sense of inadequacy, a sense of having failed to live up to their better selves.

The fundamentally repressive character of the angel myth may be most clearly discerned in a narrative poem, *The Angel in the House*, by Coventry Patmore, which for forty years or more was a perennial best-seller. Patmore was greatly esteemed by Ruskin who quoted some of his lines in 'Of Queens' Gardens' and wrote that he wished they were known to all youthful ladies of England: 'you cannot read him too often or too carefully; as far as I know he is the only living poet who always strengthens and purifies.' Tennyson, a close friend of the poet, did not share Ruskin's respect and is reported to have said that in his opinion some of Patmore's lines had been 'hammered up out of old nails'. In any event, the public loved his book which went through innumerable editions and sold more than a quarter of a million copies; it was still in print and selling at the end of the century.

Patmore's intention was to write a poem which would glorify married love as fervently as the romantics had glorified chivalrous love, or the mystics chastity. He chose to realize this sublime ambition through the medium of the modest events that made up the story of his own courtship, engagement, wedding and honeymoon.

After an absence of six years during which he was at Cambridge (wrangler and prize poet) and travelling on the Continent, Felix Vaughan, the hero-narrator and Patmore's *alter ego*, returns to Salisbury to take up his leisurely responsibilities as country squire and landlord. He lives comfortably in a handsome Tudor house standing in its own parkland, his tenant farmer pays him six hundred pounds a year, and he plans to make a name for himself as a writer. He calls on his father's old friend, the Dean, and his three daughters who used to be his playmates, and falls in love with Honor, the eldest.

In his opening description of Honor, Patmore puts to use the same chivalric hyperbole that Ruskin was later to employ; Vaughan actually refers to her as a queen, and swiftly takes up, in his own mind at this stage, a position of abject prostration before her – 'he

merits not to kiss the braid upon her skirt', etc. This heady combination of self-deprecation and histrionic idolization provides the
keynote of the early courtship episodes. Honoria is adored by
Vaughan with a knight-like devotion, of which Ruskin no doubt
wholeheartedly approved, and, as the poem's title implies, she is
also invested with religious significance. In a chapter called 'Going
to Church', Patmore unequivocally states that to love the angel is to
love her Maker:

> I loved her in the name of God,
>   And for the ray she was of Him;
> . . . Him loved I most,
>   But her I loved most sensibly.

Furthermore, he sanctifies Vaughan's erotic response to her by
arguing that he is not attracted to her mere flesh, but to the embodiment of the Holy Spirit itself:

> Her beauty was a godly grace;
> The mystery of loveliness,
>   Which made an altar of her face,
> Was not of the flesh, though that was fair,
>   But a most pure and living light . . .

And he is at pains to affirm that falling in love is not a simple
indulgence of the senses, but rather a celebration of the soul:

> My joy was no idolatry
>   Upon the ends of the vile earth bent,
> For when I loved her most then I
>   Most yearn'd for more divine content.

Honoria gives him her arm and he walks her into church. They sit
next to each other, and during the service she exercises over him the
influence traditionally attributed to beloved women, that of con-
ducting her man to a higher moral sphere (she is at this point
specifically described as an angel):

> And, when we knelt, she seemed to be
>   An angel teaching me to pray.

His spirit rejoices and is borne aloft by 'the bright spring-tide of
pure love'. Not many days later, he proposes and, to his ineffable
delight, is accepted.

Up to this point Patmore has concentrated on Vaughan's attitude to love in general and his feelings for Honoria in particular, which as we have seen are of the loftiest character. Once they are engaged, however, Vaughan's thoughts turn to the question of how husbands and wives should conduct themselves in relation to one another and, predictably enough, for all his passionate reverence of her holier qualities, he reveals himself to be a confirmed believer in feminine submission.

It is also at this stage that Patmore first provides us with an insight into Honoria's mind, the mind after all of an angel. In a chapter entitled 'The Changed Allegiance', he analyses the quality of love experienced by the newly engaged fiancée and discloses that, unlike his, her emotions are by no means divinely inspired, unless fiancés may be termed a species of divinity; for, Patmore tells us, 'she loves him for his love of her'. Indeed, she barely understands his love and has to turn to the mirror for enlightenment:

> And oft she views what he admires
> Within her glass, and sight of this
> Makes all the sum of her desires
> To be devotion unto his.

She has, however, grasped the fact that she is exchanging one master for another and, although she isn't quite used to the idea – his lightest touch still leaves her 'dizzied, shock'd and flush'd' – she is nevertheless bravely determined to offer her husband the same unstinting allegiance her parents have previously enjoyed:

> Her will's indomitably bent
> On mere[1] submissiveness to him;
> To him she'll cleave, for him forsake
> Father's and mother's fond command!
> He is her lord . . .

It is safe to say that, far from being a contradiction in Patmore's mind, the combination of angel and vassal seemed to him an entirely natural and proper one, and it would be easy to fill a page with quotations illustrating this point. He believed that the woman's function was to inspire in her man a thirst for nobler moral feelings, but he also believed that her contribution to this process took effect at a spiritual, not an intellectual level. By simply being what she was, she edified, but the metamorphosis could not be completed without a conscious, voluntary effort on his part.

Thus, although Patmore granted Honoria the highest possible symbolic status, he assessed her emotional capabilities at the lowest rate. In a chapter called 'In Love', he describes the state of her feelings towards Felix during the happiest period of their engagement:

> A rapture of submission lifts
>   Her life into celestial rest;
> There's nothing left of what she was;
>   Back to the babe the woman dies,
> And all the wisdom that she has
>   Is to love him for being wise.

'A rapture of submission' might well have served as an alternative title to this chapter; it precisely captures the frame of mind most desired by men in their women during this period.

Nasty Knowledge

'Knowledge need not necessarily be nasty', wrote a contributor to the *British Medical Journal* in 1894, 'but even if it were, it certainly is not comparable in that respect to the imaginings of ignorance.' The knowledge he referred to was that which, in his opinion, every woman should possess when she entered upon married life. Not only were the majority of middle-class women ignorant of the fate that awaited them in their bridal bed, but they were also ignorant of the meaning of what had been taking place within their own bodies since the onset of puberty.

Marie Stopes (1880–1958) may be said to have lacked knowledge on a spectacular scale. As a child and teenager she read omnivorously, and among the writers who impressed her was Darwin. She was placed second in her class for zoology in her first year at University College, London, she studied botany in Munich and, having gained her doctorate, she devoted herself for the next seven years to further botanical research. Neither her very considerable intelligence, nor her extensive education prepared her, however, for the realities of marriage.

In 1911, she met and within a fortnight agreed to marry a fellow botanist, Dr Reginald Ruggles Gates. Six months after their wedding 'she began to feel instinctively that something was lacking', and with creditable common sense she went to the British Museum to find out what it was. There she discovered that her marriage had never been consummated. Soon after, she successfully sued for an annulment on the grounds that she was *virgo intacta*.

She resolved to write a book to save others from her own miserable experience, and in 1918, two years after her marriage had been finally dissolved, she published, not without difficulty, her *Married Love*. Her purpose, she declared, was to help ordinary people with 'a book on marriage and sex [which] would teach a man and a woman how to understand each other's sexual problems.' The book sold two thousand copies in the first fortnight and subsequently went through many editions. Knowledge, nasty or otherwise, was in desperate demand.

Annie Besant, an earlier heroine of the birth-control movement, also underwent a disastrous marriage. She was an intensely religious girl; as her friend W. T. Stead later remarked, 'she could not be the bride of Heaven, and therefore became the bride of Mr Frank Besant. He was hardly an adequate substitute' (Besant was a clergyman.) Theirs was not a love match. He had proposed to her and she, confused, surprised and completely inexperienced, had felt obliged to accept. Thus, as she wrote in her autobiography, 'out of sheer weakness and fear of inflicting pain I drifted into an engagement with a man I did not pretend to love.' They were married in 1867; she was twenty years old, but had no more idea of the actualities of marriage than a child of four. 'My dreamy life, into which no knowledge of evil had been allowed to penetrate, in which I was guarded from all pain, shielded from all anxiety, kept innocent of all questions of sex, was no preparation for married existence, and left me defenceless to face a rude awakening.' It was, she believed, difficult for men to realize the full depth of many girls' infantile ignorance, but she was convinced that 'many an unhappy marriage dates from its very beginning, from the terrible shock to a young girl's sensitive modesty and pride, her helpless bewilderment and fear.'

Both these women were exceptionally intelligent and well read, and yet they lived in a society which positively ensured that a qualified zoologist and botanist could go to her bridal bed without understanding what was going to happen to her, or, in Stopes's case, not going to happen. It might seem reasonable to suppose that the spread of education among women during the later decades of the nineteenth century would inevitably entail the increasing circulation of knowledge concerning sexual matters, but education does not automatically promote enlightenment. Outside medical libraries and Holywell Street (the home of Victorian pornography) sexual information was virtually inaccessible; Marie Stopes's book was a pioneering work, and yet it was not published until 1918. It is true that after 1880, thanks principally to the efforts of Mrs Besant, Charles Bradlaugh and the Malthusian League, women could with relative ease obtain birth-control literature, but these publications by no means explained in full either the reproductive system or the mechanics of copulation, although much could be inferred from them.

It was generally assumed and stated that men picked up their knowledge 'from the gutter', a largely inaccurate phrase designed to describe those places where men tended to congregate – schools, clubs, offices and pubs. This form of spontaneous education necessarily propagated innumerable myths and prejudices, none of which did anything to improve relations between the sexes, but at least it carried the inestimable advantage of introducing its students to sex as a source of enjoyment. To this day, it is not thought necessary to teach children that the most significant 'fact of life' is that sex offers human beings, as opposed to the frogs and rabbits who usually play the foremost role in such lessons, an opportunity of deriving profound pleasure. Although the Victorian man could only contemplate sex through a fog of guilt and anxiety, he could nevertheless define and identify the act of copulation in his mind – it was a realizable concept – before he had achieved any actual experience. For the majority of women, however, copulation, if not the entire sexual function, remained either a non-existent concept or a nebulous target for unresolved, uninformed speculation, until the moment of the wedding night when the sight of a semi-naked man and his minatory organ can only have made the most traumatic impact. The ignorance in which women were kept as to the workings of their own bodies was another, and one of the most destructive, manifestations of their bondage.

The primary and universal question concerning the origin of babies was answered, if at all, with misleading euphemism and fairy stories. Havelock Ellis[2] recorded some of the theories arrived at by American children based either on the misinformation they had received or their own fantasies: 'God makes babies in heaven through the Holy Mother and even Santa Claus makes some . . . mamma or the doctor or the nurse go up and fetch them, sometimes in a balloon, or they fly down and lose off [sic] their wings . . . [they also] grew in cabbages, or God puts them in water, perhaps in the sewer, and the doctor gets them out and takes them to sick folks that want them . . . they are dug out of the ground or bought at the baby store.' In England the most popular explanations proffered were that God deposited babies under gooseberry bushes or that they were brought by the doctor. Some children were told that babies emerged from their mothers' breasts, and that was held to be the reason why they were unwell. At a later age when children acquired some vague appreciation of the fact that babies emanated from their mothers' bodies, the impression was often formed that the navel was the point of exit. This belief, according to Ellis who was writing in the first decade of the twentieth century, 'is sometimes preserved through the whole period of adolescence, especially in girls of the so-called educated class, who are too well-bred to discuss the matter with their married friends, and believe that they are already sufficiently well-informed.'

Freud argued that children themselves give little credit to the tales designed for their mystification, and that they reach quite different conclusions of their own. He isolated three theories which children, in his opinion, most commonly arrive at to explain the sexual facts of life.[3] (Ellis cites them in his book.) The first and most prevalent is that there is no real anatomical difference between boys and girls; if the boy notices that his sister has no obvious penis he concludes that it is because she is too young, and the little girl herself takes the same view. The second theory suggested that babies are brought into the world by an action analagous to that of the bowels. And the third, and less prevalent, which Freud called the sadistic theory of coitus, involves the child's realization that his father must have taken some part in his production, and his conviction that his parents' relationship was fraught with physical violence.

Freud also investigated children's opinions concerning the nature of marriage itself. They generally believed it to be a state in which modesty was abolished, the most popular version of this theory being that marriage meant people could urinate in front of each other, while another version held that marriage is when people can show each other their genitals.

Ellis was convinced that 'servant-girls of the lower class' played a great part in the sexual initiation of their employers' children, and he quoted with apparent approval Balzac's somewhat melodramatic remark, 'a mother may bring up her daughter severely, and cover her beneath her wings for seventeen years; but a servant-girl can destroy that long work by a word, even by a gesture'. Those girls, however, who had not received the benefit of a word, or even a gesture, from the family maid, had no alternative but to languish in ignorance or bewilderment until such time as they were married. In the natural course of events, the childish fantasies and rationalizations which Ellis described pass away and are replaced by more realistic and informed anticipations of sexual experience to come. The mid-Victorian girl was brought up, however, in an environment where sexuality was as far as possible cauterized from the minds of children, where every mention of the reproductive process was cloaked in mystery and prohibition and where babies were treated as beings more angelic than human. As a result she was effectively marooned on the desert island of her own infantile speculations. Instead of receding in importance and giving way to maturer attitudes, her childish theories, whether compounded of fairy stories supplied by parents and nurses, or of her own concoction, were earnestly preserved and granted an unnaturally prolonged existence, for they represented the only source of information at her disposal. Mrs Besant's reference to her own mental age of four at the time of her wedding was, it turns out, no histrionic exaggeration.

In Ellis's opinion, one of the many adverse effects produced by imprisoning women in a state of 'ignorant innocence' was that they were deprived of the knowledge necessary for intelligent sympathy with other women; 'they do not know half as much about other women as a man of the most average capacity learns in his day's march'.[4] Pleading for the rejection of the idea that female ignorance guaranteed chastity, he wrote: 'we have to teach children to be a law to themselves. We have to give them that knowledge which will enable them to guard their own personalities.' Such enlightened advice had a revolutionary ring to it in 1910, and has barely been accepted in our own time; if, however, Ellis had written those words in the eighteen-fifties they would have been thought pornographic and their author would have been accused of inciting sexual anarchy.

The alienation of women from their own bodies reinforced their sense of inadequacy and contributed to their general enfeeblement. Taught to think of the female body and its reproductive functions as objects of disgust, many women understandably adopted a policy of pretending that the erotic dimension to the human character did not exist; they rigorously expelled it from their consciousness, and prohibited its re-entry by throwing a tight cordon of puritanical security around their domestic territory. It seemed that their higher spirituality was in constant peril of being soiled or completely contaminated by their lower corporeal nature, and that their only chance of salvation lay in an absolute rejection of all aspects of their physiological being. In an age when a premium was placed on large families, this rejection was bought at a destructively steep price. Whereas motherhood was extolled as the loftiest state of achievement to which a woman could aspire, a form of sainthood, the mechanics of copulation, pregnancy and childbirth were made the subject of a comprehensive conspiracy of silence. By opposing cerebral virtues to physical iniquities, women placed themselves in a position of irredeemable insufficiency; they always felt inferior to their better selves. This division of mind from body, this turning of women against themselves, served its function as the guarantor of, among other things, virginity and fidelity, for as long as women despised and disdained their physicality, they were prevented from even acknowledging their sexuality, and therefore from putting it at risk.

Any society which puts an inflated valuation upon virginity must inevitably resort to desperate measures to ensure its preservation. By teaching their women to deny their very femininity, the Victorians locked the door of sex not temporarily but permanently, rendering many women psychologically incapable of accepting sex under any but the most functional circumstances. The conventional, twentieth-century joke image of the Victorian woman lying still on her wedding night and thinking of England implies that women were repelled by their husbands' sexual demands. The real tragedy, however, behind that cliché is that women were revolted and frightened not only by their husband's intrusion but also by the exposure of that part of themselves which they had hidden and felt ashamed of since the dawn of self-awareness. They had learnt to hate themselves.

The Wound Of Love

Nowhere is the alienation of women from their femininity more vividly demonstrated than in prevailing mid-Victorian attitudes towards menstruation. During the first half of the century, it was commonly believed that the menstrual flow was provoked by an excess of nutrient within the female system; the eggs were thought to descend from the ovaries only as a consequence of intercourse. In 1832 the ovum was definitively identified; in 1845 Dr Adam Raciborski discovered that the ova were spontaneously ejected and by 1863 Dr Pflüger was able to confirm beyond doubt the theory that menstruation depended upon ovulation. In 1896 a spectacular – for its day – piece of surgery finally rendered all further speculation otiose: Dr E. Knauer found that excising the ovaries abolished menstruation, while transplanting them re-established it.

These revolutionary breakthroughs did not, however, immediately transform professional medical thinking, which displayed a marked reluctance to relinquish familiar and long-standing hypotheses. In 1879, *The Lancet* published a paper by Dr Aldridge George defending the popular explanation of menstruation which held that, since the growth of girls before puberty was more rapid than that of boys, their bodies must produce more blood which was bound to be expelled when the rate of growth dramatically decelerated at puberty. Dr George argued that the excess of blood shed during puberty is used during pregnancy to build the foetus. 'When conception has taken place,' he wrote, 'there is an outlet for the surplus nutritive income over expenditure in the growth of the foetus and uterus, and a similar outlet also exists during lactation, so the occurrence of menses during lactation is a comparatively rare event.'

It is interesting to note that, when discussing the physiology of women, medical writers often borrowed from the economist's vocabulary. Dr Mary Putnam-Jacobi, a contemporary of Dr George, believed that menstruation was 'an excess of nutritive force in the sex upon whom devolves the greatest cost of reproduction', and she correctly explained the phenomenon of amenorrhoea, absence of flow, with the suggestion that it was 'often a piece of conservative economy when the system cannot afford the loss, and that its real treatment is that of the system generally; and that the reappearance of the menses is but the evidence of the general improvement.'

To seek analogies for human biological systems, as well as moral and other systems, in economic models was a peculiarly Victorian instinct; we have already seen how the retention of sperm before marriage was characterized as a form of savings-investment. In the case of menstruation, we can see how the medical profession attempted to lend plausibility to a doubtful theory by strengthening their exposition with economic imagery: the female reproductive system is portrayed as a microcosm of an industrialized capitalist system, with blood substituted for money as the life force. Economic terminology was both familiar and redolent of security; it could therefore be profitably employed to supply credence in the absence of convincing scientific observation and deduction.

Those doctors who were slow to absorb new and seemingly improbable theories which subsequently attained universal acceptance cannot automatically be dismissed as reactionary or obscurantist. It is, however, difficult to exculpate doctors who seemed determined to obstruct progress by breathing new life into myths that had been current since the Middle Ages. In 1878 *The British Medical Journal* published a series of letters devoted to the question of whether the touch of a menstruating woman could cause hams to go bad; for six months doctors and members stepped forward to declare that on the basis of personal observation and reliable hearsay they had no doubts upon the point. Finally the editor brought the correspondence to a halt, claiming with shameless hypocrisy that he had only indulged the topic in order to illustrate the facility with which superstitions, in themselves irrational and capable of easy disproof, could retain their hold. Two decades later, Havelock Ellis referred to these letters in his book *Man and Woman* (1894) and commented that the contamination myth still commanded widespread belief.

In view of the medical establishment's willingness to entertain archaic prejudices and its persistent disinclination to embrace progressive thought, it is not surprising that the public preserved a grossly distorted view of menstruation and its effects upon women. Even George Drysdale, a staunch campaigner for birth control and social reform, whose *Elements of Social Science* (1854) became one of the most popular contraceptive books to be published during the century, was capable of writing: 'menstruation in women corresponds exactly with the period of heat in female animals, and differs only in the unessential particular, that in women there is an external sanguineous discharge'. This quotation is taken from the twenty-

fifth edition of his book, published in 1886. Charles Knowlton's
Fruits of Philosophy, another celebrated birth-control text which
Annie Besant and Charles Bradlaugh reissued in 1877 and sold to
the tune of 125,000 copies in three months before defending it
against an obscenity prosecution, contained many primitive
misconceptions and myths concerning both masturbation and
menstruation; Knowlton, who had originally written his book in
1832, believed menstruation to be preparation of the uterine system
for conception rather than evidence that conception had not
occurred.

Ellis also remarked in *Man and Woman* that women of every class
tended to associate menstruation with impurity, and that many
women regarded their period as too shameful an occurrence to be
alluded to. For the mid-Victorian girl, pubescence must have been a
profoundly disturbing and disagreeable experience. Completely
unprepared for, and totally ignorant of the significance of the
extraordinary changes which took place within and upon her body,
she must have greeted the appearance of her pubic hair, the swelling
of her breasts and the onset of her first period with a combination of
bewilderment and fear amounting to hysteria. The growth of body
hair, particularly pubic hair, may well have seemed to her the
infliction of a disfigurement rather than the acquisition of a natural
adornment.

Little girls were given no warning of the imminence of these
regrettable developments and no explanation of them once they had
taken place. In 1853 the gynaecologist Tilt (*Elements of Health and
Principles of Female Hygiene*, 1852) conducted an inquiry into the
impact made upon women by the advent of their first period. He
interviewed nearly a thousand women and found that twenty-five
per cent had been totally unprepared for its appearance, that
thirteen of the twenty-five had been very frightened and had
screamed or gone into hysterical fits, and that six out of the thirteen
had thought themselves wounded and had attempted to wash away
the blood with cold water. He reported that the general health of
those who had been frightened was seriously impaired. Dr Helen
Kennedy[5] questioned a hundred and twenty-five American high-
school girls in 1896 and discovered that thirty-six had passed into
womanhood with no knowledge whatsoever 'of all that makes them
women'; thirty-nine of the girls had an inkling of what had happened to them and had received some instruction but were hope-

lessly confused because they had not felt free to discuss it among themselves. Less than half the girls felt able to discuss menstruation with their mothers.

Girls were encouraged to behave like invalids while they suffered from 'the curse', 'the flowers' or, as Queen Victoria called it, their 'poorly time'; they were, in effect, called upon to be disgusted with themselves. In some religious communities, among the Parsees for example, menstruating women are forbidden to be seen in public, or by men, even male members of their own families, and are restricted to the women's quarters; they are also forbidden to fulfil their normal household duties, particularly those that bring them into contact with food. No such overt ritual applied in nineteenth-century Europe, but women were nevertheless obliged to act in accordance with masculine repugnance to the supposed dirt and messiness of menstruation by withdrawing to their sick-beds and by punishing themselves with the paraphernalia of illness. The fantasies with which menstruation was associated in the male mind may be discerned in Jules Michelet's sadistic account of the average period's duration: 'woman is for ever suffering from the cicatriza-tion of an interior wound which is the cause of the whole drama. So that in reality for fifteen days out of twenty-eight – one may almost say always – woman is not only invalided but wounded. She suffers incessantly from the wound of love.' (*L'Amour*, 1859.)

By the same token, invalidism held attractions for women who were not only ashamed but frightened of the apparently arbitrary and mysterious emanations of their own bodies; menstruation represented the dark, foreboding side of their physical life, and it was only natural that they should seek to escape from it. Middle-class women led an unhealthily inactive life, and their capacity to resist the smallest onslaught of pain or discomfort was in any case minimal. As we have seen, women were also led to think that physical delicacy was the token of femininity, and so they had a vested interest in advertising their submission, as opposed to resistance, to this monthly symbol of female frailty.

In later years, when middle-class women began to campaign for admission to the professions, menstruation, and the automatic incapacitation which it enforced, was ruthlessly exploited by men, with the unscrupulous assistance of the medical profession, as an argument in favour of the exclusion of women from all posts of responsibility. As the battle grew more furious, so the degree of incapacity which doctors claimed women suffered from became more histrionic. In 1869 James MacGrigor Allan addressed the Anthropological Society of London: 'At such times,' he said, 'women are unfit for any great mental or physical labour. They suffer under a languor and depression which disqualify them from thought or action, and render it extremely doubtful how far they can be considered responsible beings while it lasts. Much of the inconsequent conduct of women, their petulance, caprice and irritability may be traced to this cause.'[6] He thought it likely that in some women menstruation was a cause of temporary madness, and he did not hesitate to classify women as natural invalids. His cool objectivity won him the admiration of the Society.

It is, of course, hardly necessary to add that the controversy which raged over the question of women's competence to assume responsibility and to sustain their energies over prolonged stretches of time never extended itself to female servants, or to working-class women in general. Although the disposable sanitary towel was on the market by the eighteen-eighties, selling at a shilling or two shillings a dozen, depending on quality, the inconvenience attached to wearing the traditional 'monthly napkin' was throughout most of the century probably sufficient in itself to render most ladies *hors de combat*. By contrast, domestics, whose hours were cruelly long and duties arduous, were presumed to suffer neither from the refined disorders to which ladies were compulsorily prone, nor from the physical and practical hardships which must have weighed far more painfully upon them than their supine mistresses. This fundamental inconsistency did not play a large part in the arguments proposed by middle-class women in defence of their ability to undertake employment.

4

The Late Victorian Period

The rest of this section is largely concerned with the final three decades of the nineteenth century, and it is therefore important to have in mind the features which distinguish those years from earlier phases of Victoria's reign.

Historians are generally agreed that the late Victorian period differed profoundly from the so-called early- and mid-Victorian periods. In the concluding section of his celebrated *Portrait of an Age*, G. M. Young employed a revealing phrase to describe what he regarded as the regrettable decline in the national character that took place after 1870: '. . . fundamentally, what failed in the late Victorian age, and its flash Edwardian epilogue, was the Victorian public, once so alert, so *masculine* [my italics], and so responsible. Compared with their fathers, the men of that time were ceasing to be a ruling or a reasoning stock; the English mind sank towards [an] easily excited, easily satisfied, state of barbarism and childhood . . .' In his opinion, these men were lacking in 'intelligence, character and purpose'. Beatrice Webb, however, when analysing the mood of the ruling and middle classes, pointed to a growing sense of doubt regarding the values and principles that had been entertained by previous generations: 'There were in the eighties and nineties', she wrote,[1] 'two controversies raging in periodicals and books: on the one hand, the meaning of the poverty of masses of men; and, on the other, the practicability and desirability of political and industrial democracy as a set-off to, perhaps as a means of redressing, the grievances of the majority of the people. Was the poverty of the many a necessary condition of the wealth of the nation and of its progress in civilization?' She recalled that a new consciousness of sin was to be found among men of intellect and property; by this she did not mean a consciousness of personal sin, but 'a collective or class consciousness; a growing uneasiness, amounting to conviction, that the industrial organization, which had yielded rent, interests and profits on a stupendous scale, had failed to provide a decent livelihood and tolerable conditions for a majority of the inhabitants of Great Britain.'

Of all the differences that divided the last three decades from earlier years, it was perhaps the relative infirmity of the economy that exerted the most decisive effects upon society. Referred to by contemporary economists as the years of the Great Depression, the period from 1873 to 1896 saw a succession of disastrous harvests; prices fell consistently, bankruptcies among farmers were common during the 'eighties, agricultural wages dropped below subsistence level, the drift of the population from country to town was accelerated and the acreage of England's wheatfields was halved between 1872 and 1900. This appalling deterioration in agricultural achievement, which was as much the result of foreign competition as of bad weather and mismanagement, administered an incalculably destructive blow to the pride of a nation which considered its rural communities to be its backbone. The stable prosperity and financial confidence on which the middle classes had for so long relied was dispelled, never to be fully regained, by a series of gruelling slumps, notably in the mid 'seventies and mid 'eighties, and by a general depression of trade and industry. British exports lost their domination of the world market and were forced to give more and more ground to their competitors, particularly those manufactured in America and Germany. The dynamic thrust of industrial expansion, which had been the hallmark of the British economy during the mid-Victorian era, was dissipated, and for the first time since the beginning of the industrial revolution other countries managed to supersede British inventiveness and to improve on British technological expertise. The United Kingdom's industrial production rose by an average of over 2·1 per cent per annum over the period from 1870 to 1914, while the corresponding figure for the United States was 4·7 per cent per annum, and for Germany 4·1. The volume of British exports had for the thirty years before 1870 been rising by 5 per cent per annum, but between 1870 and 1890 it rose by only 2 per cent per annum, and by only 1 per cent per annum during the 'nineties. Over the same period, production rates per man fell, as did the rate of capital investment.[2]

In his history of England 1870–1914,[3] Sir Robert Ensor wrote: '[The] slump of the 'eighties, following so soon after that of the 'seventies and linked to it by the unlifted depression in agriculture, gave Victorian courage and optimism the severest shock it had yet received.' In this context, however, 'middle class' should be read for 'Victorian'; for in ᵗhe main it was the middle classes who suffered from the Depression and the accompanying fall in prices, interest, and profits, and it was their morale that was undermined. The working classes, on the other hand, derived some benefit from these changing conditions, and it has been calculated[4] that the real income per head in the United Kingdom increased by about 25 per cent in each of the last three decades of the century.

Middle-class morale was further sapped by the apparent disintegration of the social hierarchy on which their position and affluence depended. By the 'seventies, the trade union movement had gathered sufficient strength to organize and sustain a number of effective strikes; in 1871, for example, 9,500 Tyneside engineers endured a strike of five months before their employers finally agreed to limit their working day to nine hours. In 1889 the London dockers struck to obtain a standard wage of 6d an hour. Public sympathy was largely with the strikers, who at that time represented the greatest single mass of chronic poverty in London, and, after a month's bitter negotiating, the dock companies conceded defeat. The membership of trade unions in 1892 amounted to more than a million and a half, and by the turn of the century it had exceeded two million. In 1893 industrial stoppages of various kinds accounted for more than thirty million working days. Following the strike at Manningham Mills, Bradford, in the same year, the Independent Labour Party was founded with Keir Hardie at its head. Whatever the real political efficacy of this party, the mere appearance of a popular socialist organization with parliamentary aspirations tended to confirm in the middle-class mind its worst suspicions regarding the likely breakdown of civilization as it knew and understood it.

It would be inaccurate to characterize the mood of the middle classes over these years as one of helpless despondency, or to suggest that they languished in fearful anticipation of the collapse of the world that had previously assured them both financial and social wellbeing. Despite the economic setbacks described above, Britain remained one of the richest countries in Europe, and it continued to afford a comfortable, not to say opulent, standard of living to those who were fortunate enough to have access to the largesse. Furthermore, as Beatrice Webb emphasized, an influential section of the wealthy had themselves become convinced that the inequitable structure of society should be ameliorated. Their programme of reform, however, consisted of plans for the gradual improvement of living and working conditions, and was void of any truly revolutionary ambition; for few of the conscience-stricken went so far as to embrace even the mild brand of socialism for which the Webbs came to stand as figure-heads.

Although Britain enjoyed an enviably peaceful political atmosphere by contemporary standards, this was an age of terrorism. All over Europe extremists of various denominations, particularly anarchists, were putting into action their belief in 'propaganda by deed' by not only assassinating, or attempting to, presidents and other prominent citizens, but by also indiscriminately bombing and murdering ordinary members of the bourgeoisie. Political violence in Britain was mostly confined to Ireland, and to Irish issues, with occasional outbreaks of bombing in London, but the property-owning classes nevertheless absorbed the general air of apprehension generated by events which befell their neighbours across the Channel.

The distinction to be drawn between the preceding years and the final three decades of the century is the presence of a deeply disturbing sense of fear. Although the country was not plunged into revolution, nor submerged by financial ruin, nor even overpowered by atheists, socialists or advocates of free-love, the middle-class imagination was, however, persistently haunted by the fear that these catastrophes were about to come to pass. The old mid-Victorian world, its values and affluence, its spiritual and commercial confidence, its comforting belief in the rectitude of everyone knowing his or her place and its robust faith in its own progress, all seemed to be crumbling into chaos. The past could no longer be looked to as a source of reassuring precedent, while the future, in its turn, boded nothing but failure and despair.

It was during these same years that the principal battles in the campaign for female emancipation were fought and won. For the most part, the feminists were not animated by any desire to alter the basis of society, they simply wished to appropriate their fair share of the rights and privileges which their male, middle-class counterparts already exercised. As we have seen, the traditional concept of marriage with patriarchal husband and submissive wife, against which the feminists were rebelling, relied heavily for its preservation on a thriving economy and promoted the close association of male

1   Charles Baxter, *The Sisters* (see page 26)

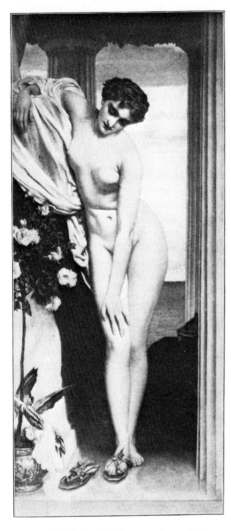

2 Frederic Leighton, *Venus Disrobing for the Bath* (see page 81)

3 Frederic Leighton, *The Bath of Psyche* (see page 83)

prowess with monetary power. It was therefore no coincidence that the attack on the established sexual hierarchy gathered strength and proved most effective at a time when men were in a state of acute anxiety brought on by the instability of the economy and their own diminished prosperity. For this reason alone, the emancipation movement must be accounted one of the forces that did most to exacerbate the prevailing atmosphere of fearfulness.

The various ways in which men struggled to come to terms with the feminist challenge are analysed later on but, before we turn to them, a brief résumé of the main phases of the development of emancipation must first be given.

The general move towards equality was not the result of a coherent policy or of a concerted effort on the part of a particular body of militant women, nor did the majority of women automatically give their support to those who fought on their behalf. Certain issues were taken up by only a handful of individuals, while others attracted the attention of the nation; some pieces of legislation were passed in the teeth of violent opposition and some came into existence merely as by-products of laws not directly related to the feminist cause. There is no doubt that the determined and courageous efforts of such women as Florence Nightingale, Josephine Butler, and Annie Besant decisively accelerated the pace at which changes in laws and customs were effected, but it is also evident that much of the progress towards fully-fledged citizenship, particularly in the fields of education, employment and civic suffrage, was prompted not so much by the activities of the militants, as by the pressure exerted by the sheer existence of an ever-increasing female population.

Throughout the second half of Victoria's reign, the laws relating to married women underwent steady, if slow, improvement. Although, as we saw, the original Married Women's Property Bill of 1857 was scuppered by the introduction of the first Matrimonial Causes Act, it was finally made law in 1870. Two further Acts followed in 1882 and 1893, the latter making it possible for Arthur Cleveland, author of *Women Under The English Law* (1896), to write – '[A married woman] can now acquire, hold and dispose of any property, real or personal, as her private property, as if she were a single woman, without the intervention of any trustee. In fact, at the present day, the law gives the husband no rights whatever over the property of his wife.' These laws also remedied a number of other disabilities: for example, wives were granted the right to embark on legal proceedings without their husbands' permission, and the right to make contracts in their own name.

In case too rosy a picture of the wife's position is inferred from these magnanimous legal gestures, it should be noted that it was not until 1891 that the judgement made in the Cochrane case of 1840 was reversed. A certain Mrs Cochrane had left her husband but had been tricked into returning to his house only to find herself incarcerated there; the courts condoned Mr Cochrane's behaviour by declaring that a husband's rights over his wife included 'enforced co-habitation and a common residence'. A similar situation arose in 1891 when a Mrs Jackson left her husband, refusing to obey an order for the restitution of conjugal rights, and was also recaptured and held prisoner. Flying in the face of public opinion, the Court of Appeal ruled that no one had the right to imprison another, and that the supposed right 'of a husband over his wife in respect of personal chastisement' could not be regarded as legally sanctioned.

The fundamentally unjust principle on which the divorce laws were founded was not altered until the twentieth century, but a number of adjustments were made to the Act of 1858. In 1878 a further Matrimonial Causes Act was introduced which gave magistrates the power to grant a separation order and maintenance to a wife on the ground of aggravated assault. This law was designed to provide protection for working-class wives who were discovered to be dying in alarming numbers at the hands of brutal husbands, particularly in Liverpool where a certain area had earned itself the nickname of 'The Kicking District'. The Maintenance of Wives (Desertion) Act of 1886, which legislated that deserting husbands could be summoned to pay £2 a week, was also intended to bring relief to the poor. Its effectiveness was, however, severely impaired not only by the usual difficulties associated with extracting money on a regular basis from disenchanted husbands, but also by the courts' reluctance to enforce maintenance orders.

One of the most significant changes to come over the middle-class wife's way of life was the reduction of the size of her family. In 1878 Charles Bradlaugh and Annie Besant won a celebrated legal victory and put a stop to the authorities' century-old policy of proscribing birth-control literature (see chapter 10). Capitalizing on their success, they proceeded to publish a sixpenny booklet written by

Mrs Besant herself which explained in simple language, but considerable detail, the various contraceptive techniques then available. With the help of the Malthusian League, Mrs Besant also set about disseminating birth-control information throughout the country. They delivered innumerable lectures, issued a monthly journal, and distributed and sold huge quantities of books and pamphlets. Mrs Besant's own book had sold 175,000 copies by 1891, and it has been estimated that between 1876 and 1891 more than a million items of contraceptive literature passed into the hands of the public. Although their propaganda was aimed directly at the working classes, it was middle-class wives who first learnt to use contraceptives. The national birth-rate fell continuously throughout the period 1871–1900, but by far the biggest drops were recorded among the middle and professional classes, whose average family sizes decreased from seven or eight to two or three children.

Most writers on the subject advised women to use contraceptives which they themselves could control; the psychological impact of this completely new dimension of independence was revolutionary. Not only were wives suddenly released from the physically debilitating treadmill of pregnancy and childbirth, but they were also free to devote much more of their time and energy to their own interests. For the first time in the history of monogamy, wives had obtained the means of liberating themselves from the tyranny of reproduction, and they could at last regard their husbands' sexual attentions as a medium of pleasure, rather than as an instrument of subjugation. By the same token, they learnt to think of their own bodies as sources of pleasure, and to respect, not fear, their sexuality. Thus, the introduction of contraception may be considered one of the factors principally responsible for the self-confidence which women increasingly enjoyed during this period.

The educational facilities available to women were transformed in the course of these years; indeed, they had scarcely existed before. In the first half of the century, such education as girls had been exposed to had been dispensed at home by governesses. In 1850, however, Frances Mary Buss started the North London Collegiate School and twenty years later effectively founded the first public day-school for girls. The Girls' Public Day School Company was then launched in order to establish schools where girls could receive as sound an education as that provided for boys in grammar schools; by the mid 'eighties twenty schools modelled on the North London

Collegiate had been opened. A number of girls' boarding schools
were also founded, following the example set by Cheltenham Ladies'
College under the headship of Dorothea Beale.

Courses were opened to women at a dozen universities, but it was
some time before they could obtain degrees. From 1879 London
University offered all its degrees and prizes to women, and it was
one of the first to do so. By 1886 Oxford and Cambridge between
them had five women's colleges; the women students were not
admitted as members of either university, but were permitted to
attend lectures and take degrees. It was not long before they began
to take high places in the class lists: in 1887 Miss Agneta Ramsay
was placed above the Senior Classic at Cambridge, and three years
later Miss Philippa Fawcett was placed above the Senior Wrangler.

The foundation of these few institutions did not of course provide
education for more than a tiny minority of middle-class girls, but
their continuing existence and the high level of performance
attained by their students enforced two vital principles: first, that
girls deserved to be educated no less than boys, and secondly, that
girls were capable of competing at the same academic standard as
boys. Schools where young ladies were taught 'accomplishments'
(flower arranging, needlework, sketching, etc.) continued to
flourish, but, as Duncan Crow, author of *The Victorian Woman*
(1971), commented, 'into the inanity of this sort of so-called education there was now injected a cadre of proper learning'.

Although the professions displayed a marked reluctance to extend
their hospitality to women, a number of women had succeeded in
qualifying as engineers by the end of the century, and 264 women
doctors were reported to be on the register in 1895. Since a feminine
tradition already existed in teaching and nursing these professions
naturally attracted the most women. The army and navy refused
admittance to women until they needed them during the First
World War, and it was not until 1922 that the first woman was called
to the Bar. Women who had neither the money nor the education to
qualify for these relatively demanding careers found jobs as clerks or
'typewriters'; the 1891 census revealed that 17,859 women were
working as clerks or secretaries. The Post Office was quick to
utilize this new work force, but it was not long before all employers
of large clerical staffs came to see and exploit the advantages of
hiring workers who could be paid less than men, but could be given
the same responsibilities.

In 1902, Clara Collet, author of *Educated Working Women*, wrote:

> More and more it is being recognized by parents that girls should be fitted to be self-supporting; and the tendency among the girls themselves is to concentrate their energies on the profession they take up, and to regard marriage as a possibility which may some day call them away from the path they are pursuing . . . there is now the least excuse for the woman who marries merely to obtain a livelihood.[5]

Her statement must be treated more as a manifesto than as an accurate account of things as they stood in that year. However, by that time, men and women alike could not escape an awareness of the fact that the days of masculine patronage were numbered. Middle-class women had gone to work, as yet only in small numbers, but the day when they would be able entirely to free themselves of the support of fathers and families was clearly foreseeable.

Mrs Emmeline Pankhurst did not form her suffragist organization, the Women's Social and Political Union, until 1903, and the struggle to secure the parliamentary vote for women belongs therefore to Edwardian, not Victorian history. Women had, however, acquired a modicum of political and civic rights during the preceding thirty years. By 1900 they were able to fill a number of public posts, including overseer, guardian, churchwarden, governor of a workhouse, surveyor of highways, inspector of factories, member of a school board and member of a parish council. From the late 'eighties they were entitled to vote in most municipal elections. But they were still not allowed to become county councillors, Members of Parliament, mayors or jurors.

Prior to the late eighteen-sixties, those women who had wished to extend their energies and influence beyond their immediate domestic province had been obliged to confine themselves to charitable and religious work, or nursing, a profession virtually invented by Florence Nightingale and for which she had won the guarded blessing of respectability. The philanthropic tradition was maintained throughout the century, and reached a kind of apogee with women like Beatrice Webb, née Potter, who assisted Charles Booth with his survey of poverty in London, and worked as a voluntary social worker in the East End, finally adopting Fabianism as her creed. But, during the period in question, women also played an increasingly energetic and forceful part in public life. A variety of causes was strenuously taken up, but none inspired the dogged fortitude and administrative flair that was brought to those campaigns that were fought over issues which most closely concerned women themselves.

One controversy in particular kept fresh for more than twenty years the subject of women and the unjust treatment they received from men, and that was the repeal of the Contagious Diseases Acts. In the early 'sixties it came to the attention of the authorities that venereal disease was rife among Her Majesty's troops, and legislation was accordingly drawn up to check and reduce the incidence of infection. In 1864, 1866 and 1869, without debate or the raising of a single objection in either House, a series of Acts was passed empowering the police and magistrates in certain garrison towns to inspect women suspected of being prostitutes and to detain in hospital those thought to be diseased. At one stage it was suggested that the whole country should be subject to these regulations. The Acts were treated as a declaration of war by feminists, and under the leadership of Mrs Josephine Butler the Ladies' National Association for the Repeal of the Contagious Diseases Acts was founded in 1869.

Mrs Butler had already demonstrated her remarkable qualities in her selfless work among prostitutes in Liverpool. She was an active supporter of women's education, married women's right to control their own property and women's suffrage, and was therefore admirably suited for the task which was to preoccupy her for the next decade and a half. The National Association's attack on the Acts was based on the conviction that certain women were being denied their civil rights and that the innocent were endangered as much as the guilty; the Association also maintained that the Acts were directed against the poorer classes and that prostitutes, rather than their clients, were open to persecution. Mrs Butler's objections were concentrated upon the moral implications of the Acts: she believed that the solution lay in curing the viciousness of men and women and not in a system which provided for the state regulation of vice. She was in no doubt that destitution was the principal cause of prostitution. Poverty among women, she argued, was the result of the lack of employment available to women and the appallingly low wages paid to seamstresses and other female workers, and these conditions, in their turn, were directly related to the absence of educational and training facilities for women. She ascribed the blame for this lamentable state of affairs to the fact that society was dominated by men, and that women were forbidden to take any part in government or public affairs.

When questioned by the Royal Commission that was set up to investigate the Association's complaints, she made it clear that, while she was almost indifferent to the efforts made to curb the disease, she was most concerned to denounce and root out the double standard of morality sanctified by the Acts. In answer to one of the Commissioners' questions, she said, 'Well, if you only give us equal laws we will not complain. Let your laws be put in force, but let them be for male as well as female, and let them include civilian gentlemen.' And in response to another question, she remarked, 'Recollect, however, that they [infected persons] cannot spread this disease except through the wilful concurrence of the person infected by a sinful act . . . Men and women can avoid that disease by voluntary self-control, and I think it is a mischief to meddle with it at all.'[6]

The government responded to the National Association's initial protests by appointing a Royal Commission to assess the efficacy of the Acts; it recommended minor adjustments which were not implemented. Mrs Butler and her allies only redoubled their efforts. In 1879 the government was forced to review the situation again; a Select Committee was set up which heard and considered the evidence of a multitude of witnesses, but found itself unable to reach any unanimous opinion. In the event, it was the minority report that proved most influential, and in 1883 the Acts were suspended.

Meanwhile, Mrs Butler had joined forces with the Salvation Army and had opened a new front by launching a formidable assault on the white slave trade. Her allegations were supported by a Select Committee of the House of Lords, and as a result a Bill was introduced raising the age of consent to sixteen. It foundered twice in the Commons. In desperation Mrs Butler turned to W. T. Stead, editor of the *Pall Mall Gazette*, who promptly exposed the trade and all its attendant horrors in a series of sensational articles entitled 'The Maiden Tribute of Modern Babylon'. Stead was sent to gaol for his pains, but not a month after the publication of his articles the Criminal Law Amendment Act (1885) was passed, which raised the age of consent and tightened up the laws relating to brothels and their owners. This Act and the repeal of the Contagious Diseases Acts a year later brought Mrs Butler's wars to victorious conclusion.

Needless to say, none of these stirring episodes was neglected by the press; the activities of the Commissions and Committees, their reports and the subsequent debates in both Houses were all dutifully reproduced in the news pages, only to be pontificated upon in editorials and redebated with fresh fervour in the correspondence columns. Nor were Mrs Butler and her Association slow to exploit any opportunity of publicizing their cause. They attracted to their side some very eloquent support, not least the voice and pen of J. Stuart Mill, and much time and energy were devoted to writing and distributing pamphlets, gathering signatures to petitions and making speeches. Their battles were by no means confined to committee rooms and the floor of the House, and their public meetings were frequently the scene of outbursts of violence – on one occasion Mrs Butler barely escaped death at the hands of a rioting mob.

Owing to the dramatic nature of so many of the incidents that formed the stormy narrative of the twenty or so years between the passing of the Acts and their repeal, no one who read a newspaper and took an interest in current events could fail to be aware of this controversy. In previous decades, the business of putting pressure on governments, getting questions asked in the House and generally adding a voice to the expression of public opinion, had been considered masculine occupations, but the Contagious Diseases debate granted conversational franchise, if no more, to any woman capable of reading a newspaper. Here was a cause that not only had for its heart the protection of women's civil liberties, but also had for its leader a woman of outstanding intelligence and unimpeachable reputation, who numbered among her lieutenants as many women as men, and who could be seen to be challenging and beating men at their own game. By provoking women into meditating upon their position in society, and by continually pointing out the iniquities of the male regime, Mrs Butler undoubtedly hastened the march of emancipation.

The years between 1870 and Victoria's death in 1901 were, as we have seen, fraught with turmoil and anxiety. Men and women alike were obliged to come to terms with changes in almost all aspects of their social and economic life; none was more disturbing and carried further-reaching implications than the radical alteration in relationships between the sexes. These alterations were experienced by women with roughly equal measures of exhilaration and alarm; for the majority of men, however, the balance fell all too heavily on the side of alarm.

5

Perseus and Andromeda

As the ratio of power between the sexes began its gradual swing towards equilibrium, a process yet to be completed, and as both men and women came to acknowledge and adjust themselves to the fact that the days of absolute masculine rule were numbered, so the character of the ideal woman and the mythology surrounding her underwent a series of reinterpretations.

During the last thirty years or so of Victoria's reign women succeeded in slowly wringing greater and greater concessions from their recalcitrant men-folk, but it would be wrong to suppose that middle-class women considered themselves to be at war with their husbands, fathers and brothers, or that men, in their turn, felt themselves to be under continual siege from the women in their families. Changes in social habits and ways of thinking do not mature at an even pace, but tend to evolve fitfully and inconsistently. Nevertheless, the inexorable trend towards emancipation did call forth from the majority of men a spirit of dogged resistance.

Discounting for the moment those who resorted to bellowing 'humbug' at every fresh outbreak of feminism, and those few who positively welcomed the dawn of liberation, let us examine one or two champions of masculine supremacy who absorbed the disagreeable exigencies of their day and yet were able to devise new schemes for shoring up the old regime.

The Painter's Image
With only a handful of exceptions, all visual images were created by men, whether they took the form of oil paintings, book, magazine or newspaper illustrations, cartoons, advertisements or even fashion plates. This factor is of course common to most cultures, including our own, but it assumed especial poignancy during the period in question, for those years witnessed the appearance of two seemingly unrelated phenomena which turned out to have a profound effect upon each other.

The Victorian public of the 'seventies, 'eighties and 'nineties was exposed to an unprecedented and ever-increasing proliferation of visual images; such was the first phenomenon. The presence of huge conglomerations of ill-educated people, potential but under-exploited consumers, had stimulated the rapid development of printing and mechanical engraving techniques which had made possible the mass production of printed materials of all kinds, including pictorial advertisements, photographs and reproductions of paintings. By the early 'eighties colour printing was able to accommodate the complex tones of an oil painting. Graphic designers, commercial artists and painters were all alerted to and exhilarated by the sudden and enormous expansion of their audience. For the first time in the history of printing, the visual image was rendered almost as powerful a medium of communication as the word.

The same generation of Victorians, recipients of this intoxicating new dimension to their culture, were also coming to terms, albeit ungracefully, with the second phenomenon under discussion – the emancipation of women.

Under these circumstances, it was impossible for an artist, no matter at what level of seriousness he was working, to create an ingenuous representation of a woman; by making an image of a woman, regardless of its specific context, he was unavoidably committing himself to the expression of his attitude to the 'woman question'. There can be no such thing as an objective image; equally, there can be no such thing as a neutral image. Very few artists have succeeded in transcending the immediate historical circumstances in which they lived and worked, and most artists, for that matter, have wished actively to comment on the social and intellectual conditions of their times. Certainly the majority of Victorian artists considered it their duty to offer their opinion on the state of society as they saw it; like their novelist contemporaries, they proceeded from a moral standpoint. During this period the question of the social role of women and their true nature was too urgent and controversial, and the performance of artists too public, to permit any pictorial treatment of woman to be anything but a contribution to the general debate.

Only by appreciating the formidable prestige enjoyed by Victorian artists can the significance of their comments on public issues be understood. It was within the reach of a fashionable painter to earn extraordinarily high sums, and this capacity alone won him much respect. At the height of his fame Millais was reputed to earn between £20,000 and £40,000 a year, and he is said to have sold his 'North West Passage' for £4,700. Holman Hunt probably achieved a record by selling a replica of his 'Light of the World' to Charles Booth for 12,000 guineas. When he died, Hunt left £163,000, every penny of which had been earned by painting, and at least three Victorian artists, Landseer, Linnell, and John Gilbert, left more than £200,000.[1] A number of artists were knighted, a few were created baronets and one was elevated to the peerage; G. F. Watts refused all offers but finally succumbed by accepting the Order of Merit. Seven artists, including the Dutch Alma Tadema, were posthumously honoured with graves in St Paul's Cathedral.

The intensity of public interest in art may be gauged by the number of galleries which were opened during the last two decades of the century. In London the present National Portrait Gallery (1896), the National Gallery of British Art (1897, enlarged 1899) and the Wallace Collection (1900) were founded and the National Gallery itself was extended (1887). In the provinces large municipal collections and galleries were established in Liverpool (1877), Manchester (1882) and Birmingham (1885). The trustees of these institutions attempted to represent all schools and nations in their collections, but it was the work of contemporary British artists which proved most popular with the public. Pictures which had been acclaimed in London were often sent on exhibition round the country and attracted lengthy queues at provincial galleries.

It was, however, through the mass-marketing of engravings that artists emphatically impressed themselves on the popular imagination. William Frith was commissioned to record the Prince of Wales's wedding for a fee of 3,000 guineas, but he is believed to have collected a further 5,000 guineas from the sale of his copyright to the dealer Flatow who arranged for the publication of reproductions and, no doubt, recouped his money many times over. Engravings of such favourites as Holman Hunt's 'Light of the World', Landseer's 'Monarch of the Glen' and Frith's 'The Railway Station' were to be found in hundreds of thousands of homes and schools. In 1879, John Millais, perhaps the most commercially successful painter of his day, exhibited 'Cherry Ripe', a portrait of a little girl in fancy dress, and the following year *The Graphic* offered it for sale in the form of a colour reproduction. 600,000 copies were sold and orders were received for a million.

As printing techniques improved and manufacturers learnt to place more and more faith in the power of graphic design to sell their goods, the advertising industry came into its own. Not surprisingly advertisers looked to painters for guidance and inspiration and it was only natural that painters, in their turn, allowed themselves to be persuaded to lease their services and popularity to this new medium. Messrs Pears, the soap manufacturers, were deeply impressed by the sales statistics of 'Cherry Ripe' and in 1885 they approached Millais and requested his permission to use his 'Bubbles', a portrait of a four-year-old boy fortuitously blowing soap bubbles through a clay pipe, as an advertisement. At first the great man demurred, not wishing to soil his reputation, but in time he relented and convinced himself that this gesture on his part would benefit 'thousands of poor people' by introducing them to real art. As a piece of publicity for both the manufacturers and the painter, the advertisement turned out to be a master-stroke: Pears was translated into a household word, and such lustre as could be was added to Millais' name.[2]

Painters, in short, were very great men, and their interpreting eye – a male eye, it must always be remembered – helped to shape the attitudes of the public who flocked to study and applaud their works.

The Olympian

Of all the great men who bestrode the Academy, the noblest by common assent was Frederic Leighton.[3]

This Titan was born in 1830 into a wealthy medical family. His father undertook his education and instilled in him a thorough knowledge of the Greek and Latin languages and of the legends, poems, and history of the ancient world. In 1840 Mrs Leighton was advised to travel for the sake of her health and the whole family embarked on an odyssey round the resorts and beauty spots of Europe. Dr Leighton lost no opportunity of introducing his precocious son to the art and architecture of the many countries they visited and, hoping that Frederic would one day take up his own profession, he instructed him in anatomy, requiring him to draw from memory, with scrupulous accuracy, the bones and muscles he had learnt to identify. At the age of fourteen Frederic disconcertingly announced that his ambition was to be an artist. His father confided this alarming news to a sculptor-friend. 'Shall I make him a painter?' 'Sir', his friend replied, 'you cannot help yourself; nature has made him so already. Let him aim for the highest, he will be certain to get there.' So positive a prophecy was not to be ignored and Dr Leighton accordingly dispatched his prodigy to the Florentine Academy. He subsequently studied in Brussels, in Frankfurt under the Nazarene painter Steinle, and in Rome.

In 1855 he submitted a picture – his colossal 'Cimabue's Madonna' – to the Royal Academy in London for the first time. It was hung in a prominent position and pronounced 'very important and very beautiful' by that scourge of mediocrity, John Ruskin. On the first day of the exhibition, however, it was accorded an even greater accolade, for it was purchased by the Queen herself for 600 guineas.

The brilliance with which Leighton made his début was to characterize the remainder of his career. He may not have been the richest English painter of the nineteenth century, although he became very wealthy, but he was probably the most handsome and certainly the most honoured. In 1864 he was elected Associate of the Academy and in 1869 an Academician; in 1878 he was both knighted and elected President of the Academy, an office he upheld with exemplary punctilio; in 1886 he was created a baronet and in 1896 he was elevated to the peerage, taking the title Leighton of Stretton. A multitude of other acclamations and dignities were showered upon him during his lifetime and when he died he was buried with much pomp in St Paul's Cathedral.

The President conducted his life on a scale of grandeur befitting his pre-eminent destiny. When not in London fulfilling his official duties and executing masterpieces, he spent his time abroad, travelling compulsively – if so extreme a phrase may be applied to so temperate a man – covering huge distances at astonishing speeds. He felt a special affinity for the Mediterranean countries, visiting them frequently and bringing home the trophies and *objets d'art* that contributed so much to the splendour of the mansion he built for himself.[4] He made many friends in England and Europe, even if none could claim him as an intimate, and he seems never to have made an enemy. He was, to borrow a phrase from Henry James, never less than 'first – extraordinarily first – essentially at the top of the list and head of the table'.

Leighton's career is easily documented; his personality, however, remains frustratingly obscure, for it is impossible to detach the man from the insignia of fame and cloaks of office. A self-portrait may reasonably be expected to throw light on the character of its creator, but Leighton's, painted in 1881 for the Uffizi Gallery, appears to have been designed in order to enhance, not unravel, the enigma. Resplendent in his presidential robes, seated before a section of the Parthenon frieze, his fine brow mantled in classical curls, Leighton majestically surveys the spectator looking up at him. The persona embodied in this portrait communicates a serene consciousness of being the object of awed speculation, and at the same time positively defies intrusive analysis. Henry James found himself both puzzled and fascinated by this absence of any discernible inner identity and he used Leighton as the basis of one of his characters, Lord Mellifont, the central figure in a story entitled 'The Private Life' (1892). He wrote of Leighton/Mellifont that he seemed to be 'all public', with 'no corresponding private life'.

Suffice it to say that his life was a flawless pattern of success. No trace of unseemliness ruffled his stately calm, no indulgence or frailty impeded his inexhaustible energy and no crisis interrupted his smooth ascent to the summit. He never married, asserting that he was 'married to his art', and no whiff of scandal or intimation of forbidden tastes has ever adhered to his name. His emotional energies appear to have been completely absorbed by his professional activities, and it was with no sense of irony that he instructed those who gathered round his death-bed to 'give my love to the Academy'.

The Neo-Classicist

While studying in Rome Leighton had dutifully inspected the sites and relics of the city and we know that he read Benjamin Robert Haydon's *Autobiography and Journals*, responding sympathetically to the author's passionate plea for a revival of the classical spirit in art. We also know that he met John Gibson, the sculptor and fanatical advocate of neo-classicism, who had been a pupil of the great Danish neo-classical sculptor Thorvaldsen. But it was not until the early 'sixties that his love for Greek art and its values kindled and took flame. He had by then visited Greece and the Hellenic Islands, an experience that left few Victorians unmoved, and had returned to look with new eyes at the Elgin marbles in the British Museum. During this period he formed a close friendship with George Frederick Watts, the 'highest' of Victorian artists and a fervent believer in the supremacy of the Greek ideal of beauty, and his influence did much to consolidate Leighton's blossoming enthusiasm. By 1864, the year he was elected an Associate of the Academy, he had wholeheartedly committed himself to neo-classicism and for the rest of his life his *oeuvre* was to be dominated by themes derived directly from Greek legends.

In 1861, following the Risorgimento, the Italian government instituted the first systematic excavations of Herculaneum and Pompeii, and Leighton was by no means the only artist to investigate the results. 'What a display it is!' he wrote, 'here we are admitted into the most intimate privacy of a multitude of Pompeian houses – the kitchens, the pantries, the cellars of the contemporaries of the Plinies have here no secret for us.'[5] His reaction was characteristically Victorian: he immediately recognized the similarities between the day-to-day life of ancient Pompeii, so perfectly preserved by the volcanic ash, and the London of his own time. Unlike certain neo-classical artists, Alma-Tadema for example, Leighton was, however, no purveyor of glamorized nostalgia. When he painted, he did so in order to inspire and teach. He extolled the perfections of classical beauty in order that they should be striven after and emulated. It was no part of his artistic purpose to provide a mirror in which his contemporaries might perceive flattering images of themselves in antique costume; on the contrary, his art comprised a series of idealized models to which he hoped the higher-minded among his public might be encouraged to aspire.

In his Presidential address of 1878 he expounded his faith in Hellenic idealism and defined its qualities: 'It is first that the stirring aesthetic instinct, the impulse towards an absolute need of beauty, was universal with it, and lay, a living force, at the root of its emotional being; and secondly, that the Greeks were conscious of this impulse as a just source of pride and a sign of their supremacy among the nations.' On another occasion he declared that he believed the genius of Greek art lay in 'its nobility and its serenity, its exquisite balance, its searching after truth, and its thirst for the ideal.' But, although Hellenic in origin, the truth he sought was Victorian by application. His ideal was that pitch of spiritual excellence exalted by all Victorian moralists, and he added to it the

4   Frederic Leighton, *Perseus and Andromeda* (see page 86)

5 Hablot K. Browne (Phiz), *Our Housekeeping* (see page 35)

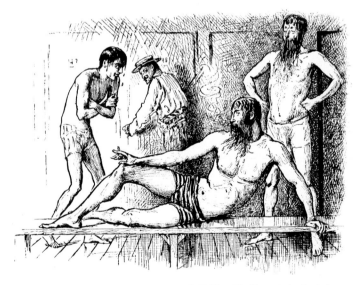

6 George Du Maurier, *Little Billee, Taffy and the Laird at the Baths* (see page 127)

neo-classical conviction that moral truth was to be represented at its most sublime, and in its most heroic form, when enshrined in the perfected beauty of the human body, specifically the nude female body. He underlined this point in a Discourse delivered in 1883, leaving his audience in no doubt as to the immediate relevance of his theme: 'In the art of the Periclean Age, of which high truthfulness was one of its noblest attributes ... we find a new ideal of balanced form, wholly Aryan and of which the only parallel I know is sometimes found in the women of another Aryan race – your own.'

Victorian Venus

One of his first attempts at presenting woman in idealized form was his picture, 'Venus Disrobing for the Bath' (see illustration), which he painted in 1867. Apart from a piece of drapery looped around one arm, his Venus is naked. She is in the act of slipping off her right sandal with her left foot. Her right arm rests awkwardly on a high wall roughly level with her head, while her left arm lies across her abdomen as her hand steadies her knee. This pose is completely contrived and cannot be held without discomfort for more than a few seconds; it has the effect of painfully twisting her body around the axis of her waist, so that her rib-cage, breasts and shoulders which form one plane appear to have been wrenched away from the other plane formed by her pelvis and hips.

Far from creating an image of serenity and exquisite balance, the qualities he had so deeply admired in classical statuary, Leighton had constructed a pose remarkable for its fractured ungainliness. In most classical renderings the Venus holds up her head so that her gaze can confront that of the spectator. Leighton, however, has made his Venus look down at her feet. Those classical versions of Venus, supposedly based on the Cnidian Venus by Praxiteles, in which the goddess carried a piece of drapery with one hand and held the other in front of her pelvis, were designed in such a way that her pelvis was not concealed, but simply shielded. But Leighton has obliged his Venus to clamp her left arm rigidly across her genitals, ensuring the total obstruction of the spectator's view. Furthermore, this arm provides the dominant line of the picture, its strength being reinforced by the angle of her gaze and the combined downward power of the pillars which frame the scene. All sense of harmony is dispelled by the positioning of her arm, which instead of protecting, effectively splits her body. The unnatural disposition of her shoulders and arms brings into prominence her breasts, placing them on display, and at the same time obliterates her genitals.

Why did Leighton choose to compose his picture in this way? Why did he create a symbol of sexuality – Venus was after all the goddess of love – which amounted to a destruction, not a glorification, of the female body? The female breasts and sexual organs are the two major foci of male desire, but they stimulate different emotional responses. Breasts are the exteriorized, visual emblems of maternity, and therefore of femininity; their softness and roundness, their appearance of having been added to the basic human form, serve as a reminder of woman's comparative physical frailty. In an age which seeks to confine women by stressing their weakness in relation to men and their dependence on men, breasts assume a crucial significance as the symbols of female vulnerability. The pubic area, however, represents an interiorized possibility; the sexual function of the vagina is to be penetrated, it promises to enclose the male organ and, in this respect, offers a challenge, for its promise cannot be fulfilled unless potency is achieved and sustained. In an age when men wish to subjugate women, but doubt their ability to do so, the female sex organs acquire a threatening character, and artists tend to castrate the women they portray by eliminating or masking their pubic areas. This is generally effected either by excising the *mons veneris* through the agency of a piece of drapery or foliage, or, more perniciously, by making the woman cover herself and thereby convey a sense of shame calculated to soothe male fears and gratify the masculine thirst for superiority.

It was in such an age that Leighton lived and worked. Although in 1867 masculine authority over women in law and custom was virtually absolute, it was by no means universally accepted as a valid principle. The long-subdued power of women was beginning defiantly to assert itself. The battle was scarcely under way when Leighton painted his Venus, and as yet men had been forced to concede very little, but nevertheless a virulent sense of anxiety had already been injected into the male sexual consciousness, a sense which over the next thirty years was to attain epidemic proportions. Something of the doubts and fears felt by men at this time are reflected in Leighton's adaptation of the classical Venus. He concentrated attention on the fragile, vulnerable part of her body – the breasts – while disuniting them from the dangerous, minatory part. He rendered her sexuality absolutely powerless by driving a shaft (her arm) through the centre of her body. And he rendered her not only physically but psychologically powerless by twisting her head so that she is forced to survey her own, self-inflicted castration.

The female body and its sexual potential exercised a compulsive hold over his creative imagination for the rest of his long and productive life; he devoted the majority of his works painted after 1867 to the portrayal of the nude or semi-nude figure, generally choosing as his subjects mythological heroines and goddesses. Indeed, the neo-classical revival that took place in late nineteenth-century England, of which Leighton was the acknowledged leader, distinguished itself from earlier revivals by the obsessive frequency with which its exponents, notably Lawrence Alma-Tadema and Albert Moore, depicted the female nude. It was Leighton, however, who developed and expressed the loftiest notion of the painter's role and duty to the public. In answering the charge that his pictures lacked passion, he sternly pointed out that the task of the artist was to maintain a sense of responsibility in relation to the emotional impact of his work; the more conscientiously he fulfilled this obligation, the greater his opportunity of elevating rather than depraving his spectator. He had specifically stated that he saw a direct line of inheritance between the faultlessly formed women of ancient Greece and the female members of his own, Aryan race. Through the medium of his goddesses and heroines he placed before his audience an idealized vision of woman; this he urged on his female spectators, while encouraging the men to seek it in their wives and inculcate it in their daughters. But like most models recommended to Victorian women for their edification, Leighton's appeared to confer sublimity while in reality it sought to preserve traditional submissiveness.

His true intention is immediately exposed when the mythological episodes he selected are examined *en bloc*. By and large they fall into two definable categories: one type of picture depicted women in states of defenceless but self-observing nakedness, and the other depicted them in states of helpless dependence on masculine enterprise.

His most explicit articulation of the first theme was contained in a picture exhibited in 1890 entitled 'The Bath of Psyche',[6] (see illustration) which according to Ernest Rhys was one of his most popular and widely reproduced works. The design of this painting is reminiscent of the 1867 'Venus': the figure of the goddess is framed between two pillars, a dark curtain hangs between them and above it a summery sky can be seen. Psyche stands at the brink of a pool; she is lifting her white robe above her head and, as she does so, she turns to look at her reflection mirrored on the surface of the water, twisting her torso towards the spectator to display the length of her naked body. The mood of the picture is relaxed and peaceful; the goddess studies her reflection with evident pleasure.

In his book *Ways of Seeing* John Berger wrote that the mirror was often used in pictures portraying nude women as a symbol of their vanity. He contended, however, that the moralizing involved was mostly hypocritical: 'You painted a naked woman because you enjoyed looking at her, you put a mirror in her hand and you called the painting "Vanity", thus condemning the woman whose nakedness you had depicted for your own pleasure. The real function of the mirror was otherwise. It was to make the woman connive in treating herself as, first and foremost, a sight.' We can feel the force of this argument when we apply it to Leighton's 'Psyche', particularly since he has provided so enormous a mirror in the form of the pool. He frequently employed this device; it can be seen in 'The Frigidarium', for instance, where an unnamed girl dressed in a diaphanous robe simply stands beside a pool looking at her own reflection, and in 'The Bracelet' where it is exploited more insidiously – a little girl holding a box with a mirror in its lid sits at the feet of a woman who is preparing to undress.

Berger also showed that behind most nude paintings of women lay the implication that the subject is aware of being seen by the spectator, and that the spectator is presumed to be a man. 'Everything is addressed to him. Everything must appear to be the result of his being there. It is for him that the figures have assumed their nudity . . . Women are there to feed an appetite, not to have any of their own.' A glance at Leighton's pictures confirms the truth of Berger's observation: his women are invariably posed for the benefit and delectation of a presence outside their depicted situation and in front of the canvas. The effect of painting a woman who is conscious of being looked at and who indicates her acquiescence is to render her a willing prisoner, an effect Leighton undoubtedly wished to create.

Leighton was anxious to impress on his audience his belief that women should lay down their arms, which by 1890 they were wielding with lethal skill, and resume their traditionally passive social and domestic role. This he idealized by invoking the spirit of classical legend. If women identified themselves and were identified with the mythological heroines he so glamorously recreated they would once again learn to take a pride in their beauty and in men's desire to contemplate it. He was always at pains to stress that beauty was by no means a simple fleshly phenomenon but, on the contrary, a moral quality. His 'Psyche' exemplified the attitude he wished women to take towards themselves: she exposes her body to the spectator and at the same time collaborates in the treatment of her body as a spectacle by looking at herself with unmistakable satisfaction; in Berger's phrase, she connives. She obediently, but willingly, surrenders herself to the inspection of the male spectator whose authority over her she tacitly endorses.

Both the context and the significance of the legendary scenes he evoked would have been immediately understood by his middle-class audience whose education had been based on the study of classical literature. It is therefore worth briefly rehearsing Psyche's story. She was the youngest and fairest daughter of a certain king and queen. Her beauty excited the jealousy of Aphrodite (Venus) who instructed her son Cupid to inspire in Psyche sudden love for some unworthy creature. He unfortunately bungled the job by wounding himself with his own arrow and falling in love with his intended victim. Time passed and her sisters got married, but the lovely Psyche remained unwooed. Her parents, understandably distressed, consulted an oracle and were told that Psyche's husband, a monster, was waiting for her on the summit of a nearby mountain. She insisted on meeting her fate and was accordingly deposited on the mountain top whence she was whisked away to a flowery valley and a palace more splendid than her father's. Although she saw no one, she heard soothing voices inviting her to bathe and eat. This is the moment that Leighton picked for his picture: Psyche is un-dressing to bathe and prepare herself for the husband whose name she does not know and whose face she is not permitted to behold.[7]

There is no need to do more than point to the obvious parallel between Psyche's plight and that of many a Victorian bride, and note that Leighton explicitly endorsed the situation by investing his Psyche's face with an expression of narcissism.

The picture which best illustrates Leighton's use of legend to

depict women in states of dependence on masculine initiative is his
'Perseus and Andromeda' (see illustration); it was exhibited in 1891
(the year after Psyche).[8] Andromeda was the daughter of a vain queen
who provoked the wrathful Poseidon into sending a sea-monster to
ravage her husband's kingdom. An oracle declared that the monster
could only be appeased by the sacrifice of their daughter. Andromeda was duly taken to a rock jutting out to sea and bound to it with
heavy chains. As luck would have it, Perseus was flying by at the
time and caught sight of her hair waving in the sea-breeze. He was so
struck by her beauty that he decided to rescue her from the clutches
of the monster. First, however, he struck a bargain with her parents
who agreed to let him marry her if he succeeded in saving her.
Leighton's picture shows the naked Andromeda writhing pitifully
in her bonds, shadowed by the monster's scaly wing, while Perseus
on his winged steed hovers above firing off arrows.[9]

Andromeda's arms are tied behind her back, her body is twisting
as she struggles and her clothes have fallen from her, leaving bare
her shoulders, breasts, abdomen and right leg. As in his 'Venus',
the plane formed by her breasts and shoulders appears to have
been torn from the lower half of her torso. Leighton has exploited
to the full the scene's inherent sadism. The point of the picture is
clear enough: without the intervention of a man, without his
protection, courage and capacity for decisive action, she would be
doomed. By 1891, women could no longer be relied on to recognize
the wisdom of looking to men for succour and support, and consequently the gospel of male superiority called for increasingly melodramatic modes of expression.

The troubled atmosphere and tortured composition of his 1867
'Venus' are not to be found in his later work which is characterized
by technical suavity and unquestioning confidence. It is also
significant that prior to that date and his neo-classical period he
chose as his subjects women notorious for their sexual aggression –
'Salome' (1857), 'The Fisherman and the Syren' (1858),[10]
'Samson and Delilah' (1859), 'Jezebel and Ahab' (1863). In the
years following the crisis that may be inferred from his 'Venus', he
consistently selected legends that either featured women who
underwent humiliation, grief, imprisonment and so on, or, on a
happier note, women who were chosen by gods and heroes for their
beauty. It is safe to say that after 1867 he never depicted women
who were other than the victims or playthings of fate. Lack of space

precludes a comprehensive list, but the following examples are representative of his use of classical mythology: 'Ariadne Abandoned by Theseus' (1868) is a study of a woman betrayed and deserted; the portraits of 'Nausicaa' (1878) and 'Psamathe' (1880) are examples of women whose mythological role was confined to possessing beauty that attracted male attention; 'The Last Watch of Hero' (1887) and 'Rizpah' (1893) are portrayals of women afflicted by grief – Hero looks out over the Hellespont where her lover, Leander, has just drowned, and Rizpah is seen protecting the bodies of her murdered sons; 'The Return of Persephone' (1891) depicts Hermes delivering Persephone, whom he has just escorted from the underworld, into the arms of her mother; 'Captive Andromache' (1888) shows the imprisoned wife of the recently slain Hector mournfully brooding as she stands in line waiting to perform the ignominious task of drawing water.

Leighton was fascinated by the goddess Clytie whom he painted in 1892 and again in the year of his death. Clytie was a beautiful maiden who fell in love with Apollo, the sun god, and spent her every day following his course across the sky; despite her ardour, she failed to win Apollo's interest and finally the gods took pity on her and turned her into a sunflower. Leighton's paintings concentrate on the moment of greatest poignancy, when the girl is at her most pathetic – the sunset. 'I have shown the goddess in adoration before the setting sun, whose last rays are permeating her whole being', he gleefully told an art critic who interviewed him only months before he died. 'With upraised arms she is entreating her beloved one not to forsake her', he said, and it is difficult not to hear a cruel note in his voice. A woman on her knees beseeching an indifferent lover was evidently an image he relished.

Leighton's eloquent expressions of what must have seemed in the 'eighties and 'nineties a fast-vanishing spirit of traditional femininity were designed to console and reinvigorate his beleaguered male audience, and to reillumine in the mind of his female audience the ideals and values enshrined in classical legend. By portraying women – goddesses and heroines all – in situations of the kind described above, he hoped to communicate to his huge public his vision of the true nature of women. The death of man, he preached, was ennobled by woman's love; though despised and rejected, her loyalty lent grace to the name of love; in a world made dark by man's bloodthirsty selfishness, her beauty radiated moral inspiration and kept alight the flame of pity. Only in an Andromeda – chained and helpless – or in a Clytie – devoted but ignored – could true femininity be found.

6

Male Self-Defence

Leighton's career spanned some forty-five or more years, but as far as his attitude to women is concerned his ideas do not appear to have greatly changed after his decisive meditations in the late eighteen-sixties. From that time onwards, the same themes are sustained with obsessive constancy and his handling of them only altered in that it steadily grew more sophisticated and confident. By studying Leighton, it is not possible to discern the radical transformations that overcame relations between the sexes during the period of his maturity, although it is possible to infer an ever-hardening determination on his part to repudiate all notions of female emancipation.

In this chapter three other examples are provided of men who fought to withstand the erosion of male supremacy. Patrick Geddes, a biologist whose most influential work was published during the eighteen-eighties, positively instructed women not to abandon their traditionally submissive social role, but like Leighton he sought to render their old enslavement attractive by subjecting it to a form of deification. Havelock Ellis, the sexologist, and Grant Allen, the biologist turned best-selling novelist, both wrote during the mid-eighteen-nineties, and both represent examples of men who acceded to the pressure of their times by attempting to grant the New Woman her due, but who in fact lent force to the old-fashioned concept of woman's essential inferiority.

The selection of these examples is not so much designed to furnish a history of the metamorphosis of man's defensive response to the feminist challenge as to indicate the degree to which male self-esteem had been shattered over the course of the forty years that separate Leighton's imperious gesture of castration made in 1867 and Ellis's cautious, even surreptitious efforts to undermine the feminists' position, which he could only effect under the guise of a flawed scientific objectivity.

This discussion opens with Darwin's summarized account of the differences between the sexes; his assessment of women's basic capabilities may be taken as that generally accepted by the laymen of his day.

Pugnacious Man – Tender Woman

In 1871 Charles Darwin published his *Descent of Man and Selection in Relation to Sex*; during the period 1871–1901 the book was revised once and reprinted twenty-four times. By the time this second, major work was completed, the *Origin of Species* had been in circulation for some twelve years and, although his theories had by no means achieved universal acceptance and were still considered controversial in many quarters, he was regarded as a figure of considerable authority.

In the final section of *Descent of Man*, which deals with man's secondary sexual characteristics, Darwin declared that 'With mankind the differences between the sexes are greater than in most of the Quadrumana,[1] but not so great as in some, for instance, the mandrill.' In describing these differences he did not confine himself to analysing the two sexes' relative physical capacities, he also defined the distinctions between their mental powers. It was not possible to do such a thing in 1871 without treading warily, and he was quick to point out that he realized that some writers doubted the existence of inherent differences; he, however, was persuaded by the analogy of the lower animals – 'no one doubts that the bull differs in disposition from the cow' – and believed that sexual selection had played an important part in the creation of these differences. 'Man', he wrote 'is more courageous, pugnacious and energetic than woman, and has a more inventive genius', while woman differed from him chiefly 'in her greater tenderness and less selfishness'. Prompted by her maternal instincts, woman displays these qualities towards her children in an eminent degree; therefore, Darwin argued with a hesitant switch of tense, 'it is likely that she would often extend them towards her fellow creatures'. It is generally admitted, he wrote in the same paragraph, that powers of intuition, rapid perception and 'perhaps' imitation are more strongly marked in women than men.

The biggest difference between the intellectual powers of the two sexes lay, however, in man's ability to do whatever he took up better than woman, whether it required 'deep thought, reason, or imagination or merely the use of the sense and hands'. He was content to infer from the law of the deviation of averages that, if men are capable of a decisive pre-eminence over women in many subjects, 'the average of mental power in man must be above that of woman'.

Primitive man had been required to engage in a series of struggles in order to gain possession of a mate, defend his family and provide them with food; the victorious outcome of these tests was dependent not on simple physical strength but on a whole range of higher mental faculties – 'courage, perseverance and determined energy' combined with 'observation, reason, invention and imagination'. These faculties have been developed in man 'partly through sexual selection – that is through the contest of rival males, and partly through natural selection – that is from success in the general struggle for life.' Although modern man no longer fights for his wife, and this particular form of selection has passed away, man does nevertheless undergo a severe struggle in order to support himself and his family which, Darwin reasoned, tends to maintain or even increase his mental powers, and also to preserve the present inequality between the sexes.

The burden of Darwin's book was to show that the human species had evolved from some less highly organized form, and to demonstrate the manner of its evolution. He devoted only a few pages to his discussion of the differences between the mental powers possessed by the two sexes, and it would be absurd to hold him up as a champion of male supremacy. He must, however, stand accused of having allowed the prejudices of his day to affect his estimation of women's intellectual capacity.

The advocates of female emancipation argued that if women were given the opportunity of putting themselves to the test they would immediately exhibit the very qualities which Darwin had ascribed exclusively to men. History has proved them correct. But, even as he wrote, millions of women were daily giving the lie to his assessment of the two sexes and their relative capabilities. The working-class inhabitants of all large towns undertook a struggle for existence, not dissimilar in its bleak and elemental simplicity to that undertaken by our savage ancestors, in an environment which owing to a complex combination of industrial and economic factors placed the responsibility for providing the family's sustenance and cohesion, not on the husband, but on the wife. Thus, nineteenth-century urban conditions extracted from working-class women those precise characteristics – courage, perseverance, determination, etc. – that Darwin had nominated as peculiar to man.[2]

Although Darwin handled the question of the fundamental differences between the sexes with gingerly restraint, he clearly felt no compunction at having accepted the stereotypes which had served throughout the century to magnify men and diminish women. By the 'eighties, however, such blithe traditionalism was inaccessible to writers, particularly to scientists. Darwin had made it clear that he had no desire to join in the feminist fight, but those who were eager to lend their scholarship to the counter-revolution were obliged to adopt positions of greater and greater extremism as increasing numbers of women proved themselves capable of fulfilling an increasing number of functions which previously had been held to be beyond their capability.

The Flagellate Sperm

Patrick Geddes,[3] a Scottish biologist, dedicated himself for nearly a decade – 1880–9 – to the task of synthesizing what was known about sex-differences and interpreting the social and economic significance of this knowledge. He was convinced that the true nature of man and woman could be seen arising from a basic difference in cell metabolism. He argued that the physical laws governing the conservation and dissipation of energy applied to all living things; at the level of the cell, maleness was characterized by the tendency to expend energy, and femaleness was distinguished by the capacity to store and build up energy. 'The hungry, active cell', he asserted, 'becomes flagellate sperm, while the quiescent, well-fed one becomes the ovum.' This theory had deeply gratifying implications for those who were offended and disturbed by the emancipation movement and by the growing reluctance of women to keep their place, for Geddes had invoked the might and wisdom of science to prove that male and female roles had been ordained in the lowest form of life; the fundamental temperaments which had developed from these original functions were, he insisted, immutable and could not be affected or altered by the temporary whims and fads thrown up by mere political or technological change.

It should not be thought that Geddes was either a crank or a nonentity; nor can he be condemned as a blind and stubborn reactionary. He falls into that category of imaginative men, with which this chapter is concerned, who acknowledged that women had a fair claim to a new social position, but who attempted to offer them an identity which, though revised, was in effect only a glamorized reinterpretation of their old inferior status.

His scholarly credentials were unimpeachable: he trained for four years under Thomas Huxley, the great popularizer of science and Darwin's most energetic apologist, served as a senior demonstrator in practical physiology at University College, London, and pursued research in the fields of botany, zoology, biology, and histology. In 1879 he planned an ambitious expedition to Mexico where he hoped to gather biological specimens; shortly after his arrival, however, he was attacked by blindness and, gravely disappointed, was forced to return home. Though he recovered his sight, he was unable to use a microscope and had no choice but to reconstruct his career: he chose to apply himself to the study of society by bringing to it a synthesis of the many branches of scientific knowledge with which he was by then equipped. The result of ten years' work along these lines was his book *The Evolution of Sex* (1879).[4] In the course of his long, closely argued work, he touched briefly on the technique and function of contraception, and inadvertently acquired a measure of notoriety, a fate common to all who so much as mentioned the existence of this inflammatory topic. Three editions were published and Geddes was able to start a summer school in Edinburgh where he lectured on evolutionary ethics. His ideas reached a large audience and were much debated; he achieved special prominence in America thanks to the efforts of his follower and popularizer, Jane Addams.[5]

His plans for future social developments based on a scientific study of sex differences were contained in the penultimate chapter of *The Evolution of Sex*, which was entitled *Psychological and Ethical Aspects*. He opened the chapter by asking his readers to admit the common ground that lay between animals and men in most of the emotions and simpler intellectual processes, pointing out that it was particularly noticeable in those emotions associated with sex and reproduction. It was, he believed, generally accepted that love – 'in the sense of sexual sympathy, psychical as well as physical' – exists among animals in many degrees of evolution, and although he conceded that humans possessed a greater emotional range, he was not prepared to agree that they had access to a correspondingly greater emotional intensity. Vague sexual attraction among the lower organisms had evolved into a definite reproductive impulse, a desire of such power that it often took precedence over even the instinct for self-preservation, and this 'enhanced by more and more subtle psychic additions' had in its turn developed into the love of the highest animals and of the average human individual.

Nor did the possibilities of evolution by any means end there. He understood that some of his readers might shrink from a comparison of human love with its animal analogies, but he argued that if we refuse to recognize the possibilities of individual and racial evolution we are forced to resign ourselves to defining 'the poet and his heroine' as exceptional creations, beyond the reach of ordinary folk. Whereas, if the idea of evolution is accepted, humanity is entitled to hope, indeed is logically compelled to embrace the assurance that 'these rare fruits of an apparently more than earthly paradise of love (such as poets sing of) . . . are yet the realities of a daily life towards which we and ours may journey.'

Putting aside the fact that neither his premises nor the reasoning behind his argument are acceptable today, it is possible to credit Geddes with an exceptionally progressive view of sexuality and its potential ability to enhance the human condition. Victorians were accustomed to thinking of the sexual emotions as dark, primeval forces, anarchic and explosive instincts, knowing no values, no morality and having no sense of good and evil, which, unless rigorously controlled, would overthrow the finer sensibilities; progress from savagery to civilization depended on the subjugation, not the release and aggrandisement of sexuality. Geddes may be counted among the first to propose sexuality as a vehicle of the nobler, humanitarian emotions, rather than of those that were atavistic and anti-social. His doing so may be seen as one of the innumerable revolutionary consequences attending the application of Darwin's basic theories to society at large.

His rhapsodic vision of an earthly paradise of love did not, however, encourage the blurring of his perception of sex-differences, and with some haste he issued a trenchant reminder of the 'deep' distinctions that separated men from women. These differences might be exaggerated or lessened, but in order to obliterate them it would be necessary to have evolution over again on a new basis. 'What was decided among the prehistoric Protozoa', he thundered, 'cannot be annulled by Act of Parliament.' He deplored the contemporary trend towards economic *laissez-faire* between the sexes on the grounds that it did no more than promote inter-sexual competition for subsistence, a piece of folly that could only have ruinous effects upon family life. The notion of equality had done good service in exposing some of the old tyrannies inherent in established sex castes, but it too must be overthrown and replaced by a 'complex and sympathetic co-operation between the differentiated sexes'. The time had come to re-emphasize, with the authority of science, not dogma, the biological factors that regulate sexual relationships – 'The social order will clear itself, as it comes more in touch with biology' – and to recognize that the sexes are complementary and mutually dependent.

'It is generally true', he wrote, 'that the males are more active, energetic, eager, passionate, and variable; the females more passive, conservative, sluggish and stable.' And yet, although males may be more active and benefit from a wider range of experience, and although they may have bigger brains and more intelligence, females, especially mothers, have a larger share of 'the altruistic emotions' and excel in the constancy of their affections. Common experience, he assured his readers, verified that men have greater variability and therefore originality, while women have greater stability and therefore more common sense. Female passivity is expressed in greater patience, more open-mindedness, greater appreciation of subtle details and consequently more rapid in-tuition. Man thinks more; woman feels more.

Through their nurture of the young, females had unrivalled opportunities of developing their capacity for social feeling, their altruism, and he expected that their increased participation in social and political life would result in a redirection of social change towards a co-operative society. On no account must woman abandon her passivity: not only would this be a transgression of the laws of biology, but it would also be flying in the face of the grand march of evolution. He drew a diagram to illustrate the steps in the evolution of egoism and altruism (see diagram over).

The two divergent lines stand for practical and emotional activity – egoism on the one hand, and altruism on the other. These find 'a basal unity' in the primitively close association between hunger and love. Each plane of ascent marks a widening and ennobling of the activities, while the actual path of progress is represented by the more and more intricate mingling of the two complementary functions. 'Sexual attraction', he wrote, 'ceases to

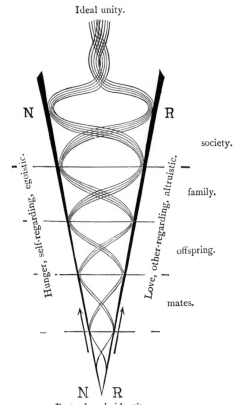

Ideal unity.

N R

society.

Hunger, self-regarding, egoistic.

Love, other-regarding, altruistic.

family.

offspring.

mates.

N R
Protoplasmic identity.
Diagrammatic Representation of the Relations between Nutritive,
Self-Maintaining, or Egoistic, and Reproductive, Species-
Regarding, or Altruistic Activities.

be wholly selfish; hunger may be overcome by love; love of mates
is enhanced by love for offspring; love for offspring broadens out
into love of kindred. Finally, the ideal before us is a more harmonious blending of the two streams.' With these heady words, he
concluded his chapter.

The nurture of altruism was woman's special evolutionary
responsibility: if she neglected her duty to the species, the ideally
harmonious blending of egoism and altruism would never come
about and humanity would be consigned to a lower rung on the
evolutionary ladder than it was actually capable of attaining.

The enormity of woman's obligations, as conceived by men like

Geddes and Leighton, to her sex, to the opposite sex, to her race, and even to her species, is a measure of the profound psychological disturbance caused by the emancipation movement. Confronted by rebellious woman, both men instinctively turned to what they believed to be indisputable authorities – Geddes to the laws of nature as revealed by Darwin, Leighton to the moral perfection of classical Greece – and sought from them confirmation of their right to sexual superiority. In her study of Geddes, Jill Conway contends that the significance of his contribution to English evolutionary thought lies in his conviction that social improvements could be expected to ensue from the enlargement of the sphere in which women's sex-determined mentality operated. While agreeing that he clung to the romantic stereotype of the passive, intuitive woman, she claims for him that he did persist in raising important questions concerning the emergence of women from the confines of Victorian domesticity. It would no doubt be wrong to quarrel with her judgement, it would certainly be absurd to present either Geddes or Leighton as the machiavellian agent of masculine propaganda, ruthlessly dedicated to the frustration of feminine aspirations to liberty. The purpose of this chapter is, however, to show the way in which certain men contrived to rationalize their fears of insurgent woman through the projection of a fantasy world order where women were placed in a position of disguised inferiority, one which accorded them an apparently heroic status, but at the same time carefully preserved their traditionally submissive characteristics.

Geddes's view of woman's evolutionary task can only be understood if it is recognized to be an elaborate piece of myth-making designed to confine her by loading on her shoulders an entirely imaginary burden, that of bringing about the fulfilment of her species through the refinement of her capacity for altruism. He insisted that her altruism resided in her passivity, and he solemnly warned her that to abandon her passivity was, in effect, to betray humanity.

It was not until 1901 that the discovery was made that sexual characteristics were linked to sexual chromosomes, and not until 1903 that the workings of hormones in human physiology were understood. These developments obliged Geddes to revise many of his theories, and he appears to have done this without reluctance, but his vision of woman's social role remained unaffected. In 1914,

he wrote[6] that at her best woman was a 'eupsychic' inspirer, a
eugenic mother and an orderly home-planner and citizen; he was
convinced that her guidance of consumption would direct the aims
of industry down beneficial paths and transform utility into art.

We cannot fail to notice the fundamental similarity between the
angels of earlier generations, Ruskin's queens, Leighton's goddesses
and Geddes's biological superwomen; all had been incarcerated in
prisons whose walls had been assiduously painted by their jailers
with scenes of glorified freedom.

An Unprejudiced Statement of the Precise Facts

In 1894 Havelock Ellis published a 'little' book entitled *Man and
Woman*, which was intended as an introduction to his six-volume
magnum opus, *Studies in the Psychology of Sex* (1897–1910); he
wrote that he had felt it necessary to clarify those issues relating to
the secondary and, as he termed them, tertiary sexual characteristics before dealing with the more important psychic functions
with which the *Studies* were concerned. In his preface to the
original edition he declared that he had been collecting data
concerning the constitutional differences between men and women
for twelve years; he had been inspired to do this by the realization
that these differences lay at the root of many social questions and
the discovery that 'no full and unprejudiced statement of the
precise facts' existed at that time.

Ellis was born in 1859. His mother was a devout evangelical and
he grew up with the ambition to be a preacher. In his teens he went
to Australia and became a teacher. Here, however, he lost his
Christian faith but experienced a revelation of his destiny: that he
should become a doctor in order to prepare himself for his life-
work, the study of sex. He duly returned home and enrolled as a
medical student at St Thomas's. While studying, he augmented his
grant by literary work; he edited the Mermaid edition of Eliza-
bethan and Restoration dramatists and wrote the first book in
English on criminology. He also became a founder member of the
Fellowship of the New Life, a libertarian organization which
proved to be the seed-bed of the Fabian Society.

In his middle twenties he led a double life: as a public figure he
was a radical among radicals, particularly in his attitudes towards
sex, but in private he was shy 'to the point of impotence';[7] his
affair with Olive Schreiner, author of *The Story of an African Farm*

and a passionate advocate of free love, was never consummated. While he was gathering material for *Man and Woman*, he met Edith Lees, a writer, free-thinker and fellow member of the Fellowship of the New Life. They were attracted to each other and she found him a sympathetic and understanding confidant. Her life had not been happy: her childhood had been blighted by the early death of her mother, the cruel temperament of her father and a stepmother whom she loathed, and as an adult she had found it difficult to form relationships with men, but had been in love and had physical relations with a number of women.

Over a period of two years she and Ellis grew closer and closer; finally he proposed that they should become lovers and live together now and again. Despite her free-thinking principles and beliefs, she firmly rejected the suggestion, and in December 1891 they were married. 'The union', he says in his autobiography, 'was fundamentally at the outset ... a union of affectionate comradeship, in which the specific emotions of sex had the smallest part.' They did not live together immediately: Ellis stayed in London to be near his work in the British Museum, and Edith went to Cornwall with a friend and rented a cottage. In March 1892, she wrote to him confessing that her relationship with her friend had blossomed into a love affair. Somewhat to their astonishment, he reacted by giving their liaison his blessing: 'I am perfectly happy that you should be so close to Claire. I feel very tender to her. Give her my sweetest love.' (8 March 1892.) He claims he felt no jealousy, only resentment that Edith's love for Claire involved diminished tenderness for him. After Claire, Edith had a succession of intimate women friends. 'I never grudged the devotion,' he wrote, 'though it was sometimes great, which she expended on them, for I knew that it satisfied a deep and ineradicable need of her nature. The only test I applied to them was how far they were good for her.'

In May 1893, he himself developed an affection for Amy, a girl he had known since childhood; they kissed, but no more. He hid nothing from Edith who was, however, furious. The injustice of her response stung him and, as he put it, 'stimulated a firmness the emotional impulse itself might have been too weak to attain ... that one kiss became a germ that slowly grew more vital during many years that followed.' It was not until 1894, when he took rooms of his own in London, that their relationship 'ripened into intimacy'. He wrote that, although his dangerous adventure with Amy, and

Edith's with Claire, undermined the original and largely conventional beliefs in which they had believed when they had married, scarcely a year before, they now began to struggle towards ideals which were truer to their natures; their 'deeper union', far from being destroyed by these experiences, was consolidated.

Such were the circumstances in which Havelock Ellis set about composing the 'unprejudiced statement' embodied in *Man and Woman*.

His declared intention (Chapter 1) was to examine the nature of those differences between the sexes that were not artificial but fundamental. He proceeded to weigh and measure each part of the male and female body at various stages of development, the infant, the child, the adolescent and the mature person. Three general conclusions emerged: women were more precocious than men, there was an earlier arrest of development in women, and the proportions of women tended to approach those of small men and children. He believed that the influence of the last factor 'vibrates to the most remote psychic recesses'. He then devoted an entire chapter to an examination of the skull and decided that there was no valid ground for declaring the skull of one sex to be morphologically superior to the other. He adduced evidence to show that the absolute weight of the male brain was larger than that of the female. He also pointed out that women possessed a relatively larger mass of nervous tissue, a characteristic they shared with children and short people generally, and one that did not automatically imply intellectual superiority. 'From the present standpoint of brain anatomy and brain physiology' he wrote, 'there is no ground for indicating any superiority to one sex over another.' Next he turned to the senses and concluded that although the balance of advantage was on the side of women – keener tactile sense, and sharper senses of smell and taste – it was less clearly on their side than popular prejudice had led him to expect. In complete contrast with general opinion, however, was his conclusion that women were less manually dexterous than men: they could sew with greater speed and accuracy, but they could not, for example, operate a telegraph key as efficiently as men.

Up to this point Ellis appeared to preserve a more or less disinterested attitude towards his subject; he offered an enormous range of evidence relating to each topic which he reviewed impartially, discarding prejudices that posed as scientific deductions and arriving at his own conclusions in a manner which suggested that the discovery of the truth was his sole concern. As the book progressed, however, an unmistakable strain of bias began to intrude itself, although his magisterial tone of objectivity was rigorously sustained.

In his next chapter, 'The Intellectual Impulse', he assessed the aptitudes of school children and decided that there were no significant differences, except that girls displayed greater precocity. He did, however, point to some pronounced differences when he came to discuss rapidity of perception. 'The masculine method of thought', he declared, 'is massive and deliberate, while the feminine method is quick to perceive and nimble to act. The latter method is apt to fall into error, but is agile in retrieving error . . .' In its finest form, this latter quality is called tactfulness.

He then discussed deceptiveness in women, remarking that the method of attaining results by ruses (a method common to most weaker, lower animals) is so habitual among women that in them deception is 'almost physiological', a phrase he borrowed from Lombroso, a criminologist of great prestige in those days. No one will doubt, Ellis asserted, the persistency of this habit of mind. But, he added hastily, it would be irrational to attribute the caution and indirectness of women to innate wickedness, for these characteristics result inevitably from 'the constitution of women, acting in the conditions under which they are generally placed. There is . . . no civilized country in which a woman may safely state her wishes, and proceed openly to seek their satisfaction.'

Lombroso and Ferro had, he said, *admirably* (my italics) analysed feminine deceptiveness and had traced seven causes: weakness – cunning and deception are the necessary resort of the weak and oppressed; menstruation – this function is treated with disgust, therefore women try to conceal it; modesty – any demonstration of love which has not been invited by a man is regarded as immodest, whence a training in deception; sexual selection – a woman instinctively hides her defects which may injure her in the eyes of men; the desire to be interesting – this leads to simulated weaknesses and a supposed need for protection; suggestibility – the greater suggestibility of women renders them less able to distinguish between the real and the simulated; and the duties of maternity – the education of children by mothers largely consists of a series of lies designed to hide from their children facts of life considered to be unsuitable for them.

Ellis concluded this astonishing catalogue of prejudice and nonsense by stating that the deception and dissimulation of women was not to be confused with untruthfulness. Women were, he said, if anything more truthful than men: '. . . careful observations today show that in the ordinary affairs of life, *in which their own emotional tendencies are little called in question* (my italics), women are quite equal, and perhaps superior, to men in devotion to truth.'

His verdict on the relative qualities of intelligence in men and women was that, though they were not of identical character or value, they fairly balanced each other. Men are better able to apply what they have learnt and are more inclined to supplement their learning by reflection or further independent investigation; they also tend to adopt more reasonable methods of study. Women, on the other hand, 'dislike the essentially intellectual process of analysis; they have the instinctive feeling that analysis may possibly destroy the emotional complexes by which they are largely moved and which appeal to them. Women dislike rigid rules, and principles, and abstract propositions. They feel that they can do the right thing by impulse . . .' These are not defects, Ellis insisted, but differences. 'In all the ordinary affairs of life the intelligence of women, whatever sexual differences may exist, proceeds side by side with that of men.'

The way in which Ellis presented his argument in this chapter may be taken as typical. He disdained any suggestion of relative inferiority among women, and acted as if he had put to rout those who were short-sighted or dishonest enough to countenance such a pernicious abuse of the facts. However, licensed as it were by these forthright disclaimers of bias, he did not shrink from parading the manifestly one-sided opinions of other writers, nor did he refrain from entering his own brand of insidious bigotry. We may note that, although his final word on the subject of the Intellectual Impulse was that the intelligence of women proceeds side by side with that of men, he nevertheless affirmed that women possessed a relative lack of intellectual curiosity, that they were less keen and less skilful in solving problems, that they felt a relative lack of interest in scientific problems, and that they showed less intellectual aptitude than men when they were not prompted by emotional motives, a factor which made it 'less easy for the average woman than for the average man to become devoted with success to the deliberate and disinterested pursuit of knowledge.'

In 'Morbid Psychic Phenomena' (Chapter XV) he discussed suicide along with criminality and insanity. Here he was up against the disobliging but unavoidable fact that more men than women killed themselves – in Europe suicide was at that time from three to four times more frequent in men than women – but he was able to turn even this unpromising material to masculine advantage. He conceded that, while the suicidal impulse was not necessarily morbid, it did imply a degree of psychic abnormality; he did not, however, draw the inference that the relative infrequency of suicide among women indicated a lesser tendency to succumb to 'abnormality'. He concentrated instead upon the marked predominance of female over male suicides among adolescents. It was difficult, in his opinion, not to connect this with the stress resulting from their precocious physical development. 'Probably', he wrote, 'an often hidden factor in the frequency of female suicides in early life generally is shame at the prospect of becoming a mother.'

But it was when he turned to the different methods employed by the two sexes to kill themselves that he was able to give full rein to his desire to dispel any hint of masculine inadequacy in this sphere of activity. He cited statistics which established that, broadly speaking, men hanged, shot and stabbed themselves, while women favoured drowning, poisoning and jumping from great heights. He then commented that men preferred to adopt *active* (his italics) methods which were usually more deliberate and repulsive (what else would one expect from a sex whose thought processes were 'massive and deliberate'?) whereas women preferred *passive* methods which were more decorous and required less resolute preparation. Being run over by a train presented something of a problem to him since it was an indubitably passive method which was incongruously selected by three men to every one woman. He dispensed with this apparent contradiction, however, by arguing that it was a method that called for a degree of determination beyond the reach of the average female suicide, and, in any case, it offended 'against women's sense of propriety, and their intense horror of making a mess'. And then, in an unguarded moment, he revealed his true partiality by stating that 'if it were possible to find an easy method of suicide by which the body could be entirely disposed of, there would probably be a considerable increase of suicides among women.'

'Is the comparative immunity of women from the suicidal impulse real or only apparent?' he asked himself. Not surprisingly, he was able to satisfy himself that their immunity was only apparent. The higher ratio of male suicides had been explained by the suggestion that women were more sheltered in the struggle for existence, that they were more adaptable, more self-sacrificing, more resigned and more influenced by religious scruples, but Ellis quoted another writer who believed that the disproportion would not have been nearly so great if all those who contemplated suicide could be taken into account: 'Many more women than men desire, or think they desire, but have not the courage to cause their own death.'[8] Ellis himself then commented:

> That women very often contemplate suicide is probable, and it may be added that a very large number of women fail in their attempts at suicide. If in determining the suicide-rate we could include unsuccessful attempts at suicide, it is probable that women's share would be larger. The passive methods of self-destruction are not always available, and they are also liable to miscarry; moreover, when a woman adopts a more energetic method of self-destruction she is more likely than a man to miscalculate from ignorance, violent methods of destruction being more within man's province.

Once again he had found it possible to establish the superiority of man. Despite the unfavourable first impression created by the suicide statistics, further examination swiftly revealed that women thought about killing themselves far more frequently than the figures implied, but lacked the necessary skill and courage to see the business through. Men, of course, abounded in skill and courage and therefore killed themselves with far greater dispatch and proficiency. And so, it was in a tone approaching the congratulatory that he wrote the final sentence of this section: '. . . there seems every reason to believe that the suicidal impulse, in European races at all events, is somewhat stronger in men than in women.'

When he came to sum up in his concluding chapter, he was able to declare that the small group of women who wished to prove the absolute inferiority of the male sex, and the larger group of men who wished to circumscribe rigidly the sphere of women, must alike be ruled out of court. Nevertheless, he felt constrained to point to certain differences between the sexes which had forced themselves on his attention with such consistency that he was obliged to regard them as fundamental. One was the greater variability of the male, and the other was the precocity of women and their tendency to diverge to a lesser extent from what he called the child-type. This was by no means to say that woman was 'undeveloped man'; on the contrary, the line of evolution led directly from the infant ape and not from some adult male simian. The human infant presented in an exaggerated form the chief distinctive characteristics of humanity – the large head and brain, the small face, the hairlessness, the delicate bone system. Once the position of the child in relation to evolution was realized, it was possible to take a clearer view of the natural position of woman. She bore the special characteristics of humanity to a higher degree than man, and she represented more nearly than man the human type to which man was approximating. 'Throughout the whole course of civilization', he wrote, 'we see men following women and taking up their avocations, with more energy, more thoroughness, often more eccentricity.' Primitive cultures had been predominantly militant, or masculine in character, while modern civilization was becoming industrial or feminine.

Pursuing this line of thought, he reaffirmed that all discussion of the alleged inferiority of women must be considered foolish and futile, and explained that wherever a special feature could be distinguished as the particular possession of one sex, it was invariably counterbalanced by special features belonging to the other sex. Nature, whose laws were paramount, had devised a scheme of mutual compensation. Thus it was that 'in the intellectual region men possess greater aptitude for dealing with the more remote and abstract interests of life', whereas, 'women have, at the least, as great an aptitude in dealing with the immediate practical interests of life'.

'Women', he wrote, 'remain nearer than men to the infantile state; but on the other hand, men approach more nearly than women to the ape-like and senile state.' Like Geddes, Ellis had managed to apply Darwinian theory in such a way as to confer on certain characteristics, which he designated the exclusive property of women, an evolutionary significance; Geddes had nominated altruism as the vital factor on which the future of human development depended, and Ellis, in his turn, selected proximity to the child-type. No less an arbiter than Nature herself, he assured his readers, had decreed that woman, through her closer affiliation to the infant state, should be the sex to advance the human species along the path of ever-increasing civilization, which was its evolutionary destiny. While scorning all imputations of inferiority, he nevertheless attributed to the more childlike of the two sexes a host of qualities that bore an uncanny resemblance to those very inadequacies on which the advocates of male supremacy had been insisting throughout the century: she was less active than passive, she showed a greater inclination than man to adapt or resign herself to the conditions in which she was placed, she was more easily affected by her emotions and was more suggestible, she was more intuitive than objective, more instinctive than analytic, she was less capable than man of sustained thought or action, and so on.

Ellis's prejudice in favour of his own sex seems to have forced itself upon him in direct opposition to his stated and no doubt sincerely held intentions; it is perhaps reasonable, therefore, to suggest that his unconscious fears of women had seeped through his determination to maintain strict impartiality and had warped his judgement in a way that he could not himself recognize. In any event, it is impossible to read his *Man and Woman* today without seeing it as part of that Victorian tradition which sought to assign to women a social role secondary to that of men. The degree to which that tradition had atrophied may be gauged by the frequency and zeal of Ellis's assertions that he had no time for 'the alleged inferiority of women' (his phrase).

The Woman Who Did

In 1898 the suspicions of the police were directed towards a little avant-garde society calling itself the Legitimation League whose members were dedicated to the belief that marriage ought to be replaced by a formal acknowledgement of union between free partners. Keen to propagate their ideals, they attended meetings, gave lectures and contributed articles to their organ, a magazine boldly entitled *The Adult*. The League's nerve centre was the home of one of its officers, George Bedborough, which also served as a bookshop where, among such titles as *Suitable Food, Wise Sex–Love and Immortality* by Fräulein Lepper, Havelock Ellis's *Sexual Inversion*[9] could be purchased at the price of ten shillings

The authorities, inspired by the advice of a planted informant, arrived at the conclusion that the League was not all it seemed, and that it was in fact a front for the seditious activities of anarchists. Accordingly, they decided it had to be smashed. They selected as their target the unfortunate Bedborough, arguing that the League would be rendered harmless if it was deprived of its publisher and bookseller. 'Convinced that [they] should at one blow kill a growing evil in the shape of a vigorous campaign of free love and Anarchism', they instructed their agent to purchase one of the books in Bedborough's shop and arrest him for selling an obscene publication. The book chosen was *Sexual Inversion*.

Bedborough's indictment, among many other terrifying items, maintained that Ellis's book contained 'divers wicked, lewd, impure, scandalous and obscene libels', and that it was the cause of 'manifest corruption of the morals and minds.' of Her Majesty's subjects. When the news of this outrage broke, a member of the League immediately formed the Free Press Defence Committee and enlisted the support of a group of assorted free-thinkers and socialists, among them Bernard Shaw. In the event, the Committee was not required to act, for Bedborough, thoroughly unnerved by his ordeal and quite unwilling to don the martyr's mantle, did a deal with the police. He pleaded guilty to three charges, the remaining eight against him were dropped and he was bound over, having given an assurance that he would have nothing further to do with the League. Ellis, in his turn, gave an assurance that he would never again publish sex books in England. *The Adult* was silenced and the League destroyed.

It is interesting to speculate how the fight on Bedborough's behalf would have developed if it had taken place, for it seems probable that in Shaw the League would have found a formidable ally. He recorded his attitude to Ellis's book in a letter to Henry Seymour, the Committee's organizer:

> ... I have no hesitation in saying that its publication was more urgently needed in England than any other treatise with which I am acquainted. ... It is almost invariably assumed that this idiosyncrasy (homosexuality) is necessarily associated with the most atrocious depravity of character; and this notion, for which there appears to be absolutely no foundation, is held to justify the infliction of penalties compared to which the punishment of a man who batters his wife to death is a trifle.

Another member of the Committee was Grant Allen, author of the best-selling and controversial novel *The Woman Who Did*, which John Lane published in 1895. Although married, and happily so if the inscription in his book is to be believed (To my dear wife to whom I have dedicated my twentiest happy years), he was nevertheless in agreement with the basic tenets of the Legitimation League. His affiliations with the anarchists, on the other hand, were remote. He had no personal connection with the author of *Studies in the Psychology of Sex*, but it is not surprising that he pledged his loyalty to Ellis's cause for their work, though in different fields, had for a brief period run parallel. While Ellis had been brooding in 1893 over the nature of the two sexes in preparation for his *Man and Woman*, Allen had been confronting similar issues in the composition of his notorious novel.

What Herminia Barton, the heroine of Allen's novel, did was to have a baby by a man whom she loved but refused, on principle, to marry. Herminia is clearly intended by her author to stand as a portrait of a free woman, one who by throwing off society's shackles has inherited and full-bloodedly embraced the true nature of her sex. But, just as Ellis' scientific objectivity with regard to the real capabilities of the female species was fraught with prejudice and hesitation, so Allen's concept of woman's essential nature was severely distorted by masculine pride and fearfulness.

Miss Barton, tall and dark, with abundant black hair and a 'rounded figure', is introduced to Alan Merrick at a garden party. He is a barrister, in excellent chambers, and son of the famous gout doctor to whom royal dukes flock. She, he is informed by his hostess, is the Dean of Dunwich's daughter. He is struck at once by her face which is 'above all things the face of a free woman'. He is impressed by her frank and fearless glance and by her beauty – 'Some hint of every element in the highest loveliness met in that face and form – physical, intellectual, emotional, moral'. They hit it off immediately, for, as the author put it in a characteristic phrase, 'he was true man, and she was real woman'.

Soon enough they are pacing the lawn deep in earnest conversation. She expounds her views on female emancipation which prove to be extremely radical; she also explains that the question of social and moral emancipation interests her far more than the merely political one. The following day they meet again and during a walk she confides in him her philosophy of life, which is to know the Truth and to act upon it freely.

Heedless of gossip, they proceed to spend day after day in each other's company. Love blossoms. One afternoon, as they lie on a carpet of sheep sorrel, looking out across the pastures of Sussex, he addresses her as Herminia. Her heart gave a delicious bound. 'She was a woman, and therefore she was glad he should speak so. She was a woman, and therefore she shrank from acknowledging it.' After some preliminary gulpings in the order of 'Am I worthy of you?', 'Ought I to retire as not your peer?' and so on, he finally declares his love for her. She immediately declares hers for him and all is bliss. Then he coos into her ear, 'Dearest, how soon may we be married?' 'Never!' she cries, a flush of shame and horror suffusing her face. 'Don't tell me, after all I've tried to make you feel and understand, you thought I could possibly consent to *marry* you?' Surely, he pleads, she doesn't carry her ideas of freedom to such extremes. She does. What does she propose? That they live together. Her attitude to marriage is implacable: 'I know what marriage is – from what vile slavery it has sprung . . . I can't pander to that malignant thing.' 'Take me', she says, 'but not my life, not my future, not my individuality, not my freedom.' He advocates a series of compromises, but she rejects them summarily: 'It never occurred to me to think that my life could ever end in anything else but martyrdom . . . Every great and good life can but end in a Calvary.' He wants to save her from herself. She begs him to take her on the only terms on which she can give herself up, but he asks for a day to think. As they part, she reaffirms the horrors of marriage: 'I know on what vile foundations your temple of wedlock is based and built, what pitiable victims languish and die in its sickening vaults.'

He spends a sleepless night arguing the pros and cons with himself. He feels convinced that it is the man's place to protect and guard the woman, even from her own higher self, and yet he is dazzled and overwhelmed by her: 'He saw how pure, how pellucid, how noble the woman was; treading her own ideal world of high seraphic harmonies.' With these angelic tones ringing in his head, he sets off to their rendezvous.

They meet and he takes her to a grassy bank where they can talk. She lets him lead her. 'She was woman enough by nature to like being led. Only, it must be the right man who led her . . .' He suggests that they wait and see, but she insists they decide that very day: either he accepts her terms or they part for ever. Her face at this point is crimson with maidenly shame. He reminds her that he is a man and begs her not to play too hard on those fiercest chords in his nature; she tells him that it isn't those chords she wants to play on, it's his brain. In the end, of course, he cannot resist: 'You have confessed your love to me. When a woman says that, what can a man refuse her?' he demands in a final burst of casuistry.

A week later he is knocking at the door of her little cottage in the backwastes of Chelsea; she has arrayed herself in 'the white garb of affiance' for her bridal evening, and her cheek is aglow with virginal shrinking. He kisses her forehead tenderly, 'and thus was Herminia Barton's espousal consummated'.

At her insistence they do not live together, she values her freedom too highly, but they see each other very frequently. In due course she is pregnant. He decides that she should leave her job and that they should go abroad. For once he is adamant, 'and Herminia was now beginning to be so far influenced by Alan's personality that she yielded the point with reluctance to his masculine judgement.' During the course of the book, he manages to persuade her to compromise, to abandon her principles, only twice: once on this occasion, and later when she gives way to his 'greater worldly wisdom' and 'masculine common sense' by agreeing to travel as Mrs Merrick. The author's commentary on her first compromise is highly revealing:

> It must always be so [that women yield to men]. The man must needs retain for many years to come the personal hegemony he has usurped over the woman; and the woman who once accepts him as lover or as husband must give way in the end, even in matters of principle, to his virile self-assertion. She would be less a woman, he less a man, were any other result possible. Deep down in the very roots of the idea of sex we come on that prime antithesis – the male, active and aggressive; the female sedentary, passive and receptive.

They travel to Italy and enjoy an idyllically happy week; then, in Perugia, Alan is struck down with typhoid and dies. Heartbroken, Herminia stays to have her baby which proves to be a girl – 'the baby that was destined to regenerate the world'. The author does not waste his opportunity and remarks that every good woman is by nature a mother and finds in maternity her social and moral salvation; motherhood, he asserts, is the full realization of woman's faculties, the natural outlet for woman's wealth of emotion.

Too proud and principled to accept help from Alan's father or to seek it from her own, she faces 'her terrible widowhood' alone, scraping a living from journalism and translating. Her only happiness is her daughter Dolores whose babbling lips and pattering feet make heaven in her attic. Alan's death has left her ship rudderless; her mission has failed. She lives now for Dolly to whom she has given the noble birthright of liberty and who is destined 'to the apostate of women'.

Dolly, however, grows up to disappoint these lofty dreams: the older she gets the clearer it becomes to her mother that her mind is incurably snobbish, that she entertains the most regrettable admiration for birth, wealth and position and, worst of all, that she has not the slightest regard for righteousness. 'In short, she was sunk in the same ineffable slough of moral darkness as the ordinary inhabitant of the morass of London.'

When Dolly is seventeen, 'a pink wild rose just unrolling its petals', she meets, falls in love with and becomes unofficially engaged to Walter Brydges, a handsome fellow with all the glamour of a landed estate and an Oxford education. But then Walter gets wind of her illegitimacy and, although he still loves her – 'nothing on earth could make me anything but grateful for and thankful for the gift of love you're gracious enough to bestow on me' – he cannot prevent her breaking off their engagement. Burning with shame, she returns home to demand the truth of Herminia, who tells her all. Dolly rejects her mother – 'You are not fit to receive a pure girl's kisses' – and throws herself on the mercy of Alan's father, the great gout doctor, who promptly adopts her. She writes to Walter telling him they are once more engaged but that they cannot marry while her mother lives.

Herminia, learning that she is an impediment to her daughter's happiness, resolves to kill herself. She writes a letter to Dolly: 'I set out in life with the earnest determination to be a martyr to the cause of truth and righteousness . . . Nothing now remains for me but the crown of martyrdom . . . Good night, my heart's darling.' She puts on the dress she wore on her self-made bridal night, inspects herself in the mirror – 'she was always a woman' – and drinks a phial of prussic acid.

The last line of the novel reads 'Herminia Barton's stainless soul had ceased to exist for ever.'

The key to *The Woman Who Did* lies in its author's use of the word 'nature' as applied to women, and Herminia in particular. J. S. Mill wrote of women that 'no other class of dependants have had their character so entirely distorted from its natural proportions by their relations with their masters'; Allen's heroine may be taken as his representation of the woman who had successfully over-thrown the tyranny of her masters, repudiated her dependence on them and won for herself the freedom to cultivate her character's natural proportions. By the time she meets Merrick her emancipa-tion is complete, she has an answer for everything: 'she had de-bated these problems at full in her own mind for years, and had arrived at definite and consistent conclusions for every knotty point'. We may assume therefore that Allen's delineation of Herminia's character reflects his view of the quintessence of woman, of woman as she is 'meant' to be if nature were permitted to run its course; he is presenting his vision of woman purified.

We can surely expect something glorious and inspiring from this bold experiment? Surely the author will reveal woman to us in a new and wonderful light, as she steps from the pages of his book, like Venus, free, uncontaminated and every inch herself?

Sadly, we are to be disappointed. Herminia certainly possesses an exceptionally powerful character and her sense of independence is unusually well developed, but whenever her nature, the true nature of all women, manifests itself, it proves to be a commonplace and familiar thing. It turns out that 'by nature' women like to be led; they *must*, we are assured, yield to man's virile self-assertion; in contrast with the active and aggressive male, women are sedentary, passive and receptive, and they only fully realize themselves in motherhood.

At one point, Allen even implies, albeit inadvertently, that her nature and her much vaunted principles, far from being inter-dependent, are in fact hostile to each other. During her widowhood another man proposes to her and, although she cannot accept him, she is sorely tempted – 'sick at heart with that long, fierce struggle against overwhelming odds, [she] could almost have said *yes* to him. Her own nature prompted her; she was very, very fond of him.' Allen proceeds to use this incident to confirm another anti-female myth. Herminia's lover, unable to bring himself to live with her, swears that if he can't marry her, he will marry no one else. She is appalled – 'To be celibate is a very great misfortune *even* [my italics] for a woman; for a man it is impossible – it is cruel, it is wicked.'

Critics were perplexed and disgusted by Herminia Barton, but the public, if sales figures are anything to go by, was fascinated by her; at all events, neither had anything to fear from her. No doubt Allen shocked some readers, but perhaps he reassured a great many more, for he was able to show them that emancipated woman – dreaded figure – was not so bad after all, nor so different from the ordinary woman.

Indeed, he went to considerable pains to underline her harmlessness. During her first conversation with Merrick, she distinguishes between political and social/moral emancipation and tells him she is interested only in the latter. Later, when her second lover tells her he is to be married, she broods bitterly on the monopolistic instinct in man as it evinces itself in the monopolies of patriotism, proprietorship, capitalism and marriage (the passage is eight pages long); it does not, however, occur to her that emancipated woman has any part to play in eliminating these vices – she seems content to set an example. She is harmless because she does not communicate. We are told that, while she was a teacher, prior to her pregnancy, she led her pupils down the path of reason, but that she did it 'unobtrusively'. She is a journalist, but she never writes about the great issues which dominate her life and ultimately drive her to suicide. She is quick enough to preach her gospel at a garden party to an attractive young man, but she never picks up her pen to proselytize. Finally, we are told that when Alan dies she feels rudderless and acknowledges that her mission has failed; here her creator demonstrates his bias a little crudely, for her mission was well under way before Alan came into her life and, now he is gone, she is still eminently capable of expressing her opinions, particularly since she has lately taken up the profession of journalism.

It must have been a relief to Allen's readers to discover that neither political radicalism nor belief in propagandism were part of woman's essential nature.

Allen also guaranteed Herminia's harmlessness by adopting a more traditional technique: he canonized her. As is conventional in Victorian love stories, the hero experiences a dramatic moral elevation under the influence of the heroine. Alan thinks of Herminia as an angel whose white wings he feels himself unworthy to touch, he tells himself that it is her better, her inner self he is in love with, not the mere statuesque face, the full and faultless figure and he wonders whether he would be right to bring her down from the pedestal whereon she so austerely stands. As we have seen, there was a considerable advantage to be derived from dressing up women as angels and placing them on pedestals, preferably good, high ones, because once up there they were out of both their husbands' and harm's way. This treatment is, however, hardly suitable for Herminia who is proposing to live with her lover and have his child. Instead, the author transmutes her from human into martyr. He continually reminds his readers that this is to be her fate, and he puts innumerable speeches to that effect in Herminia's own mouth – 'it never occurred to me to think that my life could ever end in anything else but martyrdom', she tells Alan as she turns down his proposal. By making his heroine a martyr-to-be Grant Allen neatly excuses her from doing anything concrete about her cause; she simply lives under sentence of death.

The Woman Who Did was published in 1895; this was also the last year of Leighton's working life. Although he was already suffering from the illness to which he finally succumbed in the January of 1896, he was not prevented from painting one of his most characteristic and effective pictures, 'Flaming June' (46×46 inches).[10] It shows a long-limbed, red-headed girl curled up asleep on a marble bench; behind her, stretching away to the horizon, lies the sea, burnished silver by the sun. Through her diaphanous orange robe, her flesh can be quite clearly seen. Jeremy Maas has described the picture as 'a luscious yet unlascivious essay in voluptuousness, redolent of slumbering warmth'. No greater contrast could be imagined than Allen's treatment of his high-spirited heroine and Leighton's of his nameless, dormant model, and yet the purpose behind each creation was by no means dissimilar.

'Flaming June' is the embodiment of passivity. We recall that female passivity was a key quality in the minds of those who defended the concept of masculine superiority. Geddes had insisted that women who abandoned their passivity were not only breaking the laws of biology but were also putting at risk the evolution of the species, and Ellis had repeatedly emphasized the male tendency to take an active initiative as compared with the female tendency to adopt a passive stance. Leighton's girl is passive and vulnerable, her body is completely open to the spectator's gaze; no element of connivance has been introduced here, she simply sleeps and is observed. She is beautiful and powerless, the epitome, by Leighton's criteria, of woman as she ought to be. At the same time, there is a monumental look about her: though perfectly proportioned and graceful, her body has been constructed on a substantial scale. By this means, the impression of defencelessness attains an additional dimension; for the power of the spectator is enhanced by his freedom to inspect an exposed female body which is both statuesque and impotent. In a word, Leighton's picture confirms the supremacy of the (male) spectator.

Herminia Barton's character, on the other hand, betrays no hint of passivity; her attitude to her own existence is positive, determined and fiercely independent. The wretched Alan Merrick is overwhelmed and dominated by her 'physical, intellectual, emotional [and] moral' loveliness. Hers is the more profoundly developed personality, hers is the stronger will. On all crucial questions of principle it is she who insists and he who compromises; it is he who is compelled to adapt himself to her scheme of life, and to accept her scale of values. Nor is the author's approach to her any less worshipful than his hero's: no note of ridicule, or even of the gentlest irony, is audible when he speaks of Merrick seeing Herminia tread 'her own ideal world of high seraphic harmonies'.

At first sight, it would appear that Grant Allen was inviting his readers to join with him and his hero in their adulation of Herminia, but, as we have seen, he in fact intended to achieve a quite different effect. In earlier decades the worship of women had been conducted from a position of strength and had, on the whole, been designed to reinforce that position. By attributing to women the possession of certain saintly virtues, men ensured that in the process women were prevented from exercising their more practical capabilities, and from indulging their earthier emotions. By the 'nineties, however, such a policy was no longer appropriate, for women had claimed for themselves and were strenuously exploiting their right to govern their own destinies. Allen's response to these changed circumstances was deviously realistic: he created a heroine whose character personified emancipation taken to its logical conclusion, and he presented her in a way which provoked the reader's admiration, not his derision. But, by exaggerating her independence of mind, he was able to show up all the more clearly her essential femininity, and he was also able to demonstrate that the price of absolute liberation was self-destruction.

Leighton was the older man, and he worked in an older idiom, one which he had perfected over thirty years of assiduous practice. Although Allen's attitude to women appeared to be more conciliatory, the difference between them was in effect only one of method: Allen's was more attuned to the times. The extent to which the male position had been weakened by the 'nineties may be measured by comparing Allen's assessment of women's intellectual capacity with that of Darwin, Geddes or even his contemporary, Ellis, who emerges from this discussion as a rather old-fashioned figure. By the same token, the determination on the part of men to shore up and conserve their privileges may be judged by the persistency with which they adhered to the myths relating to women's inferiority and the skill with which they adjusted them to accommodate an increasingly unfavourable reality.

7

Fear of Women

Although their respective attitudes no doubt furnished him with a measure of reassurance, Leighton's sublime pedagogy and the ingenious theorizing of Geddes and Ellis were hardly typical of the average man's response to the feminist challenge. The artist and the two scientists were exceptional in that they were able to achieve, through the manipulation of their different disciplines, a gratifying sense of control over this explosively disruptive force. They were, however, representative of their time in so far as they found it difficult, and ultimately impossible, to adapt to new conditions, and resorted instead to rationalizing their anxieties by refurbishing old arguments in support of male supremacy. It was perhaps Grant Allen, with his double-edged idolatry of Herminia Barton, who came closest to striking the characteristic note of his decade, the 'nineties.

It was a rare man indeed who did not feel in some way disconcerted by the unending sequence of alterations that took place in the relative positions of the sexes, and a still rarer one who felt able to offer women an unqualified welcome to that territory hitherto considered the exclusive preserve of his own sex. The majority of men did not know what to make of the rapidly changing circumstances in which they found themselves; no sooner had they come to terms with one aspect of female metamorphosis, than another, if not two or three, sprang into its place to confront and disturb them. Fathers were defied by daughters who insisted on smoking cigarettes, riding bicycles, wearing outrageous clothes, voicing opinions that broke every canon of femininity and educating themselves to as high a standard as their brothers; husbands were defied by wives who claimed the right to make wills, to control and own their own property, to earn their living, to obtain divorces on the same grounds as men, and generally to exercise an unprecedented degree of autonomy; and men as a whole were defied by women who demanded access on equal terms to the universities, professions and even the polling booths.

The evolution of woman from serf to citizen was, in effect, a process of continual rebellion, and the myriad struggles of which it was composed were undertaken as much by individuals on their own domestic battle-grounds as by groups and organizations in the public arenas. Men displayed an understandable reluctance to surrender their age-old privileges without a fight, and it was difficult for them, even for those who were inclined to be sympathetic to the feminist cause, not to interpret female victories as male defeats. The traditional concept of masculinity had relied on universal acceptance of the principle of female inferiority, and it was only natural that many men should feel themselves to have been emasculated, or at least threatened with emasculation, by the feminist destruction of this vital tenet. Every expansion of feminine power involved, or so it must have seemed, a corresponding diminution of masculine prestige.

By the late 'eighties and the 'nineties, women had decisively demonstrated that, however fiercely the march of emancipation might be resisted by men and by those traditionalists among women who chose to defend the mid-Victorian position – a far from ineffective faction – the era of female submissiveness was on the decline and waning fast. The cumulative effect of this bewildering, and often humiliating, revolution was to induce in men a profound sense of fear. This fearfulness involved an acute apprehension concerning their capacity to withstand the 'new woman's' aggression, as they saw it, and an intense dread of the new, and previously inaccessible dimension to sexuality that was being introduced by women who were no longer content to confine their role to that of the willing or unwilling victim of male rapacity, but who were now yearning for the chance to participate in sexual relations on equal emotional terms with their husbands.

The Queen Can Do No Wrong

In 1891, Rudyard Kipling published his only adult novel, *The Light That Failed*; he was then aged twenty-six and, it can be inferred, in a state of considerable fearfulness regarding women.

It told the story of Maisie and Dick who as children had been placed by their respective guardians in the care of the same sadistic foster-mother, and had come to care deeply for each other. The opening scene describes Maisie's last day at their foster-home, during which, after a prolonged battle with boyish embarrassment, Dick blurts out a declaration of love for her. That night, he dreams that he has won 'all the world' and has brought it to Maisie, only to have his offering spurned. The dream proves to be prophetic.

Years later, when Dick has become a highly successful painter of battle scenes, they meet again by chance. She too has taken up painting, but is still under tuition and finding it hard to sell her pictures. She confesses that her life is grey and full of disappointment, but impresses him with her determination to persevere. He finds that he is still in love with her and proposes to her on the spot, only to be flatly refused. She explains that she must do her work; he suggests that they can work together, but she is adamant: 'No, I couldn't. It's my work, – mine, – mine, – mine! I've been alone all my life in myself, and I'm not going to belong to anybody except myself.' His confidence is however unimpaired: 'We've both nice little wills of our own, and one or other of us has to be broken.'

During this conversation he coins the phrase 'the queen can do no wrong', and it is on this masochistic principle that he conducts his relationship with her. He takes to visiting her on Sunday afternoons at her studio where, under the baleful eye of her flat-mate, a red-headed impressionist for whom he conceives a deep loathing, he advises her on her painting and bites back his frustration. After enduring three months of this unrewarding ritual, he is annoyed to discover that she is going to France for a sketching holiday. She announces her plan to paint an ambitious picture based on the theme of Melancolia – 'a woman [who] suffered a great deal, – till she could suffer no more. Then she began to laugh at it all . . .' He deplores the idea, telling her that she lacks the power to do it justice, and leaves in a temper. Alone in the park, he decides he will paint his version of the picture: 'I'll make her understand', he swears to himself, 'that I can beat her on her own "Melancolia". Even then she wouldn't care . . . All the same I love her; and I must go on loving her; and if I can humble her inordinate vanity I will.' He sees her off at Dover and once again asks her how she feels about him. She gently tells him that nothing has changed. He claims the right to a kiss, which she grants, but he overdoes it, forcing her to wrench herself away. Standing on the quay, watching the boat pull away towards Calais, he observes to himself that there is 'nothing in the wide world to keep us apart except her obstinacy'.

Events then take a tragic turn; for Dick discovers that he is going blind. An old wound, contracted in the Sudan, is affecting his optic nerve, and nothing can be done to save his sight. His determination to complete his Melancolia before 'the light' fails develops into an obsession. He finds that only whisky will keep at bay the encroaching darkness and, some weeks later, when the friend with whom he shares rooms returns from a trip, Dick is seen to be 'a drawn, lined, shrunken, haggard wreck'. The picture is, however, finished, and Dick is well pleased with it. His friend Torpenhow admires it – 'She's seen the game played out,' he says, '– I don't think she has had a good time of it, and now she doesn't care . . . She's a beauty.' Within a day of its completion, Dick finally goes entirely blind. He breaks down in delirium, blabs the history of his love for Maisie to Torpenhow, from whom he has so far kept it a secret, and relapses into a coma. When he recovers consciousness, he can do nothing but sit in his room, turning over and over in his pocket the unread letters which Maisie sends him from France.

Acting on his own initiative, Torpenhow crosses the Channel to go in search of Maisie. He finds her, tells her all, omitting no detail of the miseries recounted by Dick during his delirium, and instructs her to return immediately to London and to 'kiss his eyes, and kiss them and kiss them until they got well again'. Twenty-four hours later, she is in Dick's studio.

Not unnaturally, she is filled with pity at the sight of him, and begins to sob. Through her tears she is heard to whine, 'I can't – I can't . . . I do despise myself – indeed I do. But I can't. O Dickie, you wouldn't ask me to, would you?' He nobly reassures her that there is nothing she can do for him, and that he would rather she never saw him again. She is about to depart when he suddenly remembers his 'Melancolia', which he proudly displays. This is, or is intended to be, a moment of high poignancy; for Dick does not realize that the picture has been defaced by the embittered Bessie, the girl he had used as his model, who has taken revenge on him for having sabotaged her affair with Torpenhow. Maisie cannot disillusion him, and is obliged to simulate heartfelt approval. She then runs out of the house. Kipling abandons her in her drawing-room to brood guiltily on her misdeeds: 'Not until she found herself saying, "Well, he never asked me", did she realize her scorn of herself.' No more is heard of Maisie.

After a period of lugubrious self-pity, Dick pulls himself together and begins to put his life in order. He then discovers that his 'Melancolia' has been spoliated and that he has been made to look ridiculous in Maisie's eyes. He has nothing to hope for now; his self-respect can never be revived. Torpenhow, a foreign correspondent by profession, and all his other friends have decamped for the Sudan where another war has broken out, and he realizes that there is nothing he wants so much as to be back at the front, in the thick of the action, with his comrades. Accordingly, he makes out a will leaving everything to Maisie and embarks for Port Said. Once in Africa, he commandeers a camel and a guide, and strikes out into the desert. One morning, at dawn, he staggers into the British camp and, to his delight, the 'fuzzies' commence their attack at that moment. Finding Torpenhow, who notices that his hair is grey and his face is that of an old man, he asks to be put in the forefront of the battle. A 'kindly' bullet puts an end to him; he expires in his friend's arms, under the lee of a dead camel.

An unmistakable air of childish fantasy pervades this book: anyone who can remember himself hurling at a heedless adult world the dread incantation 'I'll break my leg, and *then* you'll be sorry', will have no difficulty in identifying the motive that animates Kipling's account of Dick's failure to secure Maisie's love. Kipling lavishes pity on his hero on such an extravagant scale that it is impossible for the reader to raise even a glimmer of sympathy. But, whatever its literary qualities, *The Light That Failed* does serve to help us understand the state of male sexuality during the final phase of Victoria's reign.

It should not be thought that Dick is an example of the weedy aesthete type; on the contrary, Kipling establishes at the very beginning of the book that he is manliness itself, at least according to the author's criteria. He has fought in battles and seen men die, he has penetrated every corner of the imperial globe, he has experienced poverty, hardship and many a tight corner, he is no stranger, it is darkly hinted, to life's pleasures, he is shrewd, courageous, practical and industrious. While being a bluff, no-nonsense sort of chap, he is at the same time an artist, and one of considerable talent. In short, he is a catch for any girl. The girl in question, however, turns out to be quite impervious to his copious virtues; she does not want him or anything he has to offer, she simply wishes to be left alone to get on with her work.

Maisie herself is not proposed as the acme of femininity; on the other hand, she does presumably typify Kipling's idea of the modern girl. She is self-sufficient and independent; marriage holds no attraction for her, but represents instead a positive threat to her liberty and her chances of professional success. Kipling evidently subscribed to the commonly held belief that women who dedicated themselves to what were then thought of as male pursuits, in Maisie's case her career, would inevitably sustain some damage to their sexuality. He implies that Maisie's inability to respond to Dick's emotional pleas is unnatural, and he condemns her for the short-sighted selfishness that goes with her ruthless attention to work. In this context, it is interesting to note that his male characters all fear and deride the destructive effects on men's capacity to work which, in their experience, invariably ensue from entanglements with women. 'She may throw him out of gear and knock his work to pieces for a while', remarks one of his friends when they learn that Dick is seeing a girl. Later, when his involvement is seen to be deepening, Torpenhow complains: 'She'll spoil his hand. She'll waste his time, and she'll marry him, and ruin his work for ever. He'll be a respectable married man before we can stop him, and – he'll never go on the long trail again.'

Dick will not accept that Maisie does not love him, and obstinately places himself in the most ignominious position. Traditional roles are neatly reversed: he is the one who worries about her neglecting herself, catching cold, not eating enough and working too hard. 'I'd give everything', he tells her, 'for the right of telling you to come out of the rain.' He fits in with her routines, he allows his own painting to go to pot while he frets about hers, and he willingly submits to her slightest whim. And yet, this is a man who would as soon slay a 'fuzzy' as sketch him. His addiction to his watchword 'the queen can do no wrong' provides an indication of the degree to which relations between the sexes had swung round: he is not using the term 'queen' as Ruskin did, to promote woman to a glorified rank where she could do no harm, he is using it in its true sense of sovereign – one who commands and will be obeyed.

In his quest to locate the key to her heart, Dick discovers to his dismay that none of the conventional masculine attributes, of which he possesses a superfluity, impress her; if anything, they excite her disdain. He is finally forced to resort to winning her esteem through a demonstration of his sensitivity – he determines to paint a finer

'Melancolia' than hers. As things fall out, his attempt to do this is foiled by another woman, although by then blindness has intervened to render the exercise meaningless. The self-recrimination Kipling obliges Maisie to endure after her last meeting with Dick can only be regarded as a piece of authorial double-dealing; the contempt she feels for herself is not merited, and quite out of character, but it does make sense if it is interpreted as the resolution of the infantile fantasy referred to above – now he is blind, she is sorry. The fact is that her position throughout their relationship could not be more straightforward: she does not want to marry him and, whatever Kipling may make her say during her final scene in her drawing-room, she frequently tells him so. From the beginning, Kipling visualizes this one-sided courtship in terms of a battle of wills, and there can be no doubt as to whose was the victory; Dick's blindness, which may be seen to stand for a number of things, is the means of providing him with an honourable defeat.

When looked at in a broader perspective, the novel may be taken as an expression of Kipling's fear, one that he was by no means alone in feeling, that his masculinity was insufficient to stir the blood of the young women who were his contemporaries. Maisie is a far cry from those languid, listless and inert young ladies of an earlier generation, to whom a suitor with but a tithe of Dick's accomplishments would have seemed like Byron himself. She has put puddings and stockings behind her for ever: she lives away from home, free of all parental authority, she is financially independent (her income is given precisely – three hundred a year deriving from capital securely invested in Consols) and she leads a productive existence of her own choosing. In short, she is her own woman. This is not to say that Kipling considers her an admirable or enviable figure; for he is at pains to point out that there is something sterile about her nose-to-the-grindstone approach to her work, which he contrasts unfavourably with the dash and spirit of the men (Dick's friends are all foreign correspondents or military artists) who are ready to drop everything at a moment's notice if a 'row' (war) breaks out. He also makes it clear that Maisie's pictures lack the vision and emotional richness of Dick's best creations, and that Dick has a greater depth of soul – a traditional distinction between the sexes, and one in this instance that only bestows on the hero the doubtful privilege of suffering more intensely than the heroine. Maisie is, nevertheless, presented as a woman who sees herself as a whole person, not one who is waiting to be completed by a husband; and here is the focus of Kipling's fear.

His fearfulness finds its symbol in Dick's blindness and his subsequent pursuit of death – his trip to the desert is, in effect, an act of suicide. Freud ascertained, through his study of dreams, that blinding was a symbolic substitute for castration,[1] and Kipling's treatment of his hero certainly accords with such an interpretation. Ostensibly, Dick's loss of eyesight is the direct result of a head wound received in the Sudan a year or so earlier, but it manifests itself at the very moment when his relationship with Maisie reaches the point at which no further progress can be made. Dick has offered her everything he has, and she has remained obdurate; we can never know whether she would have been swayed by his 'Melancolia', but it is safe to say that if, on seeing it, she had acted consistently with her past behaviour, she would still not have acceded to his proposal. In any event, the whole force of the novel is generated by Maisie's implacable resistance to Dick's entreaties. When Maisie departs for her holiday, Kipling is obliged to put into action some solution to the deadlock he has built up between his characters. He could perhaps have arranged for Dick to withdraw gracefully, but this was clearly a compromise he never contemplated; instead, he resorts to more drastic measures. By blinding Dick, he removes him from the sexual arena altogether; as soon as the darkness encloses Dick, he abandons all hope of gaining Maisie. 'When she finds that I don't write she'll stop writing', he tells Torpenhow. 'It's better so. I couldn't be any use to her now . . . I'm not going to beg for pity.'

It is significant that his decision to seek out his own death is provoked by the incident in which the final spark of his sexual vigour is kindled and put out. Some weeks after his final confrontation with Maisie, he runs into Bessie, the girl who destroyed his picture; feeling sorry for him, she suggests that she keep house for him, and he, no longer too proud to accept a little pity, agrees. Her interest in him helps to restore his self-respect. One afternoon, she gives him an affectionate kiss, and he puts his arm round her: 'Ye gods!' he exclaims, 'it's good to put one's arm round a woman's waist again.' She has no objection to this development, and lets him kiss her again; 'He was beginning to learn, not for the first time in his experience, that kissing is a cumulative poison. The more you get of it, the more you want.' Unfortunately, she chooses this moment to confess to him that she has vandalized his 'Melancolia'. His immediate reaction is to shake his head 'as a young steer shakes it when the lash of the stock-whip across his nose warns him back to the path to the shambles that he would escape.' Within minutes he makes up his mind to go to the Sudan, and within two days he is on his way.

Kipling leaves the reader in no doubt that Dick desires his own death. Although the rest of the men lie down when the fighting breaks out, Dick remains upright on his camel. Bullets are flying everywhere. Torpenhow tells him to get down. He refuses – 'No. Put me, I pray, in the forefront of the battle' – and is instantly shot through the head. Thus, the nature of Dick's castration finds its true form by being self-inflicted.

Kipling's emotional response to the challenge posed by the feminist women of his day – he was, we recall, only twenty-six when the novel was published – was expressed through his treatment of his hero. By having Dick go blind, and by having him commit suicide, Kipling was issuing a threat but, like a child's threat, it was inspired not by strength but by fear. 'See what will happen to us men,' he seems to be saying, 'if you persist with your indifference.' He did not adopt the course, as Leighton or Geddes might have done, of administering a lecture to young women by holding Maisie up as an example of a girl who had sacrificed her sexuality on the altar of independence; he makes Dick pay the price for her self-determination. Kipling was in no position to issue lofty admonishments; for he was obsessed with a fear of being unable to live up to the demands which he imagined the educated, liberated, self-supporting young women of 1891 would place upon a man if he was to achieve sexual success.

Man-talk and Tobacco
In a world turned into quicksand by feminine perfidy, Dick can at least rely on the loyalty and love of his friend Torpenhow. And an excellent sort of love it is too: 'Torpenhow . . . looked at Dick with his eyes full of the austere love that springs up between men who have tugged at the same oar together and are yoked by custom and the intimacies of toil. This is a good love, and, since it allows, and even encourages strife, recrimination, and the most brutal sincerity, does not die, but increases, and is proof against any absence and evil conduct.'

This moment occurs on the evening following Dick's first meeting with Maisie; Torpenhow divines that Dick is out of sorts and that a woman is at the bottom of it. With something like relish, he warns Dick of the calamitous consequences that are bound to ensue from such folly: he tells him he is in for 'a tremendous thrashing' and a 'hammering'. Kipling's perception of relationships between men and women is fraught with struggles for power, breakings of will and the clash of irresistible forces meeting immovable objects, while his descriptions of male friendship are, by comparison, positively lyrical. After his return home from a sea-side excursion with Maisie, the first entire day he has spent with a woman, Dick experiences a deep yearning for man-talk and tobacco, which is hardly surprising since the men in his life, particularly Torpenhow, show him a tenderness and consideration that most women would be hard pressed to rival.

Nor are his friend's attentions confined to mere verbiage. Whereas Dick has the greatest difficulty in persuading Maisie to let him kiss her, once, on the cheek, he is for ever being hugged and held by Torpenhow; these embraces are, of course, of the manliest character and nearly crack his ribs, but they are nonetheless delivered with great feeling. When Dick goes blind and becomes delirious, Torpenhow nurses him with a mother's care: he holds his hand, or rather thrusts out 'a large and hairy paw' for Dick to clutch, he soothes him and puts him to bed, and when at last he is quiet he kisses him lightly on the forehead 'as men do sometimes kiss a comrade in the hour of death to ease his departure'. During his delirium Dick addresses his friend as Maisie – a meaningful confusion – and it is only fitting that when he dies, he does so in the arms of the devoted Torpenhow.

These homosexual undertones are by no means exclusive to Kipling's novel; the fiction of the period abounds with male characters whose emotions only find their deepest satisfaction in male friendship. Du Maurier's *Trilby* (1894) provides a revealing example, and is worth examining because the author's overt intention, like Kipling's, was to write a study of a tragic love affair.

It should be remembered that Du Maurier's book, unlike Kipling's, became a best-seller, and precipitated what Du Maurier's biographer has called a Trilby 'boom'. Du Maurier received a huge fan mail after the book was published: some of his correspondents simply wished to congratulate him, some wrote to inquire the true identity of his hero, but most were eager to confide in her creator their adoration of *la belle* Trilby. Requests were made to patent 'Trilby' songs, shoes, and even a kitchen range. A proud father informed Du Maurier that he had named his daughter Trilby, and demanded to know if he was the first to do so. In 1895 the book was dramatized and staged with great success at the Haymarket by Beerbohm Tree who made the part of Svengali, Trilby's evil genius, his own.

The ramifications of the novel's plot need not concern us. Suffice it to say that it is set in the never-never land of *La Bohème*, and that its central characters are three young Britons who have come to Paris to study painting. Talbot Wynne, alias Taffy, a giant of a Yorkshireman, distantly related to a baronet, and possessor of kind but choleric blue eyes, biceps as strong as iron bands, and an immense pair of Piccadilly weepers, has recently bought himself out of his cavalry regiment in order to pursue his true vocation. Sandy, nicknamed for no very good reason the Laird of Cockpen, but in fact the son and grandson of good and pious Dundee solicitors, is studying to perfect his speciality, toreador pictures. William Talbot, who is referred to throughout by the arch soubriquet Little Billee, is the youngest of the trio and the novel's hero. On him Du Maurier lavishes a wealth of flattering detail: he is small, slender, graceful, and well-built, his forehead is straight, white, and blue-veined, his eyes are large and dark blue, his hair is coal-black, and his hands and feet are very small. The inattentive reader may be forgiven at this point for imagining that he has just read a description of the heroine, so closely does Little Billee's appearance tally with the conventions of Victorian beauty.

These three are great pals, but the language Du Maurier uses to describe their friendship contains the same undertones we detected in Kipling's handling of Torpenhow's affection for Dick. Little Billee, who consistently adopts a submissive, filial attitude towards the other two, especially Taffy, looks on them as guides and philosophers, thinks them simply perfect and wonders 'if any one, living or dead, had ever such a glorious pair of chums as these'. Taffy and the Laird, for their part, 'were as fond of the boy as they could be'; they love him for his 'almost girlish purity of mind . . . his affectionate disposition, his lively and caressing ways'; they admire him 'far more than he ever knew'; in short, they love him 'very much indeed'.

It is, however, in Du Maurier's presentation of his heroine that the strongest homosexual note is sounded; for just as Little Billee's physique is confusingly similar to a girl's, so hers most closely resembles that of a man. On her first appearance – in a French infantry soldier's greatcoat – the reader is told that Trilby has a portentous voice of great volume that 'could have belonged to either sex', that her feet are 'uncompromising and inexorable as boot trees', her chin is 'massive', her teeth are big and British, and that her height was equal to a gendarme's – she was not a giantess, the author hastens to add, just very tall. Taffy declares her to be a trump, and confides his admiration for her to the Laird. 'Why, she's as upright and straight and honourable as a man.' Du Maurier himself adds to the trans-sexual confusion by commenting that she would have made a singularly handsome boy.

Contrary to the impression that might be formed by this description, Trilby is regarded as a great beauty, and all four male protagonists – the three Britons and Svengali, the villain, to say nothing of the odd subsidiary character, fall in love with her. Although the novel is set in the mid-century period of Du Maurier's youth, he is at pains to establish that Trilby's is a modern kind of beauty: 'Trilby's type would be infinitely more admired now than in the fifties.' He contrasts her with the women of an earlier generation who had been valued for their oval faces, little aquiline noses, heart-shaped little mouths, and soft dimpled chins, and asserts that she would have greatly appealed to Sir Edward Burne-Jones or Sir John Millais, two of the leading painters of the 'nineties.

If the popularity of his book and in particular of his heroine is anything to go by, Du Maurier was correct in his estimation of Trilby's attractiveness. In his book *Bestseller*, a study of some of the most-read books to be published between 1900 and 1939, Claud Cockburn wrote that the best-seller lists provide an indispensable guide to people's state of mind at any given time; for

> you cannot deny that if Book X was what a huge majority of book-buyers and book-borrowers wanted to buy or borrow in a given year, or over a period of years, then Book X satisfied a need, and expressed and realized emotions and attitudes to life which the buyers and borrowers did not find expressed or realized elsewhere . . . of all indices to moods, attitudes, and, above all,

aspirations, the best-seller list is one of the most reliable. There is no way of fudging it.

By the same token, it seems reasonable to suggest that the characteristics with which Trilby had been endowed presumably represented a type of sexuality that was in accord with public taste. And yet, Du Maurier had created a beau idéal whose sexual charisma chiefly lay in her boyishness, and occasionally even in her manliness.

Kipling had responded to his fear of the New Woman and the distressing sense of inadequacy she unleashed by seeking refuge in 'the austere love that springs up between men', and by indulging in self-pitying fantasies of mutilation and impotence. Du Maurier, however, though no less fervent a believer in the virtues and rewards of comradeship, was able to propose a more sophisticated form of reassurance, one that evidently struck a chord in the public's imagination: he imposed upon his heroine the insignia of masculinity, and made these the very qualities which most endeared her to her lovers.

It is reasonable to suppose that men will place an especially high value on the emotional satisfaction to be derived from male friendship during periods when they feel that their prowess is being threatened, rather than flattered, by women. Undoubtedly the late 'eighties and 'nineties was such a period, and it can be no coincidence that books which featured male trios and duos acting as collective heroes enjoyed great popularity during those years. A desire to celebrate the joys of male companionship and to glorify the code of male solidarity may be clearly discerned in such novels as *King Solomon's Mines* (Allan Quartermain, Sir Henry Curtis, and Captain John Good, 1885) by H. Rider Haggard, *Three Men in a Boat* (1885) by Jerome K. Jerome, *Stalky & Co.* (Stalky, M'turk, and Beetle, 1889) by Kipling himself, *A Study in Scarlet*, etc. (Holmes and Watson, 1887), and *Raffles, The Amateur Cracksman* (Raffles and Bunny, 1899) by E. W. Horning.[2]

If Trilby is examined in this context, her incongruous tendency to manliness and the adulation she aroused become more comprehensible. Du Maurier had invested her with none of Maisie's belligerent egotism, and this alone must have recommended her to the average male reader. As a chum, she is invariably loyal, eventempered and sporting; although an artist's model and a bohemian she retains an admirable sense of decency; and, as a woman, she never fails to behave towards men with a submissive willingness to be led that would have earned her Maisie's hearty contempt. However, not only did she evince a gratifying respect for the rules of conduct regulating relations between the sexes, but she also offered a brand of sexuality which guaranteed emotional safety and freedom from humiliation. She was a kind of honorary man and, as her creator was at pains to emphasize, when it came to love one could rely on men. Far from manufacturing a freak, Du Maurier had succeeded in launching a sex-symbol.

The Killer Woman

Although in many ways dissimilar to the other two novels, Grant Allen's *The Woman Who Did* shares one important feature in common with *Trilby* and *The Light That Failed*, and that is the death of its hero. A positive holocaust takes place at the end of *Trilby*, for Du Maurier had contrived a climax which entailed the deaths of Trilby herself, and of both her principal lovers, Little Billee and Svengali. But in all three books the deaths of the men are seen to be the direct result of their involvement with women. This phenomenon is highly characteristic of the period's literature, and there would be no difficulty attached to compiling a lengthy list of novels dating from these years in which it can be found. For the sake of brevity, however, the present discussion is confined to the three books already reviewed and one other source – *The Yellow Book*.

Notorious in its day for its 'lubricity' (*The Times*) and now famous largely for having had Aubrey Beardsley as its art editor and designer, *The Yellow Book* was a quarterly magazine, bound in hard covers, published by John Lane between April 1894 and May 1897. Each issue comprised a miscellany of poetry, essays, short stories, and illustrations. Among its contributors were Henry James, Ernest Dowson, George Gissing, Max Beerbohm, Arthur Symons, Richard Le Gallienne, Kenneth Grahame, Arnold Bennett, and H. G. Wells. Aubrey Beardsley contributed some of his best work, as did Wilson Steer (see Chapter 8). The bulk of its material was, however, provided by writers of both sexes who, though then well known, have been virtually forgotten today.

Whatever its merits or inadequacies, *The Yellow Book* may be said fairly to represent a cross-section of 'nineties writers, and the themes that preoccupied them may reasonably be presumed to reflect the concerns and anxieties of the class to which they belonged.

It is therefore interesting to discover that a large proportion of the stories published in the magazine contained the very phenomenon that links the three novels under discussion. One example will have to stand for the rest[3] – Ella D'Arcy's *A Marriage*.[4] (Next to the editor, Henry Harland, this authoress was the most prolific contributor, with eleven stories to her name; she also acted as Harland's editorial assistant.)

Catterson, the hero of *A Marriage*, decides to ignore the advice of his friends and to do the decent thing by his mistress and marry her, even though he realizes that a drop in social status, if not ostracism, is likely to be the result. Prior to the wedding, the girl is thought by all a model of domestic virtue – capable but unassuming; once married, however, this paragon transforms herself into a virago. She domineers her hapless husband, offends his friends, persecutes their son while indulging their daughter, develops social pretensions, and successfully disguises her humble background. The scales fall from her husband's eyes and his health begins to fail. He takes one of his old friends into his confidence and complains bitterly of his wife's new character – 'Perhaps if I had never married her – who knows? Women require to be kept under, to be afraid of you, to live in a condition of insecurity; to know their good fortune is dependent on their good conduct.' His wife, he confesses, is cold, cruel, mean, neglectful, narrow, and empty-minded, and his life is miserable. Hectic spots glow in his cheeks and a hollow cough punctuates his conversation. His friend is upset to see him in such poor condition, but as he leaves the house he reflects that death is at least a fate preferable to the one Catterson is obliged daily to endure in his own house. He then discovers he has left his hat in the drawing-room, and returns to overhear Mrs Catterson discussing a choice of dress-materials with a neighbour – shall it be the green or the black? Catterson's cough is heard echoing up the stairs, and Mrs Catterson remarks decisively '. . . it would be more prudent I suppose to decide on the black'.

Ella D'Arcy left her readers in no doubt that the wretched Catterson was to die of nothing more nor less than psychological enervation; his wife had turned out to be a woman of invincible selfishness, and he was simply not equal to the struggle. Fatal repercussions of this kind occur again and again in *Yellow Book* stories when women take the emotional initiative in relationships with men, particularly in marriage, and proceed to assert themselves.

Few of the stories that follow this pattern unequivocally champion either the male or the female cause; on the whole, they merely expose the issue. But the fact that as many of these stories were written by women as by men gives an indication of the dilemma in which the average middle-class wife placed herself when she strove to upset the traditional balance of power between the sexes. It would appear that women, no less than men, were haunted by the conviction that the right to exercise a measure of autonomy within marriage could only be obtained by putting at risk their husbands' masculinity. However highly they valued their liberty, they assuredly did not wish to reduce their men to the pitiable state so grimly outlined by Ella D'Arcy.

The deaths to which the male characters in these stories so frequently succumb were seldom more than sketchily described, and their precise causes were generally left unspecified; but then they were more symbolic than real. Death provided the only euphemism sufficiently grandiose to substitute for the condition with which the writers were actually concerned; for death was capable of representing castration, impotence, etiolation, or plain spinelessness, in short, any of the states to which they feared men might be brought if women took up arms against the sexual hierarchy.

Although the heroes of our three novels meet with ends that are narrated in more detail and more elaborately explained, their destinies, like those of the men in the *Yellow Book* stories, are nevertheless entirely predetermined by women; either they expire under the treatment of women, even when it is well-intentioned, or they act as secondary victims to fates that befall women. No sooner has Alan Merrick been persuaded to commit himself to a free union with Herminia Barton than he is laid low by typhoid. Little Billee hovers perilously on the brink of the grave and almost loses his reason when Trilby breaks off their engagement. In the final chapter, his death is brought on by grief for Trilby: she is buried on one page and he is dead, after a lengthy and painful illness, at the end of the next. As we saw earlier, Dick's blindness and subsequent death are depicted as the psychological, if not physiological, results of Maisie's steadfast refusal to fall in love with him.

This obsessive pairing of death with feminine self-assertion may be interpreted as a symptom of the fear aroused in the minds of men and women alike by the prospect of women exploiting their new-found sexual role. This fear was formally and publicly expressed through the vigorous opposition with which Parliament, the law courts, and the authorities in general invariably greeted any fresh move towards emancipation, but these novels and stories furnish the modern reader with an insight into the fear that stalked ordinary middle-class homes, and the effect it had upon ordinary marriages.

As the female stereotype began to shift and change, men were not only obliged to adjust themselves to a new style of sexual relationship with women, they were also prompted to contemplate their own sexuality in a new light. They came to see that, far from being an enemy to be vanquished, or a more or less bestial urge requiring occasional gratification, their sexuality was in fact a dimension of their nature which held an exhilarating promise. An equation between sexual pleasure and emotional fulfilment crystallized in their imagination. It was, of course, as yet impossible for them to free their ideas concerning sex of the guilt that had acted as an all-too effective censor for so many decades, and it was inevitable that they should at first associate this equation with illicit sexuality.

At the same time, however, men were profoundly apprehensive of the new possibilities inherent in their sexuality. They had previously been accustomed to treating their sexual instincts as an aspect of themselves that was best suppressed and forgotten, and although it is true that a certain licence had been permitted, they had understood this too to be a part, a regrettably necessary one, of the process of suppression. The sublimation of male sexuality into other activities had involved a gross underestimation and neglect of women's emotional needs, but women were now making it plain that they no longer accepted the ignominious relegation of their sexuality. By demanding the right to play a fully-realized part in their relationships with the other sex, women automatically placed on men the obligation to expose and explore that part of their being which they had learnt to hide and shackle. Those men who sought the fulfilment of their sexuality set themselves a painful and demanding task, so demanding indeed that many abandoned the attempt in despair. One such victim was the painter, Wilson Steer.

8

Steer

Philip Wilson Steer was born in 1860, the son of a portrait painter. During his twenties he studied in Paris, fell under the influence of Degas and Monet and developed a style which owed much to Seurat's neo-impressionist theories. He returned to England where he lived for the remainder of his long life and won for himself a paragraph in the history of art as one of the few British impressionists and as a notable painter, in both oil and water-colour, of landscapes. He was awarded the Order of Merit and died in 1943. In books and memoirs dealing with his period, his name is frequently coupled with Sickert's (1860–1942); both were founder-members of the New English Arts Club (1866) and both painted in the impressionist vein at a time when the work of French artists was either ignored or despised. Sickert's was, however, the more flamboyant personality, and he is generally regarded as the more important painter.

In middle age Steer was by all accounts diffident, cautious, retiring, and not a little old-maidish. After the death of his mother in 1898 he bought a house in Cheyne Walk, Chelsea, which he occupied until he died. For many years he was looked after by his old nanny. He never married and his circle of friends was largely composed of bachelors – Henry Tonks, George Moore, John Singer Sargent, and Henry James. As he grew older he was gripped by a mania for collecting; pictures, furniture, engravings, Japanese prints, porcelain, Chelsea china, brass Persian salvers, Chinese bronzes, medals, and coins congested every corner of his house. He also fell victim to hypochondria, never going downstairs without a hat for fear of the change of temperature between floors. Once a year between June and October he took a holiday devoted to outdoor painting in one of England's counties, and every year he tormented himself with anxiety concerning the arrangements for at least a month beforehand. He kept a cat, painted in his drawing-room and not in a studio, allowed himself to grow fat, and was lazy in all matters save painting at which he worked obsessively. He wrote few

letters and expressed fewer opinions. He took no part in the controversies that invigorated his profession. In short, he closed his door
on all that was turbulent or distressing, opening it only to those
people and ideas that would not disrupt the smooth running of his
cosily secure existence.

A friend once wrote of him:

> Oh poor old W.S.
> Your thoughts I'd like to guess,
> You are so deep.
> But, ere you sleep,
> Do you, like us, undress?

George Moore, who knew him well and saw him frequently, also
hinted at something sterile in the comfortable complacency of
Steer's demeanour when he described 'seeing Steer in my thoughts,
fat and sleek, in his armchair, his hands crossed piously over his
belly's slope, his cat curled in an armchair on the other side of the
fireplace, both carefully screened from the danger of draughts.'[1]

It is not easy to see in this staid and moribund old man the author
of one of the boldest attempts in the Victorian period to bring a
sense of flesh and blood reality to the portrayal of female sexuality,
and yet that is the task to which Steer, as a young man, dedicated
himself.

Between 1885 and 1892 Steer, painting in his impressionist style,
executed a large number of canvases in which children, mostly little
girls, are seen playing on beaches. The colours in these pictures are
vivacious and crisply handled; their mood is generally peaceful and
carefree. Occupying the foreground of one of the best known of this
series – 'Children Paddling, Walberswick' – are four girls, aged
about twelve or fourteen; they are dressed in the obligatory beach
costume of the day: straw hats decorated with ribbons, cotton
dresses reaching to their calves, and long, white bloomers. Their
black stockings lie discarded on the shingle. On the left of the
picture sits a girl drying her legs with a towel, near her another
bends down to stare into the water which laps around her ankles;
the other two have begun to wade out further, holding hands;
one holds up her skirt, the other has daringly tucked hers into her
bloomers. George Moore wrote of these children, in his review of
Steer's one-man exhibition in 1894, that they had forgotten 'their

little worries in the sensation of sea and sand, as I forget mine in that dreamy blue which fades and deepens imperceptibly . . . they are as flowers, and are conscious only of the benedictive influences of sand and sea and sky.'

Steer's own age during the years he was painting his girls ran roughly from twenty-five to thirty-two, although by then he had contracted a far more potent obsession. He was by no means exceptional in his preoccupation with pubescent girls, but he did differ from his more morbid contemporaries, Ernest Dowson for example, in portraying his nymphets in their gayest mood. Whether running in the evening sunlight across Walberswick pier, playing knucklebones on the beach, leaning over the pier to investigate a passing yacht, or bending down to inspect a sandy pool left behind by the tide, Steer's girls are always completely absorbed in their own activities; they bask blithely in the timeless calm of a summer holiday. Steer was one of the few Victorian artists to portray children indulging in ordinary childish games, free of any mawkish overtone. He seems to rejoice in their vigorous insouciance.

However, he also rejoices in something a little less wholesome, for an undeniable whiff of the sea-side voyeur infuses his treatment of his innocent subjects. His girls are gawky, leggy and tall; they are unmistakably feminine but at that age when the female character-istics have barely obtruded save to breathe a sinuous pliancy into their slender forms. Their faces are never individualized and are frequently shown as sun-tanned masks. Because they are young and innocent their behaviour on the beach is not expected to match the strict decorum sustained by their mothers and older sisters; they tuck up their skirts, disdain their stockings, show their legs, flaunt their bloomers, stick out their bottoms as they bend to pick up a shell, and generally display themselves provocatively.

Steer, the onlooker, is fascinated by their uninhibited gambols and no painter has more successfully portrayed the supple freedom of adolescent movement. It comes as a shock, therefore, to see how woodenly he modelled the figures in a picture called 'A Summer's Evening' (see illustration). At first sight it appears to be a typical Steer creation: three pubescent girls on a stretch of beach dotted with yellow poppies preparing to go home as the sun sets, painted in char-acteristically vibrant colours. A number of curious features, however, distinguish it from others in the series, of which the most striking is that the girls are naked. One sits with her back to the viewer pinning up her hair, the second is lying on her back, an arm supporting her head, her long red hair trailing over her shoulder, and the third stands, her arms stretched above her head, getting ready to pull on a white shift. The face of the standing girl is, as usual, not characterized by features but is painted a fiery red. Her body is skinny and gauche, its slightness accentuated by her arms reaching upwards. Her breasts are scarcely delineated, but her nipples are picked out in scorching orange, as is her *mons veneris*. Her pose is far from natural: she looks uncomfortable, painfully immobilized, like a model who has been asked to hold her position too long, as indeed was the case.

The shore line, which stretches away towards the cliffs in a long, curving line, is deserted except for the girls. It would, of course, have been difficult for Steer to have painted naked girls in anything but a completely private setting, but the sense of isolation created by this huge expanse of empty beach lends the painting an eeriness quite at odds with his other pictures, which all exude a bustling vitality. By leading the eye away from the foreground this long, curving line also creates a feeling of uneasy ambivalence, implying that Steer did not wish to commit unequivocally his viewer's eye to the three naked girls; it is as if the artist himself, already embarrassed by his choice of subject, is assisting the viewer to look the other way.

'A Summer's Evening' was a studio painting on which Steer worked for two or three months during the winter of 1887–8. All three girls have red hair and it is thought that they are drawn from the same model. The picture certainly has a far more laborious and calculated air than his other sea-side scenes but, considering the cultural conditions in which he was working, it is not surprising that he took extraordinary trouble when he came to depict nudity.

During the latter thirty years of Victoria's reign, the nude was not in itself unacceptable to Victorian taste; indeed, providing certain restrictions were acknowledged and respected, it was enthusiastically welcomed. Nor was the sensual treatment of the nude necessarily forbidden; many of Alma-Tadema's later and most popular paintings contained nude figures that were clearly designed to titillate and would today be classified as soft pornography. As a neo-classicist, Alma-Tadema was, however, able to take advantage of the irreproachable respectability with which that tradition had been invested by its other practitioners. Their unquestioned sincerity of purpose, their invariably edifying choice of theme, the high position they occupied in the hierarchy of their profession and their formidable personal prestige bestowed on their school of painting a special licence with regard to the nude that was not readily accessible to artists working outside their privileged territory.

A handful of painters did occàsionally paint nudes without the benefit of a high-minded excuse, but none made any determined effort to challenge the code of propriety to which the great majority of British artists willingly subscribed. For example, Whistler, no respecter of his fellow-painters' standards, executed a number of exquisite nudes, but unfortunately he only took up the subject towards the very end of his life. During the 'nineties Charles Conder also painted a few nudes, but they offered no serious threat to the canons of decency and have been described as 'beautiful generalities basking in a silken twilight'.[2] Aubrey Beardsley drew a series of unashamedly erotic illustrations for an edition of Aristophanes' *Lysistrata* but they did not become generally available until many years later.

Late Victorian art abounded in nudes, but apart from a very few isolated exceptions, all were created within the sanctified context of a classical or mythological *mise en scène*; no tradition existed of painting nude women for their own sake. Since William Etty's death (1849), no artist had devoted himself to painting ordinary women in ordinary surroundings, free of allegorical trappings. Those painters, like Leighton, who had endeavoured to express their attitude to physical female sexuality had been unwilling to do so without resorting to the protection of established convention, a manoeuvre which had necessarily imposed a measure of distortion.

Such was the domestic situation when Steer took up his brushes to paint the naked red-heads in his 'Summer's Evening'. But other influences had already made their mark on his style, and it would have been strange if he had not at least considered putting to use the examples set by his French masters. While studying in France, and particularly while studying Degas, he must have come across innumerable portrayals of naked women unencumbered by the moralistic paraphernalia required of his compatriots. Since the eighteen-sixties French artists had looked for no excuses, classical or otherwise, for painting nudes: Manet had stripped a woman at a picnic in the company of correctly dressed gentlemen ('Déjeuner sur l'herbe'); Courbet had shown that models were, in reality, solid masses of feeling flesh and not marbled goddesses ('l'Atelier du peintre'); Degas himself had put his girls into the bath to wash those parts of themselves which many English husbands had never seen on their wives, far less in pictures; Renoir had celebrated the glowing amplitude of a girl fresh from a swim in the river ('la Baigneuse blonde'); and Gaugin had painted his maid who looked after his children simply sitting naked on her bed, darning her clothes ('The Seamstress').

Steer would certainly have examined these pictures, or the work of these artists while he was in Paris, and he must have been struck by the profound differences that lay between the French and British treatments of the naked female body. Although he was able to absorb and put into practice many of the impressionists' technical principles, their psychological approach to the nude was considerably less easy for him to imbide.

Apart from having to overcome the handicap of lacking a domestic tradition of painting the nude under natural conditions, Steer had to gird himself to wrestle with a truly terrifying adversary. Painting the naked body of a girl to whom one was attracted was for a Victorian no mere academic exercise. It is true that by the standards of their day artists enjoyed an almost unique access to nakedness since society chose to turn a blind eye to their drawing 'from the life', always providing that the model was not a lady. But this privilege in itself did not make the labour he had set himself any the less daunting to one of Steer's timorous and reserved temperament.

In distinguishing between the terms *naked* and *nude*, Kenneth Clark has written, 'the naked body is no more than a point of departure for a work of art'. He acknowledged that 'the desire to grasp and be united with another human body is so fundamental a part of our nature, that our judgement of what is known as "pure form" is inevitably influenced by it', but he believed that 'the amount of erotic content which a work of art can hold in solution is very high'. He explained how the nude throughout history has satisfied a multitude of human needs other than the purely 'biological'. The Victorians, however, were unable to share his cool and sophisticated attitude; for them a naked body was, unavoidably, a point of arrival. The desire to grasp and be united with another human body was just as fundamental a part of their nature as of any other nation's at any other time, but their desires and their willingness to acknowledge them were so throttled and distorted that they could only stomach the smallest quantity of overtly 'erotic content' without succumbing to nausea.

Steer was not only familiar with his countrymen's inability to consume the naked body, he suffered from the same disease himself; being an artist did not bestow upon him immunity from his society's ills. At the same time he was determined to give expression to his sexual yearnings. His proclivity for pubescent girls at this stage of his life appears to have been generalized and unfocused: none of the girls in his pictures has an identifiable face and all share the same lanky, coltish physique. It was the type that attracted him, not a particular individual, but when it came to painting the naked body of a type, the demands on his courage were such that his style lost all its customary naturalness and gaiety, and he could not avoid drawing hysterical attention to the very parts about which he was most apprehensive.

To paint a body is to establish a relationship with it; Steer's relationship with the bodies he so laboriously painted during the winter of 1887 was that of an onlooker, albeit an onlooker experiencing feelings of impassioned longing. But 'A Summer's Evening' remained an impressive achievement for, without resorting to disguise or convention, Steer had publicly declared his attraction to a certain kind of sexual beauty, and had been honest enough to depict his girls in their authentic setting – not the steps of some apodyterium,[3] but the sea-shore at Southwold Bay.

In 1888 Steer ceased to be an observer of adolescent girls in general by becoming a devotee of one in particular: she was called Rose Pettigrew and when he first met her she was twelve years old. Miss Pettigrew has herself written a colourful though tantalizingly incomplete account of their affair.[4] She describes how she and her three sisters were brought to London by their recently widowed mother to earn a living as artists' models; Rose was eight at the time. The three Pettigrew sisters were evidently very beautiful for they had no difficulty in finding employment with the leading artists of the day. Rose describes herself as the ordinary one of the three, 'tiny, with bushels of very curly bright gold hair, a nose which started straight but changed its mind, by turning up at the tip, a rose-leaf complexion, and a cupid's bow mouth, which most of the big sculptors have cast; I had an extremely pretty figure.'

First to put the sisters' striking looks to use was Millais who

incorporated them in his 'An Idyll of 1745'. Once launched on
their career, they went from strength to strength, posing for 'every
great artist in the land: Whistler, Poynter, Leighton – whom she
did not admire as an artist – Holman Hunt, Prinsep, and Sargent'.
Rose herself became attached for a while to the Whistler *ménage*,
then located at The Vale, Tite Street, and grew especially fond of
'the real' Mrs Whistler (Beatrix Godwin whom Whistler married
in 1888). She says she loved to be in the house when Oscar Wilde
called, although she recalls one disagreeable incident: 'I was
looking at a book one morning when he came in; I had my curly
hair tied back with bright ribbon, as all small girls did in those days;
Oscar pulled one of my curls and said "I would look beautiful if I
wore my hair like that." I felt disgusted . . .'

'My next adventure', she wrote, describing her first meeting
with Steer, 'was a most important one.' Invited by an older girl-
friend, aged fourteen – Rose was 'nearly twelve' by this time – to
meet 'the best looking man in Chelsea', she agreed, as a lark, to go
to Steer's home. The friend claimed that he was 'very keen' on her.
Rose was not disappointed in Steer, whom she thought 'the tallest,
thinnest and best looking man' she had ever seen. On this occasion
he was busy, and eager to be rid of them. Before they departed,
however, he kissed the other girl, but only looked at Rose, remarking 'I'd kiss you too, if you didn't have pimples.' She was humiliated
but curious, and took immediate steps to banish the offending
pimples. As soon as she deemed her face presentable, she put on her
very best frock, one that Mrs Whistler had made for her, and went
straight back to her hero's house. He answered the door and she
asked if he would like to paint her, adding that she was accustomed
to posing for all the big painters. He disapproved of the dress but
was taken with her. He asked her age and she lied, saying fourteen.
She posed for a little while, more to give him the opportunity of
taking a good look at her than of achieving anything artistic, they
flirted together, and she departed in high spirits.

It was not long before she was posing for him regularly, and at a
cut-rate – an unnecessary, if generous gesture for, as she discovered,
he had a comfortable private income. The Whistlers were upset by
her sudden switch of loyalty; Mrs Whistler asked if she was in love
with him, and if he knew her age. She replied that she was not in
love with him and that he did not know her age, but that she thought
he was a great artist who would one day be very famous Steer for his

part was clearly infatuated; except for a few society portraits, he painted no one but her.

It is not easy to gauge the passage of time from her narrative, but she then writes, 'by this time [?] he had become as much in love with me as I with him; he asked me one day if I'd let him kiss me; I said I didn't mind, but didn't show much eagerness, not nearly as much as he was evidently used to.' She makes no further comment on this incident, but goes on to say that she let him think that she was sixteen, and that because he loved her she could not take his money and posed for nothing as often as she could – about three times a week.

She and her sisters spent many evenings with him and his friends; on birthdays chianti would be drunk from tooth mugs and cracked cups and afterwards Rose, who only drank to appear grown up, was often sick. They danced, sang popular songs – Tonks's performance of 'A pale young curate' being particularly memorable – and played guessing and word games. Although Steer's singing was notable only for being consistently out of tune, his dancing was impressive and he often took Rose to the local dance hall where they won competitions as the best waltzers, despite the absurdity of their joint appearance: 'We must have looked a very comical couple, I so tiny, and he so tall, he also had a habit of bending over as if he was going to turn a complete somersault over my head.'

She ends her story with maddening abruptness for in the very next paragraph she describes how their relationship broke up. He turned up one evening at the dance hall wearing a new velvet coat to which she took an instant dislike. He had brought her a bunch of carnations, but she refused to accept them because they clashed with her green dress. He protested that the colours were complementary. She persisted; he lost his temper and said, 'You'd make a funny wife for an artist!' She replied that she had no intention of marrying an artist, certainly not one who wore velvet coats, and returned his ring to him the next day. 'I hated parting with it,' she wrote, 'it was a beautiful carved gold one which a relation of his had left his family, he was a bishop.' Her next sentence, which could not be plainer or briefer, presumably sums up a period of great unhappiness for Steer: 'He came back with it for months, but I would never see him.'

Rose later married a musician, H. Waldo Warner, a genius in her estimation, who made her very happy; she was his widow when she came to write this account of her affair with Steer. She had no doubts that she married the right man: 'I'm sure he [Steer] loved me very much, but he owes me a great debt, for not becoming his wife; he achieved everything in his lifetime, which he would never have done had he married; we would never have been happy, our house would have been filled with babies, pretty models and velvet coats.'

She brings this touching document to an end by hoping 'that my two lovers [Steer was also dead by this time] will meet and become great friends; they were two modest simple souls.'

Rose Warner was seventy-one when she revived on paper her memories of Steer which appear to have come back to her un-marked by the passing of time. She has successfully conveyed the verve, egotism, and naivety of her former, fourteen-year-old self and it seems reasonable to suppose that she has presented the substance of the affair as she experienced it at the time. At no point does her narrative ring false; the elisions of time, the impetuous changes of subject, and her frustrating reticence concerning the personality of Steer all seem to provide evidence of authenticity, in that they ingenuously reflect the priorities and preoccupations of an adolescent girl in love.

Between 1888, the year of his meeting Rose, and 1892 there was a period of overlap when he was still painting his sea-side girls in the old impressionistic style and was at the same time painting Rose alone in a completely different and, for him, new style. After 1892 until the dissolution of their affair three years later he painted her with obsessive exclusivity, only deserting her to paint landscapes and the occasional lucrative portrait.

After painting her a number of times in conventional settings – 'Girl on a Sofa' (1891), 'Reclining on a Sofa' (1892), 'The Blue Dress' (1892), etc. – in 1894 he suddenly began a series of portraits of Rose in which he employed his new style. These portraits have none of the summery exuberance which characterized his paintings of other girls; they are sombre in colour, and intensely intimate in atmosphere. They were, evidently, of the utmost importance to Steer for he arranged to have them reproduced in the then flourishing and notorious *Yellow Book*.

Following the example of Degas – he is supposed to have been much influenced by Degas's 'Woman at a Window' which at that time was in Sickert's possession – he abandoned his colourful impressionist palette and instead restricted himself to basic tones, using a dark reddish-brown ground into which he painted the deeper shadows in dark red or black before drawing out the lights in white and pale flesh colours. In each case the emphasis of the picture falls directly and solely upon Rose herself. Steer does not utilize her as a mere model, a pretty adjunct to a piece of furniture or a length of material; she is the object and focus of his picture. His portraits of her exude an uncomfortable feeling of confinement: Steer seems to have trapped his loved one in a transparent vivarium in order to submit her to an intensive examination. Once again he is the onlooker, but this time he has firmly pinned down the object of his observation; Rose will not run away across the beach or have to be replaced by surrogates during the winter months.

This lowering, claustrophobic sense of inspecting a specimen is further strengthened by the presence of a mirror in many of the portraits: Rose is seen looking at herself in a full-length mirror, looking at the viewer via a mantelpiece mirror and is seen reflected in a mirror as she sits in a chair. John Berger maintained that the real function of the mirror, which was often used in nude painting as a symbol of the vanity of women, ' was to make the woman connive in treating herself as, first and foremost, a sight.' Steer's use of mirrors was, I believe, an unconscious device designed to excuse him for looking, and for looking so intently, at Rose. By offering an alternative angle of observation, an angle other than his own, he was attempting to expiate the guilt he felt towards the object of his observation. But the mirrors perform a more complex function than the diversionary line of shore in 'A Summer's Evening' which only led the eye away from the offending object, for they lead the eye directly back to the source of his guilt. And, by the same token, the intensity with which he studies Rose is doubled by the reflection's second perspective, and the ferocity of his gaze is magnified.

In most of the portraits Rose is dressed only in her shift; she is never naked or even half-naked, and she is seldom fully dressed. There is no indication in Rose's sketch of their relationship that he ever took her to bed, or saw her naked, and there is nothing in the pictures themselves that is inconsistent with celibacy, but these portraits are, nevertheless, far more sexually advanced than his earlier sea-side work. The girl concerned is, unlike those whose faces were but sun-reddened blurs, graphically individualized –

7   Philip Wilson Steer, *A Summers Evening* (see page 136)

8 Philip Wilson Steer, *Portrait of Himself* (see page 145)

Rose's profile is unmistakable. She has been brought into the closed environment of the studio where she can be scrutinized closely and at leisure; although not naked, she is dressed in such a way as to show to the best advantage the beauty of her long legs, elegant arms, and slim figure. She does not have to be spied on like the girls on the beach; she is content to sit and be observed. It seems reasonable to assume that by publishing these intimate portraits of a clearly recognizable girl as a series in so *risqué* a publication as *The Yellow Book*, Steer was attempting to make a statement that was sexual as well as artistic.

Steer was, however, still a long way from being able to depict freely the sexuality of the woman he loved, or of any woman. He was also still some way from being able to come to terms with a woman older than an adolescent; Rose was seventeen in 1894. One of the Pettigrew portraits eloquently expresses the vigour of the inhibitions under which he then laboured: it is the only one in which he appears and, revealingly, he called it 'Portrait of Himself' (see illustration). (It was painted *c.* 1894 and appeared in the second volume of *The Yellow Book* dated July 1894.) Rose is seated in the foreground on a plain wooden chair, wearing a white, flounced petticoat with a white bodice held in at the waist by a ribbon, black stockings, and black, dainty shoes. She has crossed one leg over the other and is adjusting her shoe. Her arms, which are bare, are very prettily modelled, and her pose seems natural and spontaneous. Her face is, however, completely obliterated by her hair which has fallen forward as she leans and turns her head to concentrate on her shoe. This is the only occasion on which Steer has hidden her features.

Once again the mirror device is used, but unobtrusively for he has painted the whole scene as a reflection. He stands very stiffly with one foot slightly in front of the other; he holds a palette in one hand and his other arm is stretched towards the out-of-sight easel; he is formally dressed in black coat and striped trousers. Behind him are a couple of tables, a picture hanging on the wall, and a window through which the light falls. The most striking feature of this picture is that Steer has neatly decapitated himself; only his white collar and an inch or two of neck twisting round to look in the mirror can be seen.

He has succeeded in getting himself in the same room as his half-dressed girl, but by making it clear that the room is a studio and not a bedroom, that the girl is sitting in her underclothes in order to be painted and not as a prelude to lovemaking, and that his interest in her is strictly professional, he has ensured that no suggestion of impropriety can be read into the situation. Although he has rendered the scene sexually harmless, he can still only paint it by preserving the anonymity of the participants. No amount of striped trouser or black jacket could eliminate from his mind the true nature of the relationship between artist and model. He has managed to exchange his role of observer/*voyeur* for that of protagonist/lover, but guilt has exacted its own stern price for this transformation by obliging him to mutilate himself and to expunge the identities of both himself and the girl.

It was not just as a joke that he called this headless study a 'Portrait of Himself' for it would appear that his love affair with Rose and the problems he faced in trying to come to terms with her on canvas entirely preoccupied him during the years 1894 and 1895. The combined evidence of the pictures and Rose's autobiographical sketch suggest that Steer's relationship with her was chaste and, furthermore, could not have been otherwise; at that stage in his life he was unable to sustain a relationship that put upon him greater sexual demands than those inherent in his continuing intimacy with and 'engagement' to the teenage and, presumably, virginal Rose. The ever-present mirrors, the oppressive sense of captivity that surrounds the invariably posed figure of Rose and the concentrated severity with which she is examined combine to render the artist's presence quite as tangible as that of Rose herself; the act of looking predominates. A critic said of 'The Mirror – Model Seated' (*The Yellow Book*, Volume V, April 1895), 'it possesses [the] fascinating power of forcing you to look out of the eyes of the painter'. This series of portraits represents a record of Steer's sexual development in relation to his emotions towards Rose: he is looking at himself looking at her, just as she is looking at him looking at her. Looking was the limit of his capability at that time, but to have expressed so succinctly on canvas the nature of his involvement with Rose was a remarkable feat.

In only one painting, 'The Japanese Gown', did Steer get even close to painting Rose naked. Before committing himself to this large canvas, Steer completed some smaller studies. In the first Rose is shown simply standing in the gown, her hand holding her chin. In the second, however, the gown has been allowed to fall open and reveal her naked stomach, but, predictably, a mirror has now been introduced and the viewer is offered an alternative angle of observation. In the final version, exhibited at The New English Art Club in November 1894, Rose's naked stomach has been modestly concealed by a long robe which she wears beneath the gown, and Steer, as if to quash any hint of sensuousness, has twisted her into a pose that looks positively painful.

After the completion of *The Yellow Book* series their relationship seems to have undergone a change for the worse; his paintings of her lacked the old intensity, his style changed and his interest broadened to include both his model and her surroundings. Rose, for her part, appears in paintings such as 'Rose Pettigrew in a Blue Dress' (1895) and 'Girl Reading a Book' to be bored and resentful; she is no longer actively contributing but merely doing as she is told. If the portraits can be regarded as reliable evidence of their emotional state of health, it is not surprising that their decisive row occurred at this point. There can, however, be no doubt that Steer was deeply hurt by the failure of their affair and by its sudden termination. George Moore implies that he never fully recovered and I believe it is possible to infer this from the subsequent pattern of his painting. 'None would guess', wrote Moore in 1924, 'that this rather fat, lazy man was once fond of dancing, and that his life was illuminated by a love story. We pitied his suffering when the lady married.'

As far as his painting was concerned, the immediate result of his separation from Rose was that he became obsessed by the nude. His treatment of this daunting subject took two forms, which he pursued simultaneously; he painted a series of unashamedly erotic pictures and another series of bleak, stiffly posed nudes.

His erotic paintings were executed in a style reminiscent of Watteau, Fragonard, and the French eighteenth-century court painters who were celebrated for their tender and witty handling of amorous themes, and his subjects were chosen from those mythological episodes traditionally exploited as excuses for sensual illustration. At that time engraved reproductions of Fragonard's drawings were widely available and much admired, and that school of painting had been further popularized by the publication of the Goncourt Brothers' celebrated *L'Art du XVIIIème Siècle*. Much debased and vulgarized, their style had been taken up and exploited by pornographic artists whose work could be purchased by the discerning in the more esoteric print shops. Steer was, no doubt, fully aware of the *risqué* connotations surrounding the style he had elected to simulate.

The subjects he selected are in themselves indicative of his frame of mind during this critical period: 'The Rape of the Sabines' (1896), thought to have been inspired by Poussin's treatment of the subject; 'The Pillow Fight' (1896), a lush bedroom scene showing two semi-naked girls locked in boisterous scrimmage among billowing pillows, sheets, and hangings; 'Sleep' (1898) (see illustration) in which a naked woman lies on a bed, one leg hanging over the side, and smilingly fondles her breast; and 'Danae or The Golden Rain', a portrait of the goddess passively but voluptuously anticipating the attentions of the disguised Zeus. All these pictures depict women undergoing various forms of ravishment or assault.

Although admiration is due to any Victorian artist who was sufficiently defiant of convention to depict women in states of unmistakable sexual gratification, Steer cannot be congratulated on having achieved much more than a sort of vapid naughtiness. And yet, seen from a biographical point of view, the pictures executed in this derivative style are of great interest. They seem to signify Steer's graduation from adolescent girls to mature women, and though no less voyeuristic than his previous works they suggest a preparedness on his part to come to terms with both nakedness and copulation. They undoubtedly represent a significant advance on his previous reluctance to go further than extracting such erotic satisfaction as he could from observing the playful or self-absorbed behaviour of partially dressed girls.

During the same period following the collapse of his relationship with Rose Pettigrew he also painted a number of other nudes in a style so markedly different it is hard to believe they were both conceived by the same imagination. Amplifying the method he had so effectively employed in the Pettigrew portraits, he created a style remarkable for its blunt simplicity and its manifest refusal to seek any reason for painting a naked woman other than nudity for nudity's sake. His austerity of purpose is borne out by the plain titles he gave these pictures: 'Nude Seated on a Bed' (1896), 'Nude Seated on a Sofa' (1896–8), 'Standing Nude' (1897), 'Seated Nude' (1897), and so on.

A model called Miss Geary ('Seated Nude, The Black Hat', 1898) is clearly identifiable in some but not all the pictures. She and the other models he used at this time share a physique that has nothing in common with either the lissom ebullience of the beach girls or Rose Pettigrew's long-legged elegance. They are short, stocky, full-breasted, and well-rounded. There is nothing girlish, far less boyish about them; they are women as surely as Rose and the red-heads were adolescents. The sketchy evidence relating to this part of his life is insufficient to support the theory that he had an affair with Miss Geary. The evidence provided by his pictures, however, does clearly imply a radical change in his sexual proclivities which can be dated with some precision as taking place soon after the termination of his engagement to Rose.

It cannot be said that the nude studies he executed in this style represent an unqualified triumph, for sadly the rigours of the cultural environment he was working in had fettered him so closely that his rebellion, when he finally made it, was all too vividly marked by the very bondage from which he was struggling to release himself. An unremitting gloom pervades these pictures: his models sit, or lie, upon their cheerless sofas, glumly resigned to assuming whatever pose, however disagreeable, their employer should dictate. They seem to be marooned upon their studio podia, damned for ever to eke out a forlorn existence amidst the hats, gloves, bunches of false flowers, and lengths of material with which the artist beautifies their docile limbs. They stare dumbly and expressionlessly into the middle distance, quiescently permitting the spectator to rake their naked bodies with his gaze. None holds herself with any appearance of ease or comfort.

Even when he came to emulate a masterpiece of relaxed self-satisfaction – Manet's 'Olympia' – he managed to invest his version with a pained stiffness all his own. Manet had placed a huge, soft pillow behind his model's head and shoulders and had decked her hair with an orchid. Exotically adorned and luxuriously propped up, she contemplated the spectator contemplating her with an alarmingly challenging expression. Steer based one of his studies for his picture 'The Toilet of Venus' (1897–8) on Manet's quizzical coquette. He, however, forbade his model a bolster, and required her to sit up on her bed in a stilted, rigid position, supported only by her arm. He stripped the flowers from her hair and banished from her room the opulent trappings that had enriched Manet's boudoir. He expanded the size of the bed, dispensed with Manet's fine linen, and left his model to squat upon a surface more like a kitchen table than a couch of love. He placed her further away from the spectator's

eye, thus diluting the uncompromising directness with which the
Olympia had outstared her audience. He attempted to recreate the
cool insolence of her expression, but achieved no more than a look of
demure bravery. Steer could not compete with the sexual sophistication that had gone into the making of Manet's picture; guilt,
inexperience, and fear of public reaction had compounded to
prevent his reproducing the warm-blooded sensuality of the original. Manet's creation is humorous and high-spirited; Steer's is
solemn and dejected.

In this series of pictures he did manage, however, to liberate
himself from the mirror device which he had employed so persistently in his Pettigrew portraits. In doing so he effected his most
impressive achievement, one that was not rivalled by any other
Victorian artist. These paintings offer no alternative angle of
observation, no divergent line escorts the eye away from the advertised subject; instead, the spectator is squarely confronted by the
nude figure. Previously he had found it necessary, perhaps literally
in Rose's case, to engage his models in some engrossing activity,
as if he wished to disguise his true motive for painting them. Now,
he abandoned all such sops to conscience and presented them just
as they were – patient and submissive objects of his unblinking
inspection. For the first time, and the last, in his career, he succeeded
in portraying every part of his models' bodies. No blur of hectic
colour was summoned to mask their breasts, nor were their pubic
hairs discreetly obliterated.

It would be reasonable to predict that the next phase of his
development as a painter would be preoccupied with the fusion of
the two styles he had evolved during the years 1896–1901 and that
he would marry the pliancy of his derivative paintings to the
honesty of his nudes, by breathing into his hitherto frigid models
some of the amorous warmth and sexual light-heartedness that had
characterized his imitations of Fragonard. The whole pattern of
his progress from the Walberswick girls to Miss Geary seems to
point to this synthesis. But it was not to be.

During the Edwardian period, he reverted to society portraits
and landscapes, abandoning the nude never to study it again.
Later, he lost interest even in portraits and concentrated exclusively
on landscapes, experimenting with and perfecting his use of water
colours. In 1916 a fashionable hostess asked him to paint her portrait; he declined, saying, 'I am not a portrait painter, but if you

like I will do a small landscape of you.' At the time of his death, it was for the pictures created in the latter half of his life that he was chiefly remembered.

It seems that with his retirement from the battle involved in perfecting his vision of the nude, he resigned himself to immaculate bachelorhood, gave full rein to his mania for collecting, and sealed himself for ever behind the impenetrable wall of his enigmatic public personality. Making speculative use of the evidence supplied by his pictures, it is possible to infer that he toyed for a year or two with the idea of allying himself to a society woman, but finally decided to extinguish and bury the passionate side of his nature and reconcile himself to the cosy celibacy which George Moore emphasized in his 'portrait'. Moore said that his friends would have liked to have seen Steer married: 'He was so happy unmarried that it was only natural that we should put his fortitude to the test.' It is, however, difficult not to regard his middle-aged, solitary 'happiness' as anything but the bloodless serenity of a man who has abdicated from life. When some enterprising publisher proposed that his biography should be written, he vehemently refused, declaring, 'nobody knows me intimately enough'. And clearly he had no intention of allowing that state of affairs to change.

His weakness as a painter, and presumably as a man, was that he never succeeded in establishing a more intimate relationship with the women he painted than that of observer and observed. The deeper intimacy perceptible in his paintings of Rose Pettigrew was the result of an exceptionally close scrutiny of his subject; his voyeurism had become fixed to one object. The painful break with Rose freed him from his obsession with adolescent girls, and released a brief spurt of sexual energy, but it did not prove sufficiently vigorous to carry him into and sustain a relationship with a mature woman. It did, however, strengthen his boldness as an observer, and he examined the nakedness of Miss Geary and his other models of that period with an honesty unmatched by any British contemporary. He never portrayed his subjects as embodiments of moral truths, nor did he use them to model antique or whimsical costumes, and his determination to paint what he saw did not waver when he finally confronted the challenge of plain nudity.

In common with most Victorian artists, he encountered the greatest difficulty when attempting to convey the personality of the

woman whose body he was painting. Although the features of some
of his models are recognizable, the nudes themselves are character-
less and seem to possess no sensual or even companionable quality.
When he did at last screw his courage to the point of taking off their
clothes, he appears to have been terrified by what he discovered
beneath, and only by depriving them of their sexual attractiveness
could he bring himself to paint them. He treated their bodies as
inanimate lumps of flesh and, as if to emphasize their sexlessness, he
frequently imposed impossible distortions on their limbs, or
required them to hold themselves in positions of ungainly painful-
ness. 'The Black Hat',[5] (see illustration) for example, shows a
woman whose right hip has apparently been wrenched away from her
abdomen. Thus, like the condemned man in Oscar Wilde's *Ballad of
Reading Gaol*, he killed the thing he loved. He had manoeuvred himself into the position of having to unsex the bodies of those whose
sexuality he desired to paint. He had not found it necessary to unsex
either his adolescents or the fanciful inmates of his borrowed boud-
oirs, but he could only come to terms with the real bodies of real
women by suspending them in a kind of pictorial formalin where
they harmlessly floated – lifeless, yet very life-like.

By 1896 Steer was able to look at female sexuality and depict its
fleshly, hairy reality, but he could not bring himself to embrace it.
He could not unite the eroticism he had borrowed from other
painters with the physical actuality of the naked bodies he stripped
and examined in his studio. This dilemma was, however, by no
means peculiar to him. The story of the development of his sexuality
and ultimate unfulfilment belongs as properly to the social as to the
art history of his period. His struggle to explore and release his own
sexuality, and to meet the sexual demands made by women exemplified the struggle that was taking place in the minds of many young
men of his generation. Nor was his failure any less representative.
By abandoning the stereotyped images of woman that had satisfied
an earlier generation, these men placed themselves in an extremely
vulnerable position. Although women had won for themselves a
significant, if limited, extension to their legal and social rights, they
still continued to shelter behind the protection provided by traditional sexual conventions; they wished to play a fuller emotional
and sexual part in their relations with men, but as yet they were
reluctant to jettison the old forms of relationship. Marriage still
furnished the only acceptable arena for sexual development, but it

was at the same time an institution serving many purposes, of which sexual gratification could claim only a low priority. Those, like Steer, who wished wholly to fulfil their sexual natures could not do so unless they were willing to go with their partners into exile from their class; not surprisingly, like Steer, the majority found this an impossible feat.

In 1911, long after he had ceased to grapple with the nude, he painted a picture which he entitled 'The End of the Chapter'. It depicted a girl kneeling before a fire-place warming her hands; on a chair behind her lies a book, face down. She is dressed in an elaborate, flowing dress, and she is evidently called upon to do little with her life save read novels and maintain a decorative appearance. The room overflows with Victorian drawing-room clutter; three pictures compete for space on the small area of wall, a sideboard staggers beneath the weight of innumerable pieces of china, the mantelpiece bears a similar load of candelabra, clocks, and pots and the fireplace bristles with ornaments, shelves, tiles, and brass implements.

Roger Fry abused the picture. 'There is no sign', he wrote, 'of any abandonment to any feeling . . . the furniture is done with the same placid, uninspired competence as the profile . . . one hopes, indeed, that it is the end of a chapter, the saddest one in a life of great and genuine achievement, and that he may have the energy to turn the page.' Fry's hopes were to be disappointed; the page was never turned. If, however, the picture is judged within the context of Steer's life, it assumes a special significance. It can be interpreted as Steer's conclusive gesture of resignation from the battle against those Victorian values which had so decisively prevented his realizing his artistic and sexual ambitions.

The girl, whose profile is poignantly reminiscent of Rose's, does not face the spectator; she has almost turned her back on him. The fire at which she warms her hands is invisible and she appears to be warmed instead by the glow of affluence and security exuded by the multitude of possessions that encumber the room. In her billowing, impractical dress, she is herself a possession, quite as decorative and quite as helpless as the china on the sideboard. The possessions, although not the girl, were of course Steer's own, and by identifying the model so closely with his collection of *objets d'art*, by then the passion of his life, he was perhaps acknowledging his submission to bourgeois domestic conventions.

The picture may be read as a formal, if ironic, declaration that he no longer sought to unveil and penetrate the sexuality that lay beneath the dress, that he no longer sought to upset the moral code that protected women from such unveilings and penetrations. He was hereafter content to leave women as they were, objects of adornment whose value could be measured on the scales of marriage. 'The End of the Chapter' was perhaps a valedictory bow to all the girls who collaborated with him, for with this picture he returned his models to the safety of their parlours and to the sovereignty of their husbands and fathers, and shut up for the last time the draughty studio where, docile, naked, and aching, they had posed and posed until their skins seemed chafed raw by his inexorable gaze.

On the day he received the Order of Merit, shortly after the ceremony, someone knocked on his front door. He answered himself, still dressed in court regalia. 'I want to buy a masterpiece,' the man said, 'I don't mind how much it costs.' 'I don't paint masterpieces', Steer replied, and shut the door.

WORKING-CLASS
SEXUALITY

9

Working-Class Sexuality

No analysis of the sexuality of the Victorian working class can be other than meaningless if it is not preceded by a description of the conditions under which the poor were obliged to live. It is far from melodramatic to say that the twentieth-century imagination cannot fully comprehend the appalling nature of these conditions, both physical and psychological, without girding itself to make a very strenuous leap of historical empathy.

Although our contemporary society[1] has not succeeded in eliminating slums, poverty, homelessness, and even starvation, and although it continues to entertain grotesque economic inequality, we can still make the hollow boast that no section of our population, however under-privileged, is forced to suffer the kind of abject and bestial poverty that represented the lot of roughly a quarter of the Victorian urban population. A social worker would have to search diligently among today's Glasgow or Liverpool to locate even ten families enduring the conditions under which literally hundreds of thousands of Victorian working families subsisted.

It is true that many aspects of Victorian urban life are readily accessible to us, and many more not actually in existence are easily reconstructed in the imagination. The shape of our industrial cities and towns, their architectural appearance, their streets, shops, institutions, and facilities are largely Victorian in origin and have not been radically changed in the course of the last hundred years. It is also true that some of today's slums are the selfsame slums that were erected to house Victorian workers, and that the inhabitants of those slums are probably direct descendants of the original occupants. Some of the same factories, docks, and mills are still in existence and still drawing on the same communities for their labour, and the same shops, pubs, and football grounds are still supplying and entertaining these same communities. But no part of this inheritance, none of these apparently shared experiences, should encourage us to assume that we can easily penetrate and

identify with the circumstances in which working families of a
hundred, or even seventy years ago really lived.

Despite legislated reform and the steady improvement of urban
facilities, the lives of the working class were governed throughout
the nineteenth century by factors that combined to imprison them
in a state of crushing impoverishment, from which the only release
was death. Far from being reduced or alleviated as the years wore
on, these factors were intensified. The poverty imposed upon them
was of a brutality that defies modern comparison; it was compounded
of severe exhaustion and malnutrition resulting directly from over-
work and grossly inadequate pay, of squalid living conditions, and
of chronic anxiety provoked by their unremitting failure to provide
for themselves and their children. Not only were their backs broken
daily by insupportable material burdens, but their spirits were also
destroyed by equally insupportable psychological burdens.

The ways in which the working classes established and conducted
their sexual relationships, the character of their family life, and the
manner in which they brought up their children can only be properly
understood in the context of these uniquely Victorian circumstances.

The Poverty Line

In 1885 Charles Booth, a Liverpool shipping magnate, read with
indignant disbelief the findings of a survey of a working-class
district in London which indicated that a million out of the capital's
total population of four million people lived in extreme poverty.
The survey had been conducted by the Social Democratic Federation, a marxist organization, and their report had been serialized
by the *Pall Mall Gazette*. Booth, suspicious of the motives inspiring
the authors of the report, could not accept their statistics; he called
on the leader of the Federation, accused him of grossly over-stating
the true position and declared that he intended to take his own
survey in order to expose and refute the irresponsible exaggerations
perpetrated by the socialists.

Booth was born in 1840 to a prosperous Unitarian family; he
worked in the shipping business with his brother and, largely as a
result of the astute purchase of the most up-to-date steam ships, he
became extremely rich. As a young man he dabbled in radical
politics, but in 1872, a year after his marriage to the daughter of
Thomas Macaulay, he suffered a breakdown from over-work and
decided to devote himself exclusively to his business affairs. But

when he moved to London in the eighteen-eighties he became increasingly preoccupied with the problems caused by unemployment, and matters came to a head in 1885 with the publication of the *Pall Mall Gazette* articles. For the next seventeen years he supervised a meticulously researched investigation of poverty in London, the results of which were incorporated in the seventeen volumes of his celebrated *Life and Labour of the People of London*. His work decisively proved that the Social Democratic Federation had in fact underestimated the degree of destitution to be found among the inhabitants of London.

Assuming that the East End would contain more areas of extreme poverty than any other part of London, Booth commenced work there and was forced to conclude that the marxist figure had erred by as much as ten per cent, for he discovered that the number of 'poor' people amounted to roughly thirty-five per cent. He then proceeded to examine the rest of London and to his amazement he found that 30·7 per cent of the total population of London lived on or below the poverty line. By the word 'poor' he meant

> those who have a sufficiently regular though bare income, such as 18s to 21s per week for a moderate family, and by 'very poor' those who from any cause fall much below this standard. The 'poor' are those whose means may be sufficient, but are barely sufficient, for decent independent life; the 'very poor' those whose means are insufficient for this according to the usual standards of life in this country. My 'poor' may be described as living under a struggle to obtain the necessaries for life and make both ends meet; while the 'very poor' live in a state of chronic want.

In 1901 B. S. Rowntree consolidated Booth's conclusions by publishing his *Poverty: A Study of Town Life*. He was eager to know how conditions in a small, industrialized, provincial town – York – compared to those in the metropolis. Taking Booth's work as a model, Rowntree was able to study the far smaller, more compact population of York with even greater accuracy and thoroughness.

He first made an assessment of the earnings of almost every working class family in the city, and then calculated the proportion of the total population living in poverty. He grouped under two headings the families he regarded as impoverished:

1. 'Families whose total earnings were insufficient to obtain the

minimum necessaries for the maintenance of merely physical
efficiency.' (Primary poverty.)

2. 'Families whose total earnings would have been sufficient for
the maintenance of merely physical efficiency were it not that some
portion of it was absorbed by other expenditure, either useful or
wasteful.' (Secondary poverty.)

He found that 9·91 per cent of the whole population of York was
living in a state of primary poverty and that 17·93 per cent was living
in secondary poverty. His total figure of 27·84 per cent compared so
closely with Booth's, and their methods of investigation and defini-
tions of poverty were so similar, that he felt no hesitation in
affirming that the proportion of the population living in poverty in
York was practically the same as in London. This was an alarming
revelation, for it was generally assumed that the scale of poverty in
London far outstripped that of any other town. Rowntree also
pointed out that the period during which he was gathering his
statistics was generally considered one of unusual prosperity. 'We
are faced', he wrote in his concluding chapter, 'by the startling
probability that from 25 to 30 per cent of the town populations of
the United Kingdom are living in poverty. If this be the fact, its
grave significance may be realized when it is remembered that, in
1901, 77 per cent of the population of the United Kingdom is
returned as "urban" and only 23 per cent as "rural".'

In his discussion of the immediate causes of poverty Rowntree
established that the average wage paid in York for unskilled labour
was insufficient to provide food, shelter, and clothing adequate to
maintain a family of moderate size in a state of bare physical
efficiency. A York labourer could expect to earn between 18s and
21s per week; he was, however, required to spend, according to
Rowntree's calculations, at least 21s 8d if he was to keep himself,
his wife and three children. This estimate of the necessary minimum
expenditure was based on the assumption that the diet enjoyed by
the labourer and his family was even less generous than that allowed
to able-bodied paupers in the York workhouse. Displaying a spirit
of human understanding to which Booth seldom rose, Rowntree
described the gruelling privations thrust on a family by inadequate
wages:

A family living upon the scale allowed for in this estimate (21s 8d)
must never spend a penny on railway fare or omnibus. They must

9 Philip Wilson Steer, *Sleep* (see page 148)

10   Philip Wilson Steer, *Seated Nude, The Black Hat* (see page 148)

never go into the country unless they walk. They must never purchase a halfpenny newspaper or spend a penny to buy a ticket for a popular concert. They must write no letters to absent children, for they cannot afford to pay the postage. They must never contribute anything to their church or chapel, or give any help to a neighbour which costs them money. They cannot save, nor can they join sick club or Trade Union, because they cannot pay the necessary subscriptions. The children must have no pocket money for dolls, marbles, or sweets. The father must smoke no tobacco, and must drink no beer. The mother must never buy any pretty clothes for herself or for her children, the character of the family wardrobe as for the family diet being governed by the regulation, 'Nothing must be bought but that which is absolutely necessary for the maintenance of physical health, and what is bought must be of the plainest and most economical description.' Should a child fall ill, it must be attended by the parish doctor; should it die, it must be buried by the parish. Finally, the wage earner must never be absent from his work for a single day.

If any of these conditions are broken, the extra expenditure involved is met, *and can only be met*, by limiting the diet . . .

The condition of the poor, he said, was 'a struggle for existence so severe as necessarily to cripple or destroy the higher parts of their nature'. Between them Booth and Rowntree forced their contemporaries to acknowledge the fact that a quarter of the population of the richest country in the world was so poor that daily life consisted simply of the fight to stay alive. In the process they also exploded some of the myths surrounding the shiftless poor, for Rowntree in particular made it clear that unemployment and low wages were the principal causes of poverty. He demonstrated that, far from languishing in idleness, immorality, and improvidence, the vices traditionally pointed to by middle-class observers seeking to explain working-class penury, the poor in fact performed miracles of thrift with their pitifully small budgets.

Housing

The proletarian districts of nineteenth-century towns and cities were characterized by acute overcrowding and squalor:

These streets are often so narrow that a person can step from the window of one house into that of its opposite neighbour, while the houses are piled so high, storey upon storey, that the light can scarcely penetrate into the court or alley that lies between. In this part of the city there are neither sewers nor other drains, nor even privies belonging to the houses. In consequence, all refuse, garbage, and excrements of at least 50,000 persons are thrown into the gutters every night, so that, in spite of all street sweeping, a mass of dried filth and foul vapours are created, which not only offend the sight and smell, but endanger the health of the inhabitants in the highest degree . . . The houses of the poor are generally filthy, and are evidently never cleansed. They consist in most cases of a single room which, while subject to the worst ventilation, is usually kept cold by the broken and badly fitting windows, and is usually damp and partly below ground level, always badly furnished and thoroughly uncomfortable, a straw-heap often serving the whole family for a bed, upon which men and women, young and old, sleep in revolting confusion. Water can only be had from the public pumps, and the difficulty of obtaining it naturally fosters all possible filth.

This passage was quoted by Engels in his *Condition of the Working Class* (1845) from an article in *The Artisan* (October 1843 issue) on the sanitary conditions of working people. It could, however, stand as a fair description of working-class living conditions in any industrial town in any decade during Victoria's reign. Although the fifty years that separate Engels from Booth saw much legislation designed to reform these conditions and much private, philanthropic energy spent in trying to ameliorate them, when Booth came to write his *Life and Labour of the People* he found himself describing a London that was, if anything, dirtier and more overcrowded than the Manchester of Engels's day.

Engels reported that a fifth of Liverpool's population, more than 45,000 people, lived in narrow, damp, and badly ventilated cellar dwellings, of which there were fewer than 8,000 in the city. In Bristol 2,800 families were found to occupy only one room each. But it was among the Irish immigrant workers in Manchester, the town to which most of his book was devoted and where he worked in the family business, that he discovered the most outrageous examples of overcrowding. He frequently came across two or more families living together in a tiny, dripping cellar, crowding into the same bed, if a heap of filthy straw or rotten sacking could be called a bed, and sharing the premises with their pigs. Many families were too poor to scrape together the rent themselves and were obliged to take in lodgers.

Writing in 1883 W. C. Preston, author of *The Bitter Cry of Outcast London*, a pamphlet designed to draw the attention of the middle classes to the state of degradation to which the poor had fallen, described a tenement house in which one cellar was occupied by a father, mother, three children, and four pigs. In another room a man lay ill with smallpox, while his wife was recovering from her eighth confinement and their children ran around naked and filthy. An underground kitchen was found to be inhabited by seven people and the corpse of a child whom no one could afford to bury. Nine brothers and sisters lived, ate, and slept in one room. Few of the tenants owned beds, most slept on rags, shavings, or straw, some simply lay down on the verminous boards. And finally he wrote of a widow who chose to occupy only her bed while she let the floor of her single room to a married couple. Engels himself discovered an old man who had taken up residence in a cow-stable which had neither windows, floor, nor ceiling but only a rotten roof through which the damp permanently seeped. He made his living by removing manure from the street in a handcart and dung-heaps stood all around his hut.

Engels summed up his findings:

... We must admit that 350,000 working people of Manchester and its environs live, almost all of them, in wretched, damp, filthy cottages, that the streets which surround them are usually in the most miserable and filthy condition, laid out without the slightest reference to ventilation, with reference solely to the profit secured by the contractor. In a word, we must confess that in the working-men's dwellings of Manchester, no cleanliness, no convenience, and consequently no comfortable family life is possible; that in such dwellings only a physically degenerate race, robbed of all humanity, degraded, reduced morally and physically to bestiality, could feel comfortable and at home.

Octavia Hill, a philanthropist who ran a number of slum-rescue schemes whereby tenements were purchased, cleaned, repaired, and decorated and then let at cheap rents on the understanding that high standards of hygiene and behaviour were upheld, described the state in which her tenants lived before she reconditioned their dwellings; 'one foul, dark room, with rotten boards saturated with dirt, with vermin in the walls, damp plaster, smoky chimney, approached by a dark and dangerous staircase, in a house with no through ventilation or back yard, with old brick drains, and broken down water-butt without a lid.'[2]

In the same article she compared the 'wynds' of Glasgow with London's courts and alleys. These were crammed together even more densely than their London equivalents; most were blocked at one end preventing the free movement of air, and together they formed a honeycomb so convoluted that access to the wynd farthest from the street could only be achieved by passing under a series of crumbling arches which led from court to court and which were located beneath the houses. The tenement blocks were taller than those in London and had been built so closely together that the gaps between were mere crevices of six or eight inches width, and it was from these 'dreepings' or 'wastings' that the back rooms derived their air and light. Over the years many of them had become completely blocked up with rubbish thrown from the windows, and had been turned into stinking hatcheries of disease.

Apart from having to occupy tiny, damp rooms in badly ventilated, dilapidated buildings the poor were also required to live literally in their own filth. Water could only be obtained from the communal pump or tap which was situated in the courtyard below the tenement block or at the end of the street and was frequently out of order or operational during limited periods. Supplies had to be carried in buckets, making it difficult for the ordinary housewife to cook and clean effectively and virtually impossible for the mother of six or the old person living on the fourth floor at the top of a rickety, lightless flight of stairs. The poor were in any event almost completely ignorant of the concept of hygiene, and had no understanding of the significance of cleanliness, nor of the dangers of allowing rotten food, rubbish, and excrement to pollute the air and water. G. R. Sims reported in his *How the Poor Live* that as a joke a boy had thrown the corpse of a cat into a water butt serving an entire tenement block and that it was six weeks before the butt was cleansed. Even if they were unaware of the risk of disease the poor had no choice but to endure the discomfort and inconvenience of living in the permanent presence of their own excreta. Lavatories of the most primitive kind were situated, generally adjacent to the water supply, at the entrances of courts or at the ends of lanes and streets, and each one was supposed to satisfy the needs of a hundred or more people. The lavatories themselves were badly designed, badly sited, and badly cared for; the sewers that lay beneath them were inefficient and seldom serviced. No writer who turned his attention to the condition of the poor failed to comment upon the fact that the unpaved roads, the alleys, passages and courts, the stairways, the hallways, the back yards, and of course the very rooms themselves in which the poor lived all bore their layer of excrement.

The Bitter Outcry of Outcast London provides one of the most vivid descriptions of the dirt with which every slum building was encrusted. The author, W. C. Preston, in a section entitled 'The Condition in which They Live', acts as an imaginary guide:

> To get into them [pestilential human rookeries] you have to penetrate courts reeking with poisonous and malodorous gases arising from accumulations of sewage and refuse scattered in all directions and often flowing beneath your feet . . . You have to grope your way along dark and filthy passages swarming with vermin . . . Eight feet square – that is about the average size of very many of these rooms. Walls and ceiling are black with the accretions of filth which have gathered upon them through long years of neglect. It is exuding through cracks in the boards overhead; it is running down the walls; it is everywhere. What goes by the name of a window is half of it stuffed with rags or covered by boards to keep out the wind and rain; the rest is begrimed and obscured that scarcely can light enter or anything be seen outside . . . Every room in these rotten and reeking tenements houses a family, often two.

Engels recalled visiting a court in Manchester on the river bank close to some tanneries which filled the entire district with the stench of animal putrefaction and finding at the very entrance of the yard, at the end of a covered passage, a privy without a door so dirty that the inhabitants passing in and out of the building could not avoid splashing through pools of urine and excrement. Octavia Hill wrote that in many of the houses she refurbished the dustbins were unapproachable and that the stairs and steps nearby were caked with the overflow; back kitchens had been used in the absence of any other receptacle as dustbins and contained the accumulated refuse of many years; in some houses the dirt on the stairs was so thick and hardened that it had to be removed with a shovel.

These scenes of horror can be culled from any book written during the reign seriously concerned with the condition of the poor. Some areas were of course cleared, rebuilt, drained, and lit, but as fast as improvements were made the working population expanded, particularly in some of the worst East End slum districts which were further crowded by immigrants, and rents went up, forcing the poor to seek out new accommodation which inevitably possessed all the old inadequacies.

Before abandoning this catalogue of miseries it is worth quoting from Booth himself, for he and Rowntree, unlike all other observers, conducted painstaking house-to-house investigations and from their books emerge detailed portraits of entire streets and neighbourhoods.

Shelton Street, for example, is described in detail in Volume II of *Life and Labour*; it lies east of Soho and south of Bloomsbury and vestiges of its former squalor may be envisaged today by the imaginative. It was just wide enough to allow a vehicle to pass either way and it comprised about forty houses in which two hundred families lived, mostly in one room each. The majority of the tenants were Irish Roman Catholics who gained their livelihood from the nearby market in Covent Garden as porters, or by selling flowers and vegetables. Fifteen rooms out of twenty were described by Booth as 'filthy to the last degree' and none was free from vermin. In hot weather the occupants did not go to bed but simply sat in their clothes in the least infested part of the room. Most of the doors stood open day and night to provide a little badly needed ventilation, and the passages and stairs gave shelter to the altogether homeless. At the back of each house was a little yard just big enough for a dustbin, privy, and water tap which served six or seven families, the water being drawn from cisterns frequently clogged with refuse.

In number 4 Shelton Street one of the ground-floor rooms – few of the rooms were larger than eight feet square – was occupied by a family of costermongers, a Mr and Mrs Shane and their four children. As tenants, costermongers were not popular for they were often obliged to bring home for the night their stock which in the case of fruit and vegetables only added to piles of rubbish and the stench and it was not uncommon for them to use the room in which they lived as a stable for their donkey or horse. Mr Shane had caught cold from exposure and was to lie in bed for nine months enduring continual pain until he finally died. His wife drank and their eldest son had already been in prison twice.

On the second floor there was a woman with four small children whose husband had gone to America. The children had no shoes and were usually hungry. Their mother had to lock them in the room each day while she went to sell oranges in the streets. On the third floor in two small rooms lived a family consisting of father, mother, a son and daughter, both adults. The daughter was married and had a child; the father was, 'in consequence of drink', paralysed, helpless, and almost speechless. The rooms, according to Booth, were filthy and the occupants lived like pigs.

Shelton Street is by no means the worst described by Booth, nor were its inhabitants the most destitute; it was merely an average street in an area occupied by the very poor.

It is true that not every member of the urban proletariat lived in conditions as bad as those described above. Some families could afford to rent and live alone in little 'two-up two-down' houses which nowadays are avidly purchased by the middle classes, some streets were provided with adequate sanitation, and some landlords were conscientious in the upkeep of their properties, but as a general rule it can be assumed that the twenty-five per cent identified by Booth and Rowntree as poor were chronically overcrowded, underfed and underpaid. To put the situation in another perspective: Rowntree records that in 1891 nearly ten per cent of London's population, more than 380,000 people, were living in one-room tenements.

Family Life

Marriage was not common among working people who on the whole obtained their wives and husbands simply by taking up residence with them. Considerations of property, dowry settlements, inheritance, and breeding which lent the middle-class Victorian wedding such dramatic poignancy, were hardly relevant to the working couple. Indeed, it seems that the sheer expense of the wedding itself prevented many couples from marrying. G. R. Sims records (*How the Poor Live*) that a philanthropic clergyman's wife who took a particular interest in a young working couple was shocked to discover that, although they were sober, decent, and

clean, and the parents of two delightful children, they were unmarried. She determined to rectify matters and succeeded in convincing the couple of the importance of legalizing and sanctifying
their liaison. A new gown was bought for the bride-to-be; frocks
were made for the little ones, and a day's holiday without loss of
pay was arranged for the groom. Finally she persuaded her husband
to perform the ceremony. The fateful day arrived, but bitter
disappointment was in store for the well-meaning matchmaker for
the groom had been offered a carting job worth five shillings and
had decided that he could not afford to miss the opportunity of
earning two days' wages in one just for the sake of getting married.

Relationships among the poor were swiftly formed and just as
swiftly broken, but the house-to-house surveys conducted by
Booth and Rowntree suggest that fidelity between couples was the
norm, not the exception, and that family loyalties and connections
were sustained over many generations. The symbolic significance
with which the middle classes had charged the institution of
marriage carried less weight with the poor who, for excellent
reasons, looked upon any binding contract between two people
with extreme misgiving. Theirs was a world fraught with uncertainty; if anything was certain in it, it was that life tended to get
worse, not better. Fundamental to the middle-class concept of
marriage was a profound faith in the stability of the future, both
national and personal. A man who married was confident that his
country was safe from invasion, that his investments were protected,
and that England could look forward to ever-increasing prosperity.
He also confidently believed that the woman he married would be
by his side for the rest of his life, that she would be the mother of his
children, that the house he built or bought would stand and shelter
him until he exchanged it for another, that his prosperity, like his
country's, would steadily grow, that his children would be worthy
inheritors of his accrued wealth and that his position in society
could only improve.

The working man by contrast was unable to share a single scrap
of this enviable optimism. The slightest tremor in the national
economy – and during the 'eighties and 'nineties the economy
underwent a series of sharp recessions – affected him dramatically,
for prices and rents rose and jobs became harder to find. His income was never guaranteed, general unemployment, illness,
accident, or merely the caprice of an ill-tempered employer or

foreman were all too likely to deprive him overnight of his wage, forcing him to pawn his few possessions and to rely on the earning power of his wife and children. If jobs were not to be had, or if his wife was unable to work he was compelled to leave his lodgings and find somewhere even smaller, cheaper, and dirtier. Penniless and desperate he finally faced the choice of either resorting to crime or submitting to the workhouse where he knew he would be subjected to indignity, made to toil at some fruitless task, and be forbidden to see his wife and children. Alternatively, if he was sufficiently callous or hopeless, he sent his wife on the streets to earn a living.

It was not unknown for husbands and wives to form criminal teams, she attracting clients to a dark alley or doorway, and he mugging and robbing them. Once embarked on a criminal life, he naturally ran the risk of being imprisoned; sentences were long and harsh in those days and wives on the outside with children to support were not slow to form new allegiances. Parents tended to look on their children as potential wage-earners and children, by the same token, grew up anxious to escape the confinement of one-room family life and eager to spend their earnings on themselves. Expectation of life among the poor was cruelly short: disease, the rigours of childbirth, the vulnerability of infants to infection, the lack of medication, to say nothing of the sheer danger inherent in many jobs, all combined to add a strain of cruel insecurity to lives already wretchedly precarious. In short, the working man could make no declaration of faith in the stability of the future when he threw in his lot with a woman, and in the light of the ominous inconstancy that clouded every aspect of their life, it is hardly surprising that marriage as such was not only unimportant among the poor, but positively unpopular.

A multitude of destructive factors laid siege to the working-class marriage, but none can have been so effective as the sheer squalor of the immediate environment. It seems scarcely possible that human beings could be capable of sustaining marital solidarity, and even harmony, when cooped up in dank, rat-infested eight-foot-square hovels, in the ever-present company of their numerous children and lodgers. But, although all contemporary observers wrote with horror of the violence, drunkenness, and carelessness which they claimed typified working-class relationships, the evidence nevertheless suggests that couples retained a formidable capacity for loyalty and perseverance.

In the course of his investigations into conditions obtaining among London trades and crafts, Henry Mayhew, the celebrated journalist and author of *London Labour and the London Poor*, took note not only of his subjects' working lives but also of their homes and marriages. Gifted with exceptionally sharp eyes and ears and a novelist's intuition for the illuminating detail, he was additionally blessed with a genius for winning the immediate confidence of people he interviewed; consequently his portraits radiate a vivid specificity not to be found in many nineteenth-century social writers who on the whole were satisfied with generalized, impressionistic sketches. His work among the boot- and shoe-makers led him to a couple who by dint of courage and determination had surmounted gruelling adversities and had succeeded in holding together their family and marriage. In this account Mayhew let the man's own words speak for themselves:[3]

> The kitchen we lived in was damp, dark and dirty. The ceiling was only six feet from the floor. The health of myself, wife and children suffered much here, with the bad quality of food we were obliged to eat, bad ventilation, and many hours of toil. My wife was kind and affectionate, and loved her children with the kind of affection a mother only can feel. We used to look on those little beings with hearts ready to break. We saw them waste day after day, almost forgetting to notice the havoc that mental anxiety and the attendant miseries of poverty made upon ourselves. [It looks as if Mayhew touched up the narrative at this point.]

At this period he was working from five or six in the morning until twelve at night, a back-breaking daily marathon that failed to produce sufficient money to buy meat for Sunday dinner, but later his job changed and his income dropped even lower. 'With this miserable work, I was obliged to set my poor wife down to sew, while bread we could not buy much of. We lived upon boiled rice and hard biscuits, sold at 2d per pound at the East-end.' Having unsuccessfully attempted to save up enough money to emigrate he was finally reduced to the solution that haunted and terrified the poor throughout its existence: the workhouse.

> My dear little ones wanted; so day after day we sold and pawned, till we became a perfect wreck. I was next advised by my friend

to seek workhouse relief . . . After many hard struggles to screw my courage to the sticking place, I *did* go. My business being a useful one, they wished myself and family to go into the house, and would not relieve us out. I would sooner have died in the street than consented to part from my family in such a way. I returned home, and cursed in my heart such a country as England, which seemed to deny me the only privilege that I felt I wanted – labour sufficiently remunerative to support my children without becoming a pauper.

This man's story provides an indication of the strength and dedication required of working couples who were determined to prevent the disintegration of their families. Neither the claustrophobia engendered by continual imprisonment in a tiny, dirty, overcrowded room, nor the crippling debilitation induced by permanent undernourishment and overwork, nor even the depression produced by helplessly watching their children slowly but inexorably deteriorate were sufficient to break the spirit of this couple. They were however not exceptional, for Mayhew's letters to *The Morning Chronicle* abound with portraits of couples displaying similar heroism in the face of similarly grim circumstances, and the observations of Booth and Rowntree, though never as colourful or penetrating as Mayhew's, confirm the impression conveyed by him that the tendency in working-class marriages was towards longevity. Interestingly, it was the writers of fiction who laid stress on the instability of working-class liaisons.

The atrocious overcrowding endured by the poor was noted by all writers with more or less indignation, but none commented on its corollary, the deprivation of privacy. Obviously, privacy was unobtainable in a room occupied by both a couple and their children or a lodger. A satisfactory sex life, however, requires privacy, for no couple, no matter how ardent or uninhibited, can fully gratify each other's desires if they are denied the freedom to behave as they wish without being observed or overheard. To copulate in the presence of others calls either for furtive cunning or brash heedlessness; on those who were inhibited, nervous, or easily upset this permanent lack of privacy can only have had the most damaging effect. Not surprisingly, for many couples sex was only possible after they had passed into a state of alcoholic oblivion.

Apart from preventing couples from simply undressing and

making love when and how they liked, absence of privacy also precluded their enjoyment of innumerable other activities. Privacy looks in two directions: it affords the opportunity of being solitary, and it permits one to be alone with another, free of intrusion. A married couple living with others in the confinement of a single, small room were denied both forms of privacy. They could not argue, fight, or cry without involving an outsider, they could not freely confide in each other, nor could they merely take pleasure in each other's company unless they left home. They could not recuperate alone after an exhausting day; they could not obtain the silence necessary for study or reading without inconveniencing the rest of the family. In short, they could make no noise or gesture without taking into account its effect on a third party. They were doomed to suffer the ever-present tension which other people, however loving or beloved, inevitably impose on a couple if continually in their company.

The Wife's Burden

In his study of poverty in York Rowntree stated that the average weekly wage of an unskilled labourer (between 18s and 21s) was insufficient to provide adequate food, shelter, and clothing for himself, his wife, and three children. It is however worth remembering that there were families whose total weekly income was considerably lower than this average. For instance, 474 families, comprising 1,589 people, were found to be earning an average weekly income of 11s 7d. The precise nature of the destitution suffered by these people can be best illustrated by showing that, whereas it would have cost £228 to provide them with food for a week of the kind eaten by paupers in the York workhouse, the aggregate weekly earnings of these families fell short of that figure by some £22. Needless to say, families who fell into this category did not remain there long: death, the workhouse, or perhaps a change of fortune soon intervened to halt the spiral of misery, hunger, and debt.

It was upon the shoulders of the wives in all working-class families, whether their incomes were below 18s or above 30s, that the responsibility for administering the family budget fell. In some mining villages it was the custom for men to bring home their wage-packets immediately after they had been paid and, in order to ensure that fair play took place, to deliver them to their wives at the cottage door in full view of the rest of the street. The wives then doled out to their husbands a share of the wage for drink and tobacco. In most working-class communities, however, the wife was simply handed a sum of money which her husband considered sufficient for housekeeping expenses. Whatever the traditions of the community the wife invariably took or was given the job of organizing family expenditure.

Rowntree was at great pains to demonstrate that no wife, however thrifty or skilful with her budgeting and shopping, could hope to stretch her husband's wage-packet far enough to provide even the bare necessities for physical efficiency, and for those wives whose husbands did not selflessly devote their entire wage-packets to family needs the situation was all the more hopeless. Having expended all her energy and ingenuity on extracting the maximum purchasing power from her minuscule exchequer, she then had to learn to resign herself to the fact that, despite her every effort, her husband and children were destined to remain undernourished, underclad, and cold. She had no alternative but to fail. At the same time, she had no alternative but to maintain the unequal struggle as long as she had a family beneath her roof.

It was possible, as Rowntree did, to calculate the gruesome discrepancy between basic minimal requirements of food, warmth, living space, etc., and the actual quantities available to the poor, but there was no scale on which the psychological damage ensuing from the continuous impact of failure could be measured. If even the most prudent housewife had to submit to a harsh regime of self-discipline in order to put the plainest food in her family's mouths and the shabbiest garments on their backs, what chance did the idle, the ill, the muddle-headed, or the extravagant housewife have of keeping herself out of debt?

Three classic solutions were available to the housewife who was determined neither to prostitute herself nor surrender to the oppression of an inadequate income, each in its way grossly punitive: she could economize on food (in other words starve herself and her children to ensure that her husband, the bread-winner, was properly nourished), she could take in a lodger, or she could take in work. If she was in dire straits she could adopt all three at once.

Rowntree demonstrated that for those families whose weekly income was less than 21s expenditure on food was generally the only item on the budget that would stand reduction. He wrote '. . . they are liable to sink into [destitution] at any moment. They live constantly from hand to mouth. So long as the wage-earner is in work the family manages to get along, but a week's illness or lack of work means short rations, or running into debt, or more often both of these. Extraordinary expenditure, such as the purchase of a piece of furniture, is met by reducing the sum spent on food'. One of the women interviewed said 'If there's anythink extra to buy, such as a pair of boots for one of the children me and the children goes without dinner – or mebbe only 'as a cup o' tea and a bit o' bread, but Jim [her husband] ollers takes 'is dinner to work, and I give it 'im as usual; 'e never knows we go without, and I never tells 'im.' The desperate housewife governed her expenses according to the principle that until you are eating nothing you can always eat less. Although husbands' needs were given absolute priority, presumably most women found it difficult to deprive their children of food and consequently forced themselves to undergo slow starvation, which radically reduced their ability to perform an already impossible task.

On the face of it taking in a lodger was the least onerous of the three choices in so far as he contributed to the rent. But in practice an extra member of the family, albeit a wage-earner, only made additional demands on her depleted energy and compounded her anxieties. She was expected to shop, cook, sew, and clean for him, to make over to him a part of her pitifully small territory, and to sacrifice what little privacy she and her husband had previously enjoyed.

Never did the trap of poverty close so tightly or cruelly upon its victims as when housewives were reduced to taking in work at home to supplement their husbands' wages. Mayhew, who had witnessed enough misery in his time to refrain from hysterical outbursts, wrote of the freelance needlewomen in London that he 'could not have believed that there were human beings toiling so long and gaining so little, and starving so silently and heroically.' It is worth knowing exactly what he means by 'toiling so long'. One example will have to suffice.

He visited a female shirt worker who lived over a coal and potato shed in a tiny room on the second floor and was 'steeped in poverty to the very lips'. The kind of shirts in which she specialized took five hours to make apiece and if she started early in the morning, around six, she could expect to make three if she worked steadily until nine at night. If however business was brisk – and she could never afford to turn down work for fear of antagonizing her employer – she often had to get up at two in the morning and work through to the evening of the following day. Occasionally she took cat-naps in her clothes, but, as she put it, 'the agitation of mind never lets one lie longer'. And what was the shirt worker paid for this labour of Hercules? She earned an average of 4s a week, not counting the cost of cotton and candles, which reduced it to 2s 6d. 'I know it's so little I can't get a rag to my back. I reckon nobody in the trade can make more than I do – they can't – and there's very few makes so much I'm sure.'

Mayhew wrote this report in 1849[4] and his words were no less relevant in the 1890s when Booth came to study conditions in the 'sweated' trades. Thomas Hood's celebrated poem *The Song of The Shirt* which appeared in *Punch* in 1843 and gave the magazine a dose of helpful notoriety made this same point no less eloquently:

> O! Men with Sisters dear!
>   O! Men! with Mothers and Wives!
> It is not linen you're wearing out,
>   But human creatures' lives!
>   Stitch – stitch – stitch,
>   In poverty, hunger, and dirt,
> Sewing at once, with a double thread,
>   A Shroud as well as a shirt.

> Work – work – work!
>   My labour never flags;
> And what are its wages? A bed of straw,
>   A crust of bread – and rags.
> That shatter'd roof, – and this naked floor –
>   A table – a broken chair –
> And a wall so blank, my shadow I thank
>   For sometimes falling there!

By taking in work at home a woman not only committed herself to inhumanly protracted periods of barely rewarded toil, but she also sapped her precious sources of energy, which had in any event already been weakened by semi-starvation. She endangered her eyesight if she contracted to do fine work and was at the same time unable to afford the best quality candles. She put her health at risk by stiffly stooping for hours at a time over her work in a dank and draughty room. Most poignant of all, she isolated herself from her family and in particular her husband if she had to start work after the children had been put to bed. The few pennies ground out of these prodigious efforts may have helped to narrow the unbridgeable gap between wages and necessary expenditure, but they can have done nothing to alleviate the leaden burden of anxiety under which working-class wives groaned.

Compounded of helplessness, hopelessness, and unremitting failure this tyrannical anxiety inflicted quite as much damage as the hunger, poverty, and squalor which had provoked it in the first place. Poverty dictated its own cruel terms: a squalid house could not expect to attract a lucrative lodger; an underfed child could only offer minimal resistance to disease; an exhausted, ragged man had little chance of winning the best-paid jobs; and a half-starved mother of four who had been at work half the night had no energy to walk to the market where the cheapest food was for sale, and no strength to carry buckets of water up to her room to wash her clothes and children. Poverty was not simply a matter of being able to afford less, it also involved irreparable degradation of the spirit and a lifetime's chronic worry.

The Sex Life of the Working Woman

A woman's sexuality must to some extent reside in her own attitude towards herself; the sexual persona she displays towards men generally and her husband in particular is an amalgamated reflection of the woman she considers herself to be and of the kind of sexual response she thinks she excites in men. A satisfactory sexual relationship cannot be achieved if both partners do not enjoy a healthy measure of sexual self-respect.

The nineteenth-century working woman's self-respect was subject to a series of devastating blows which can only have inflicted deep humiliation if they did not totally destroy it. She had to resign herself to seeing her attractiveness stripped from her in the space of a few years. Repeated childbirth and prolonged suckling, to say nothing of a continuously inadequate diet, combined to deform her figure irretrievably. Too poor to buy new clothes, far less fashionable ones, too poor to buy clothes that flattered or fitted her, too poor to buy cosmetics or perfumes or to visit the hairdresser, too poor to buy pretty shoes instead of serviceable boots, and too poor to buy jewellery or to brighten her appearance in any way, she had to reconcile herself to a lifetime's drabness.

Along with these privations, she was obliged to endure indignities of a more intimate kind. She, her husband, and their children were probably filthy, smelly, and infested with lice. Baths were difficult if not impossible to organize since they called for many arduous trips carrying heavy buckets to and from the communal tap; in any event, most families did not possess a bath. Nor could she afford eau de cologne, the Victorian equivalent of the modern deodorant. Washing clothes required large quantities of hot water, but water was difficult to obtain and fuel expensive; neither washing nor ironing were easily done in a tiny, squalid room full of small children, and it was only the determined and energetic housewife who could provide herself and her family with a regular supply of clean linen. Dentistry was not by then available to the working class and no attempt was made to educate them in dental hygiene; consequently, she knew nothing of, and anyway could not have afforded, tooth-brush and tooth-powder, both in common use among the middle class. Her teeth were decayed and unpleasantly discoloured, and her breath smelt. In short, she was not only drab but dirty, and all these miseries combined to lower if not eliminate her sense of her own sexiness.

Although her husband was no doubt quite as drab and dirty as she, her life extorted a higher physical toll and, unless he did some particularly debilitating job, her appearance was bound to decline at a swifter pace than his. The single girl of nineteen bore no resemblance to her married self of ten years later: no matter how pretty she had been as a girl, as a mother of four she could only expect to look plain, harrowed, and worn out. As we shall see, this discrepancy in the relative attractiveness of husband and wife was by no means the only pressure on the husband to seek sexual companionship elsewhere. Meanwhile, she sacrificed her sexuality to her marriage and, by a cruel irony, won for her pains no more than her husband's cooling affections.

Her life was a grim compound of anxiety, humiliation, and insupportable responsibility. She who mastered her precarious family budget and exercised effective discipline over her family's expenditure ran the risk of losing her husband through an excess of shrewishness; she who failed, and sank into debt and squalor, lost him through sluttishness. She who could temporarily allay her fear of pregnancy, whether by contraception, folly, or drunkenness, still could by no means freely enjoy her sex for it was severely curtailed, if not annihilated, by the lack of privacy and the presence of children and lodgers, by the discomfort of her immediate physical surroundings, and by the knowledge that her own body no longer held for her husband the charm it had held a year ago.

Mayhew interviewed a couple of tailors whose working day the husband described:[5] 'I must begin work at six in the morning, and sit close at it till eleven at night . . . my wife slaves night and day, as I do: and very often she has less rest than myself, for she has to stop up after I have gone to bed to attend to her domestic duties.' No great imaginative effort is required to reconstruct their sex life.

When the early carefree days of courtship and marriage were over, when the treadwheel began to revolve and bite into her physical reserves and when she first noticed the decay of her looks, these were the moments when her capacity for sexual enjoyment was critically jeopardized. Her first visit to the pawnshop, her husband's first drunken display of violence, her first black eye or broken arm at his hands, her first experience of the law, of bailiffs or of a vindictive landlord, her first eviction, her first miscarriage, her first child to die, her husband's first disappearance from home, his first bout of unemployment, and his first spell of imprisonment, all these experiences, both severally and together, inexorably withered her capacity for sexual pleasure. Sex ceased to provide excitement, relief, or peace and became only a source and focus of anxiety. In time, as these first experiences recurred for the third and fourth time and melted into a day-to-day pattern uniformly composed of degradation and squalor, her desire for her husband and for sexual coexistence with him atrophied and died.

Under these circumstances, it is not surprising that prostitution as an alternative way of life held a powerful attraction over and above the far from contemptible financial benefits it afforded. To the teenage girl on whom the prison gates of permanent employment were closing, the prospect of a life on the street may well have offered an attractive means of escape: she would have money of her own to spend on clothes, jewellery, and cosmetics, she would have the opportunity to see something of life beyond the end of her street and beyond the factory wall, and she would be able to visit dance halls and pleasure gardens where the lights were bright, the company fast, and where gentlemen congregated for the express purpose of lavishing large sums of money on pretty working-class girls. Most importantly, prostitution provided an opportunity of preserving one's self-respect. Looking at her mother and the other adult women in her family and neighbourhood, the girl may well have vowed, and with good reason, that whatever else became of her she would not follow in their footsteps; by taking to prostitution, she gambled that she would be able to prevent her figure from collapsing into the drab shapelessness of her mother's, that she would never have to slave prodigiously with her needle, as her mother did, to make a few pennies and that her attractiveness, her sexuality, would not be ground to nothing by the drudgery and labour of ordinary married life. Like any other job, prostitution carried its occupational risks, but they must have seemed minimal when compared with the certain humiliation and self-destruction that domestic life automatically entailed. It is a measure of that grim and barbarous age that for many working girls prostitution seemed to guarantee a degree of self-respect that was conspicuously absent from most other ways of life within their grasp.

While investigating workers in the cheap shoe trade, Mayhew came to the conclusion that the only means available of evading the poverty that inevitably overwhelmed them was to put their children to work as soon as they were able. He quoted the statement of a man who could barely scrape together twelve shillings a week, despite the fact that his wife and three daughters worked with him.[6]

'My daughters have to work fifteen hours a day', he told Mayhew. '. . . They seem to have no spirit and no animation in them; in fact, such very hard work takes the youth out of them. They have no time to enjoy their youth, and, with all their work, they can't present the respectable appearance they ought.'

It may well have occurred to one, if not all three daughters, that the price of exchanging such a life for that of a prostitute was negligible when balanced against the advantages; even at its most gruelling, prostitution destroyed youth and vitality no faster than making shoes under these conditions.

Walter (the author of *My Secret Life*) supplied an example of a girl who was in the throes of making just this decision. Walking through the park one summer night in a randy mood, he came across a girl whom he assumed to be 'one of the host of Paphians'. She moved away, but he laid hold of her arm and said, 'let me feel you and I'll give you some money'. 'No,' she replied, 'my sister's there, and I don't want her to catch me.' As they walked to a more secluded spot, he questioned her and discovered that she was a sixteen-year-old envelope-folder. Her sister was gay and she wanted to 'see about' like her, but her sister had caught her, driven her back home, hit her, and handed her over to their mother. The girl was nevertheless determined to imitate her sister, and when Walter told her to lie down she did so with alacrity. By the time they parted the girl had earned herself half a sovereign. He advised her to stay at work and avoid the park, but she brought the conversation to a decisive end by saying, 'I shan't [go to work], I only gets nine pence a day, and walks three miles there, and three miles back. – I'm tired on it.'

By abandoning envelope-folding the girl was undoubtedly making a sound financial move, but her desire to 'see about' like her sister, that is to escape from her background, was clearly at least as persuasive a factor as the possibility of acquiring more money.

Female Employment

By the end of the century, prospects facing the teenage working-class girl had substantially improved. Education had spread rapidly following the various Education Acts, and very few women were incapable of reading simple material and most could write more than their names. As a result, their horizons, if only the horizons of their imagination, were opened up immeasurably, and the women's pages of the popular magazines launched by Newnes and Harmsworth bore witness to their increasing literary appetite. Girls in their teens and early twenties flocked to the factories where they could earn relatively high wages. Between 1891 and 1911, the number of women employed in, for example, the manufacturing and transport industries rose by forty per cent, and most of them were unmarried. In the opinion of Peter Stearns[7] 'there was a virtual revolution in the life style of working-class women before marriage' during the period 1890–1914, for by 1911 fifty-four per cent of all unmarried women over the age of ten were employed; he estimated that the figure for unmarried women over the age of fifteen must have been as high as seventy-seven per cent. Clearly, the figures relating exclusively to working-class women, did they exist, would be even higher.

The girls, particularly those who had formerly been in service, claimed they enjoyed factory life: they found 'more life' there. By taking factory jobs they certainly escaped the confinements of home, they were able to mix on terms of equality with the men at the factory and, above all, they won for themselves financial independence. Beatrice Webb described social life among factory workers, as she saw it, in a letter to her father (1886) which, however class-bound in its outlook, could not have been written two decades earlier:

> [The hands] are a happy lot of people – quiet workers and very sociable – men and women mixing together in a free-and-easy manner – but without any coarseness that I can see . . . Parties of young men and women go off together for a week to Blackpool, sometimes on cheap trips to London – and as the women earn as much or nearly as much as the men there is no assumption of masculine superiority. Certainly this regular mechanical work, with all the invigorating brightness of machines, and plenty of fellow-workers of both sexes, seems about the happiest lot for a human being – so long as the hours are not too long.

Generally the girls lived at home and gave their mothers roughly half their wages to pay for board and lodging; the remaining half was spent on clothes – a new industry sprang up to offer them cheap, mass-produced fashions – on entertainments – music halls and picnics were especially popular – on holidays, books, and newspapers. They also saved for the future, a synonym in their case for marriage. They were, not surprisingly, keen to prolong these dog days and tended to marry a year or so later than their mothers' generation, at, say, twenty-two rather than nineteen.

Although in the long term this access to greater prosperity paved the way to an improvement in the position of working-class women generally, in the short term its effects were not so favourable, for these girls who first enjoyed the benefits of independent spending and, for that matter, independent thinking, were required to pay a bitter price when they came to marry. The young men with whom they had spent such carefree, comradely holidays were depressingly quick to assume 'masculine superiority' when they exchanged their role of workmate for husband. The working-class man entertained a very rigid, traditionalist conception of a woman's duties and her role in his life. Somerset Maugham embodied this conception in

Harry, one of the characters in *Liza of Lambeth* (1897). He believed
that

> 'A woman's plice is 'er 'ome, an' if 'er old man can't afford ter
> keep 'er without 'er workin' in a factory – well, all I can say is
> thet 'e'd better go an' git single.'
>   'Quite right too,' agreed his mother-in-law; 'an' wot's more,
> she'll 'ave a baby ter look after soon.'

And so the noose tightened around the neck of Harry's wife.

Ironically, the new prosperity enjoyed by increasing numbers of
single women only served to encumber further the already heavy
yoke of marriage: the amount of money she had got used to spending
exclusively on herself was severely reduced when she married, her
hitherto active social life suffered a similar restriction, and her world
was shrunk to the confines of her street and home. Compared to the
figures for single women at work, those for married women are
strikingly low: in 1901, in Swindon and Newcastle less than 10 per
cent of all married women and widows worked; in London,
Birmingham, and Manchester between 10 and 20 per cent worked,
and a survey made in Northampton and Reading could locate only
one family in which both husband and wife worked. (These figures
refer to women working outside home in regular employment, and
do not embrace the innumerable wives who made ends meet by
taking in washing, sewing, etc.) A working wife was a slight on her
husband's virility: only the sick, crippled, and unemployable sent
out their wives to earn. Her husband's virility was also disparaged
if she failed to produce children, and in healthy quantities.

Birth-Control: Method and Madness

Of all the strains bearing on a working-class wife perhaps the most onerous were those connected with pregnancy, childbirth, and the upbringing of small children. The joy natural to all couples when they become parents was undoubtedly mitigated, for the wife at least, by the price extorted from her by motherhood. She was deprived of her capacity to earn, if not by her first pregnancy, certainly by the appearance of the second and any subsequent children; she had to come to terms with the difficulty, perhaps the impossibility of properly feeding, clothing, and educating her children; she had to surrender the privacy she and her husband had previously enjoyed, particularly if poverty required them to share their bed with their children; and she had to endure the severe assaults on her health, to say nothing of her figure, inflicted by childbirth and suckling. Apart from being painful and frightening, childbirth was in those days downright dangerous. Gynaecology was a neglected sphere of medicine, and in any event most working women had no choice but to rely on the doubtful expertise of neighbours and relations. It is not surprising that the notion of contraception was readily embraced by working-class wives when it was put to them.

The social and economic desirability of contraception was a nineteenth-century phenomenon; medical discussion of the subject has presumably been going on since the dawn of civilization, but the doctrine of neo-Malthusianism, as birth-control was called, and its dissemination date only from the eighteen-sixties. The views of the Reverend Robert Thomas Malthus (1766–1834) were scarcely in accord with those to which he unwittingly lent his name. Not only was he an aristocratic Anglican and a fervent upholder of traditional, puritanical morality, he was also an economic pessimist who firmly believed poverty to be the inescapable lot of man. In his *Essay on the Principle of Population as it Affects the Future Improvement of Society* (1798) he argued that population will always tend to outrun the growth of production. The increase of population, he maintained, will take place, if unchecked, in a geometrical progression, while the means of subsistence will increase at an arithmetical progression. Only 'vice', 'misery' and self-restraint could curb this inexorable expansion of population.

In what Hazlitt described as 'a snivelling interpolation', Malthus propounded his remedy of 'moral restraint' which was in effect a call for the postponement of marriage, 'from prudential motives, with a conduct strictly moral during this period of restraint'. In other words he preached that, if the poor could not afford to support their offspring, they should not be permitted to marry. At the same time he strenuously disapproved of contraception by artificial means: 'Promiscuous intercourse, unnatural passions, violations of the marriage bed, and improper arts to conceal the consequences of irregular connexions, clearly come under the head of vice.' On another occasion he wrote, 'I should always particularly reprobate any artificial and unnatural modes of checking population, both on account of their immorality and their tendency to remove a necessary stimulus to industry.'

The preventatives proposed by Malthus were cruel, authoritarian, and manifestly unreal; furthermore the premise on which he founded his theories was shown to be unsound. Beatrice Webb, who worked with Charles Booth during the compilation of his *Life and Labour*, eloquently pointed out that the effect of prosperity on the London slum-dwellers of the nineties had precisely the opposite effect to that predicated by Malthus:

> To one who had been brought up in the political economy of Malthus, and taught to believe that every increment of income and security would inevitably be accompanied by additional children in working-class families, it was disconcerting to discover that the greater the poverty and overcrowding, and especially the insecurity of the livelihood, the more reckless became the breeding of children; whilst every increment in income, and especially every rise in the regularity and the security of the income in working-class families was found to be accompanied, according to the statistics, by a more successful control of the birth-rate.'[1]

It is however a measure of his influence that Beatrice Webb should be taking seriously in the eighteen-nineties an idea propounded in the previous century.

The economic philosophy of Malthus enjoyed such a prolonged period of respect largely because it conveniently provided capitalism with an apparently scientific vindication of a theory of minimal wages. Proceeding from the Malthusian principle that population will always expand to the limit of subsistence, this theory held that a man should only be paid enough to satisfy his barest needs, for the more he was paid, or for that matter the more charity he received, the more children he would inevitably breed.

In the past knowledge of contraception had been the possession of the educated, wealthy classes, but throughout the nineteenth century a number of men and women stepped forward to provide the poor with this privileged information. They were persecuted by the establishment for their pains. In 1878 Charles Bradlaugh, radical, freethinking MP and lawyer, and Annie Besant, freethinker and socialist, fought a celebrated case and in the teeth of vigorous opposition won a decisive victory for the birth-control propagandists by securing the right to publish *The Fruits of Philosophy* by Dr Charles Knowlton. This booklet argued the case for contraception and lucidly and simply described the reproductive system and the available contraceptive techniques. The social effect of the trial was immediate and dramatic. The sensational publicity surrounding the case and the energetic manner in which Bradlaugh and Besant took advantage of their success combined to bring to the attention of millions of people the possibility of contraception. From 1878–81 the Freethought Publishing Company under Bradlaugh and Besant's management sold 185,000 copies of their sixpenny edition of *The Fruits of Knowledge*; other publishers distributed other editions, and the total number of copies sold during this brief period is thought by Norman Himes[2] to be in the region of 235,000. By the same token, the circulation of other books and pamphlets on the subject must have greatly increased.

In 1879 Annie Besant published her own *Law of Population* which was designed to replace Knowlton's out-of-date work and by 1891 175,000 copies had been sold at sixpence each. The full title of her booklet was *The Law of Population: Its Consequences, and Its Bearing upon Human Conduct and Morals* and in dedicating the book she made it clear that it had been specifically written for the poor: 'to the poor', she wrote, 'in great cities and agricultural districts, dwellers in stifling court or crowded hovel, in the hope that it might point out a path from poverty, and may make easier the life of British mothers.' This and similar pamphlets were often bound together with advertisements on separate sheets telling readers where they could obtain modern contraceptive supplies.

Following the Bradlaugh trial the Malthusian League was founded along with its journal *The Malthusian* (1879–1922). With Annie Besant as its secretary the League devoted itself to disseminating information about birth-control. Initially it concentrated its energies on lectures and the distribution of pamphlets, but later a medical branch was formed which was to prove influential among doctors in England and on the Continent. Himes estimated that the result of all these efforts was the sale in England between 1876 and 1891 of not less than a million tracts furnishing elaborate contraceptive information. He thought it not inconceivable that the figure was closer to two millions. The literature to which this enormous number of people were exposed not only explained the techniques of contraception, but also preached birth-control to the working class as a gospel of freedom. Annie Besant in particular stressed the tendency of population pressure to cause poverty, misery, low wages, and child labour. It comes as no surprise therefore to discover that the birth-rate drops at a strikingly swift pace after 1876.

Predictably, though ironically, the middle and upper classes were quick to appreciate the benefits of contraception and the birth-rate among them suffered a pronounced decline during the 'eighties. It was not until the turn of the century that a similarly sharp decline took place in the working-class birth-rate, and even then the pace at which it happened varied significantly from place to place, and job to job. The birth-rate among textile workers, for instance, which was already low, dropped steeply between 1886 and 1901, while among miners it barely altered.

Apart from the publicity she invariably generated, perhaps one of the reasons why Mrs Besant sold so many copies of her *Law of Population* was simply that she was a woman writing for women, unlike all the other nineteenth-century Malthusian writers who were men, and it seems reasonable to assume that the methods she recommended to her hundreds of thousands of readers were by and large the ones they tended to use.

In the first editions of her booklet she devoted two pages to a discussion of 'the safe period' which she declared to be unsafe. On the other hand she considered withdrawal – *coitus interruptus* – 'absolutely certain as a preventative'. She also thought highly of syringing with a solution of zinc or alum, a technique advocated by Knowlton, although she commented that 'there are many obvious disadvantages connected with it as a matter of taste and feeling', adding that 'the same remark applies to the employment of the *badruche*, a covering used by men of loose character as a guard against syphilitic diseases . . .' The check that seemed to her most preferable was the sponge, for it was both certain and did not in any sense grate on feelings of affection or of delicacy. The sponge had been recommended by many writers throughout the century, notably by Richard Carlisle who as early as 1826 had discussed it in his *Every Woman's Book* or *What is Love*. It consisted simply of a small piece of sponge, attached for convenience and safety to a piece of thread, which the woman inserted into her vagina where it blocked and absorbed the spermatozoa. Mrs Besant in later editions advised women to soak the sponge in a solution of twenty grains of quinine to a pint of water. She made it clear, as had other writers, that her faith in this technique was based on the fact that it was not only reliable and unobtrusive but that its use was also entirely within the woman's control.

By the one hundred and tenth edition, which appeared in 1887, she had substantially modified her account of the available techniques. She now recommended three methods as being most reliable, the soluble pessary, the india rubber pessary (cervical cap) and the sponge. She advised women to douche with a solution of quinine (ten grains to a pint of water) in the morning before removing the cap. Quinine was also used as the supposed active agent in one of the more popular brands of suppositories. (It was not until the twentieth century that it was discovered to have only a low spermicidal power.) Many women found it acted as an irritant when applied to delicate skin. This edition of the book saw the first reference to the use of the artificial sponge which had also been consistently recommended in another celebrated and influential book, *The Wife's Handbook* by Dr H. A. Allbutt.

Her section dealing with techniques was introduced by a scathing condemnation of the medical profession's failure to play its part: '. . . further investigation', she wrote, 'of this intricate subject is sorely needed, and it is much to be wished that more medical men would devote themselves to this important branch of physiology. The main difficulty in the way is the absurd notion that prudential checks are obscene, and very few doctors have the courage to face the odium that would arise from a frank treatment of the subject.'

The medical profession was criminally slow to learn about contraception and even slower to share the knowledge with its patients. Its attitude may be gauged by a letter that appeared in *The Lancet* in 1885: 'The means by which pregnancy can be prevented *ab initio* . . . has happily not yet been introduced into an overloaded medical curriculum, and . . . is as distasteful a subject to the medical practitioner as it would be to the most fastidious divine.' The correspondent concluded by declaring that the medical profession 'must never identify itself in this matter, however indirectly'; he felt sure, however, 'that the majority of your readers will gladly assist in evoking the aid of the law to prevent the further spread of this horrible trade.' An editorial in a 1905 issue of *The Lancet* asserted that any young girl who read a certain (innocuous) birth-control pamphlet which was to be found advertised in *Myra's Journal* (a dressmaking periodical) would soon acquire 'a second-hand knowledge which would place her on an equal footing with an experienced prostitute.' This remark is all too typical of its time.

The profession's attitude towards birth-control and its advocates is best illustrated, however, by the virulence with which his colleagues attacked Dr Allbutt and expelled him from their midst. Dermatologist, freethinker, and republican, Henry Arthur Allbutt was also secretary of the Malthusian League's newly formed Medical Branch. In 1886 he published *The Wife's Handbook*, 'a decent popular medical treatise designed to diffuse among the general populace hygienic knowledge, but especially information on pre-natal care and the management of the baby'; the book contained a chapter, of less than four pages, in which he explained to his readers how conception could be prevented. True to his principles and those of the League he priced the book at sixpence and declared his intention that it was to be 'a book which could be understood by most women, and at a price which would ensure its place even in the poorest household'. He was later to insist that his motives for publishing the book were of the highest, for he earnestly believed that a popular educational campaign disseminating contraceptive knowledge among poor women could only bring to a halt the poverty, prostitution, misery, and marital discord which he identified as the inevitable results of reckless reproduction.

Soon after its publication *The Wife's Handbook* became the object of a fanatical campaign conducted by the Leeds Vigilance Association for Enforcing the Criminal Law Amendment Act and the Protection of Girls which finally culminated in the General Medical Council setting up a committee of inquiry. Here it was pointed out that the book was objectionably popular in approach, that it was accessible to unmarried women, and that it displayed a lamentable tendency to 'demoralize the world'. Allbutt was found guilty of publishing his book 'at so low a price as to bring the work within the reach of the youth of both sexes, to the detriment of public morals'. His offence was, in the opinion of the Council, 'infamous conduct in a professional respect', and his name was erased from the Medical Register.

With publicity like this the book could hardly fail, and it went on to be one of the best-selling Malthusian tracts, second only probably to Mrs Besant's own book. Peter Fryer records that 390,000 copies had been sold by 1907. Determined not to abandon the struggle, Allbutt proceeded to publish a pamphlet, *Artificial Checks*, in his own defence, and continued to practise. Although outlawed by his colleagues, he does not appear to have suffered unduly. In July 1889 he was able to write to the editor of the *Leeds Times* that attempts to destroy him had failed, for since his excommunication he had grown richer, his practice had expanded, his fees had doubled, his name had become famous and, in short, he could afford to snap his fingers at the Council.

The *Pall Mall Gazette*, one of the few newspapers to take his side, declared that the Council's decision was 'one of the most glaring illustrations of professional prejudice and human folly', but Allbutt came closer to the mark when he wrote in his vindictive pamphlet that his 'mock trial' was 'a tribunal out of touch with the real wants of the suffering – a tribunal of aristocratic physicians, whose legislation clogs the wheels of progress, and prevents medical men being the friends of the poor'. He always maintained that his only crime had been to publish *The Wife's Handbook* at too low a price; 'it was too cheap', he wrote, 'it was necessary to try and crush me'.

The contraceptive techniques recommended in *The Wife's Handbook* differ slightly but significantly from those in *The Law of Population*. The safe period, withdrawal ('hurtful to the nervous system in many persons'), injections (alum, quinine, Palfrey's Powder, quinine or vinegar solutions), sponges or tampons, the cervical cap, and the sheath ('a very certain check') were all mentioned and discussed, but Allbutt was, according to Himes, the first English author to make reference to the Mensinga diaphragm. Dr Wilhelm Mensinga, a Dutch medico, afterwards professor of anatomy at Breslau university, invented this large occlusive pessary with a watch-spring rim in the eighteen-seventies; it later became better known as the Dutch cap. Allbutt provided instructions for the use of the 'check pessary', or cervical cap, and specifically recommended Rendell's soluble pessaries. Indicative of the times was his condemnation of the internal use of arsenic and other drugs to produce impotence. He placed no faith in the method apparently favoured by some Italian women of coughing directly after intercourse in order to expel the semen.

Both Besant and Allbutt, in the tradition of the great contraceptive pioneers, aimed their propaganda directly at the working classes, specifically at the wives. Unfortunately many of the techniques they described were beyond the reach of the very audience they most wished to influence. Although cheaper than ever before and growing cheaper year by year as manufacturing methods improved and demand increased, contraceptives were by the end of the century still too expensive for the very poor. For example, The Improved Vertical and Reverse Current Syringe, complete in box, with particulars for injection and directions for use, cost either 3s 6d or 4s 6d, post free, depending on which model the customer ordered. The Improved Check Pessary – 'constructed on a common-sense principle, and strictly in accordance with the female organization' – cost 2s 3d. Both articles were advertised in the 1886 edition of *The Wife's Handbook* and were accompanied by testimonies from Allbutt himself, but even the most glowing testimony was unlikely to have persuaded a housewife struggling on a budget of 18s to part with such a relatively large sum as 2s 3d.

It was not only the lack of ready cash that prevented the poor from adopting contraception as speedily as its advocates hoped: the very environment in which they lived made it difficult, if not impossible, for them to practise even the simplest methods. Both authors laid great stress upon douching, recommending it as a method both cheap and effective, but it can hardly have appealed to those couples whose water-supply was remotely located, and perhaps even switched off at nights. Nor can either douching or some of the more cumbersome techniques have been popular with women who could not rely on reasonable privacy.

The pace at which the poor accepted contraception was largely governed by the amenities they were provided with and the pace at which they in their turn were modernized. The spread of education played a significant part in the advancement of birth-control; more and more women were able to read for themselves the relevant literature, and the primitive myths and taboos surrounding child-birth and sexuality generally were effectively, if slowly, dispelled. But the improvement of housing conditions and sanitation had an even more profound impact, for they made possible the practice of a concept which, though revolutionary in itself, was only accessible to those enjoying a certain standard of living.

The Price of Reproduction

Prior to the advent of contraception the sexual act had invariably been fraught with the possibility of pregnancy. An addition to her family was a prospect feared by the working-class woman of the nineteenth century, the sharpness of her fear being in direct ratio to the number of children already in existence. The middle-class mother also suffered in her turn during this century of voluminous families, but she at least could console herself with the knowledge that she was introducing her offspring into a comparatively comfortable world and that the man responsible for her 'delicate condition' could be relied on to maintain his family in a state of suitable prosperity. No such consolation attended the discovery of pregnancy in a working-class household.

Fear of pregnancy must have imposed a regime of virtual celibacy on many working couples. The conditions in which they lived were in any case hardly conducive to 'love-making', and the inescapable anxiety regarding the consequences of their actions which were endured by the wife, if not by her husband as well, must have been sufficient finally to extinguish any remaining spark of desire. A wife's capacity to enjoy her sex-life was, as with all other aspects of her existence, directly governed by her ability to provide materially for herself and her family; an active sex-life was an item for which few working-class budgets could cater. Before the days of manufactured contraceptives the fear of pregnancy was in itself a very potent preventative, although sadly it was only truly effective in so far as it prevented huge numbers of women from deriving any pleasure from their husbands.

According to middle-class observers and novelists, working-class marriages were steeped in physical violence, and it was a cliché of those times, no less than our own, that the enormity of working-class families was the thoughtless but inevitable product of the husbands' drunken rapacity and the wives' helpless submission. Fundamental to this cliché was the suggestion that drunkenness and violence were flaws inherent in the working-class character. The fact was, however, that couples needed to be drunk if they were to anaesthetize the anxieties and temporarily dispel the inhibitions that normally stood in the way of their making love. The wives, usually rendered frigid with worry, were perhaps, whether consciously or not, content to give in to their husbands' passion, momentarily comforting themselves with the thought that the responsibility for the consequences had been forcibly removed. Far from being natural to their character, violence was a last resort, but one which they were all too often compelled to adopt. Instinct and desire had to fight and conquer the strict frugality and self-restraint, the guarantors of their frail solvency before sex could take place. In the case of the working class to 'spend' (Victorian slang for ejaculate) was literally to spend (money), and the expenditure was in effect an irrecoverable extravagance. To squander the family savings in the pub, to be drunk every night was, in comparison with engendering another mouth to feed and another back to clothe, a sound economic policy.

The coming of contraception did not make anyone any richer, nor did it mend any roofs, nor lay any drains, but it did bestow one formidable boon: it eliminated the hitherto ever-present fear of imminent pregnancy. The neo-Malthusians believed and preached that smaller families meant greater prosperity for the labouring classes but, without actually saying so, they knew that they were not only offering their readers freedom from financial worry, they were also securing for them the opportunity of a happier sex-life. Sex could at last be contemplated in isolation from monetary considerations. It is too much to say that the working class, once introduced to the doctrine of birth-control, was at a stroke blessed with prosperity and nuptial bliss, but at least it can be said that if a couple chose to practise contraception their sex-life ceased to be a positive barrier between them and became a potential source of mutual comfort and pleasure.

Contraception did not, however, radically affect the working-class birth-rate until the turn of the century. Rowntree, making his survey of poverty in York in the eighteen-nineties estimated that for couples whose weekly incomes were 25s and below the average number of children was roughly four. It is worth recalling that he also established that the family budgets of twenty-five per cent of York's population would not properly feed and clothe two adults and one child, far less four children.

A young married couple, with only themselves to support, stood at the highest point of prosperity they had ever known or would ever know in their lives. If the wife worked, and they were both in good health, they could expect to eat reasonably well, to furnish their rooms or cottage, and to wear new clothes and shoes; they could also afford to visit the music hall, to read a daily newspaper, to drink and smoke and go on holiday to one of the many new resorts that were by the 'eighties within easy reach of most big cities. But this period of relative luxury was abruptly terminated as soon as the wife became pregnant. She was of course, at this age, at her most attractive, their sex-life was at its most active and the chances of conception were therefore at their highest.

Most women abandoned work for ever during their first pregnancy, thus halving family incomes at the very moment when expenditure was dramatically increased. Some women were able to leave their children with mothers or mothers-in-law, but employers were not sympathetic to working mothers and preferred to offer jobs to single girls. Working-class men preserved a fiercely traditionalist view of the woman's role, and those who were prepared to let their wives work when they were first married generally insisted on their staying at home as soon as there were children to look after. Women who had jobs tended for the sake of the money to delay leaving as long as possible and in the process often endangered their babies' health and their own. A lifetime's malnutrition combined with ignorance of pregnant women's special needs did nothing to enhance the chances of easy and successful births. Doctors and medicines were expensive, ante-natal clinics did not exist, and the only available literature was written for the benefit of the doctor, not the patient. A mother-to-be had no choice but to rely on the folk wisdom of the street and the experiences of other mothers, relatives, and neighbours.

Gynaecology was one of the more neglected branches of medicine in the nineteenth century and although chloroform was in use by the 'nineties the prospect of having a baby in hospital was alarming, especially if one was poor and a patient in a charity ward. Most mothers chose in preference the security of familiar surroundings and faces and, with the aid of midwives and occasionally even doctors, braved the primitive simplicity and unhygienic conditions of home.

Miscarriages and still births were frequent. If, however, the child lived to breathe the foetid air of his parents' bedroom, his continuing existence was far from guaranteed for he still ran the risk of catching one of the many diseases which throve in the ubiquitous dirt. By the end of the century the understanding of the importance of hygiene and improved medical techniques had effectively reduced the incidence of infant mortality among babies born in the bigger, teaching hospitals and in middle-class homes, but the odds against survival for the baby born into a poor home remained lamentably high.

If a mother lost neither her child nor her life during childbirth she then had to solve the problem of feeding the new mouth. Malnutrition rendered many mothers incapable of providing sufficient milk, or milk of the right strength; others contracted breast abscesses or sores which prevented them from feeding properly. In such cases, if wet-nurses could not be found, the babies died of simple starvation. On the other hand, mothers whose milk was plentiful and rich were tempted to continue breast-feeding long after it was necessary, for they were loath to dispense with a reliable source of free nourishment; many employed protracted breast-feeding as a form of contraception. These women were forced to sacrifice even their figures in an effort to save a few pennies.

Before long the cycle of pregnancy, birth, and upbringing was set in motion again; if the woman was healthy, strong, and fertile, only celibacy or desertion would bring to a halt the succession of fresh babies. It is true that childbirth tends to become increasingly easy and safe with each confinement, but pregnancy can never have lost its terror for those prone to repeated miscarriage, those who felt great pain during childbirth or for the victims of acute post-natal depression.

Equally difficult to assess is the intensity of suffering experienced by those whose children succumbed to disease or accident. A measure of immunity was no doubt derived from the fact that the death of a child was an occurrence common to most families; nevertheless few parents can have escaped the bitterness and despair that inevitably accompany such tragedies. In some cases, grieving parents may have been able to recognize that poverty and its effects, rather than some fault of their own or the will of God, had been directly responsible for the death of their children; this in itself, however, cannot have consoled them. The death of a child is harrowing under any circumstances, but the knowledge that their children died because of their inability to feed and protect them from disease can only have added to the anguish endured by working-class parents.

There were, of course, mothers who positively sought the extinction of new life. Rather than undergo the rigours of pregnancy the mother of an already over-large and underfed family, or the mother who had been told that her next child would damage or kill her might well put herself in the hands of an abortionist. Outlawed, condemned and, if caught, severely punished, the abortionist nevertheless flourished for his services were in constant demand. In every working-class district there lived a woman reputed to be experienced in these matters, or one celebrated for the infallibility of her folk remedies, or, worse, a struck-off doctor, or a half-trained nurse who was skilled in the application of hot baths, pints of gin, and long knitting needles, and who, in all likelihood, far from aborting the foetus, succeeded only in maiming the mother. To seek abortion in those days required great courage or the provocation of grim desperation, for not only was the victim exposing herself to an operation which was reliable only in so far as it was dangerous, but she was also flagrantly rebelling against any moral teaching which might have come her way.

If a child, when it was born, was unwanted but persisted in defying mortality its luckless parents had but one course open to them, infanticide. Some parents killed their children by neglect, some paid baby-farms to neglect their children for them and some found foster-parents through the agony columns who for a fee would euphemistically 'adopt' the superfluous child.[3] Each year the Thames yielded up its grisly catch of infant corpses. The Victorian cliché, to be found in countless novels, of the baby left on a rich man's doorstep, had its melancholy foundation in reality. Some parents, responding in desperation to the pressure of an ever-increasing family, abandoned or expelled those children whom they hoped were sufficiently mature to look after themselves, and it was in order to shelter these waifs of four and five years old that Dr Barnardo opened his celebrated homes. Life expectancy in the slums was miserably short, disease was rife, and death too frequent an occurrence for the sudden and unexpected decease of a child to attract much notice.

The hardships endured by the poor tested to the limit their powers of endurance and it is not surprising that some mothers concluded that it was kinder to kill their babies than to leave them in a world they themselves had come to hate. Some killed their children out of self-protection: the family budget could not be stretched to accommodate the needs of another member, the food ration could not be further subdivided, the bed could not hold another body, the family rags could not clothe another back, however small. And some killed in psychological self-defence: they could not survive another cycle of night-feeding, crying, nappy changing, and teething and at the same time retain their sanity.

The little stranger of Victorian fiction was, in reality, all too often a little terrorist who merely by his innocent existence and unwitting arrival threatened to demolish many a working-class household.

The Sex Life of the Working Man

The burden of anxiety borne by the working-class man was no less onerous than his wife's, and had no less destructive an effect upon his sexual nature. He had to live with the knowledge that no matter how strenuously he laboured – at what was probably a job of grinding boredom – he could never amass sufficient money to provide his wife with a housekeeping budget that would properly house, feed, and clothe her and their family. He knew that every drink he bought at the pub was literally food out of his children's mouths, and that every pipe he smoked had to be paid for by his wife's supplementary earnings or by her self-deprivation. As the years went by, he was obliged to witness the pathetic deterioration in health, looks, and spirits of the wife whom he had, presumably, once desired. He had to reconcile himself to the cruel effect of consistent poverty upon his children – 'stunted stature and dulled intelligence' – as Rowntree put it. He had to endure the invasion and occupation of his territory by a lodger because he could not get together the rent by his own unaided effort. He, like his wife, had to suffer the miseries of living in a single unventilated, unlit slum room.

Turning once again to Mayhew for an eye-witness report, we find the following description of a tailor who simply by falling ill had inflicted great suffering upon his family:[1]

> In a small, close, and bare, unfurnished room, stretched on a bed scantily covered, I found the poor sick slop-worker . . . I asked why the sick man was not taken to hospital. The man himself could not speak for coughing. The wife told me he could not go to hospital, his clothes were all in pledge; they had been taken to the pawnshop for the subsistence of the family. 'If it hadn't been for that we must all have starved', she said . . . 'I have pawned all my under-clothing. I have five children. I have pledged almost all their clothes, and if I could have taken any-thing else off the poor little things, I should have done it to get victuals for them.'

When investigating the boot- and shoe-makers he came across a man too poor even to provide his wife with privacy while she gave birth to his child. A neighbour described the scene to Mayhew:[2]

> 'In many houses in Monmouth Street there is a system of sub-letting among the journeymen. In one room lodged a man and his wife (a laundress worked there), four children, and two single young men. The wife was actually delivered in this room whilst the men kept at their work – they never lost an hour's work; nor is this an unusual case ... I could instance ten or twelve cases of two or three married people living in one room in that street. The rats have scampered over the beds that lay huddled together in the kitchen.'

These men were chained to failure; no effort on their part, however ingenious or diligent, would ever win the privilege of simple dignity. Every working man had to come to terms with or succumb to the knowledge of his own inadequacy. Some resigned and left their wives and families to scramble through life as and how they could; most, if the evidence of Mayhew, Booth, and Rowntree is to be believed, worked on doggedly, making the best of a fate that only had the worst to offer.

Rowntree's analysis of the average working-class family budget showed that only by dint of persistent frugality and self-discipline could a family with an income of 21s (in 1900) manage to sustain itself without falling into debt; he also showed that families with lower incomes could neither hope adequately to feed, clothe, and house themselves, nor avoid dealing with the money-lender and the pawnbroker. Rowntree's calculations were, of course, based on the assumption that the husband brought home his wage-packet intact, but the enormous number of Victorian public houses still standing in working-class districts, the grandeur of their architecture, and the splendour of their interiors, are eloquent witnesses to the fact that the average husband, far from enjoying the occasional drink when he could afford it, devoted a handsome slice of his earnings to the greater enrichment of the brewers. He also, for that matter, smoked, bet on horses, dogs, pigeons, and prize-fighters, went with prostitutes and attended football, rugby, and cricket matches; he bought newspapers, books, and magazines, and he paid dues to a trade union; he took his wife to the music-hall or dancing at one of the pleasure gardens or dance halls, he took her and their children on holiday picnics and to the sea-side and he bought her fancy hats and shawls in the street markets. The family budget catered for none of these activities, but they all nevertheless form staple components of late nineteenth-century working-class culture.

As the wage-earner a husband enjoyed a considerable advantage over his wife for he had, as long as he was in work, continual access to spending power. He could buy his escape from the physical and psychological miseries of their home, and in a world where the male word tended to be law he did not find it difficult to justify or simply enforce his right to whatever kind of oblivion he chose. He retained his spending power, however, only by withholding from his ever-desperate family a proportion of his wage, the benevolence or otherwise of his character governing the size of this proportion. Except for those who lived in communities where tradition ensured that the men handed over their wage-packets unopened to their wives, and who therefore had no choice but to spend the sum allotted to them, none can have been so saintly as to have refused himself cigarettes if he smoked, or a drink after work, or even a bet on a horse to enliven an otherwise featureless day. And, since he knew that with or without his beer money the wage he earned was insufficient for the needs of his family, he was hardly inspired to impose on himself the rigours of self-denial. The very inadequacy of his earning power in relation to the cost of living only intensified his sense of hopelessness and drove him to demand even greater sacrifices from those who depended on him.

In many professions, even the man who was determined to take home to his wife every penny he earned found it difficult to do so, for both recruitment and payment were conducted in the pub itself. Mayhew discovered that the drunkenness for which casual hands in the tailoring trade were notorious was the direct result of employers 'calling on' their labour in public houses. One of the men described to him how the system worked:[3]

'The men off trade and seeking employment are kept knocking about at the public house all the day through. The consequence of this is that the day is passed in drinking, and habits of intemperance are produced which it is almost impossible to withstand. Those who have got money treat those who have none; and indeed, such are the inducements to drink, that it is almost impossible for the tailor who is not regularly and constantly employed to remain sober.'

And so, if a casual hand was not chosen to work, he had to face his wife with the news that not only had he failed to earn any money that day, but he had also spent the little he had taken with him.

Tailors were frequently paid their wages in the pub where a pernicious system operated which almost guaranteed that they drank as much as they had earned. More than one man was generally employed in the making of a large garment, say an overcoat, but payment was made in a lump sum. In order that each should receive his share, the men would agree to take their wage at the pub where change could be readily obtained. The consequences of this procedure were explained to Mayhew:

> 'The publican often keeps the men an hour waiting for the change . . . [and] the most intemperate and improvident of the workmen spend a large portion of their wages in drink. I myself generally spend half (unless my Missus catches me); and on several occasions I have squandered away in liquor all I had earned in the week. My Missus knows my infirmity, and watches me of a Saturday night regularly.'

The system most favoured by publicans involved withholding payment, sometimes for as long as a day, and at the same time offering credit at the bar; this crude expedient ensured that many men had drunk their wages for the week, and were in debt to the publican before they had even been paid.

Thanks to the efforts of the National Temperance Society and other similar organizations, and the pressure applied by the ever-stronger trade unions, these practices had more or less been eliminated by the end of the century, but the pub still remained, as it does to some extent today, the hub of working-class community life. The wage packet, however, continued to be the target of a multitude of sharp stratagems all designed to claw back into the employer's pocket as large a part as possible of the pitiful sum temporarily deposited in the worker's hand. Some employers operated a 'company store' system whereby a proportion of the worker's wage was paid in tokens redeemable only at a shop owned or associated with the employer, where goods were sold at exorbitant prices. Some employers picked both pockets at once by situating the store on the premises of the local pub. Factories were known to institute their own criminal codes by which the most trivial offences – unpunctuality, carelessness, even talking to another worker – would incur substantial fines that could not only amount to the worker's wage but actually exceed it, so that the wretched employee, at the end of a hard week's work, found himself not only penniless but in debt.

Some employers, particularly in trades open to 'sweating', insisted that their workers lived on the premises where they were charged exorbitant sums for board and lodging. Mayhew interviewed a tailor living in appalling circumstances:[4]

> 'We worked in the smallest room and slept there as well – all six of us. There were two turn-up beds in it and we slept three in a bed. There was no chimney, and indeed no ventilation whatever. I was near losing my life there – the foul air of so many people working all day and sleeping there at night was quite suffocating . . . We were all sick and weak, and loath to work. Each of the six of us paid 2s 6d a week for our lodging, or 15s altogether, and I am sure such a room as we slept and worked in might be had for 1s a week. . . . The usual sum that the men working for sweaters pay for their tea, breakfasts, and lodging is 6s 6d to 7s a week, and they seldom earn more money in the week. Occasionally at the week's end they are in debt to the sweater.'

Married men who worked in this way were obliged to keep their wives and children in separate lodgings, or if times were bad and wages low they had no choice but to dispatch their families to the workhouse. Mayhew talked to a boot-maker who had virtually been driven to alcoholism by the squalor and claustrophobia of his lodgings:[5]

> 'I could not read by any fireside, for there was no fireside and no chair to sit on. By degrees I made a sort of home in a tap-room; and it grew and grew until I was fond of beer, and found myself a fuddler. That's a certain evil of the system. Men must find an hour of comfort, and it can only be found in the public house.'

Thrift, the great Victorian virtue, so piously invoked as the cure for all ills whenever the topic of working-class misery was under discussion, was in reality inaccessible to the working man for his thriftiness could only be practised at the expense of the employing classes who, in their turn, devoted themselves to maintaining him in a constant state of subjugated improvidence. The worker not only received a grossly unjust price for his labour and was required to work in obnoxious conditions, he was also made to undergo continual humiliation and endure persistent anxiety simply in order to get his hands on his promised wage-packet which, in all likelihood, had already been rifled. The fate of the working man was pithily described to Mayhew by a shoe-maker:[6] 'I feel degraded by the way I'm employed, and we all do, but how are we to get out of it? It's just degradation or starvation, and I'm not quite ready for starvation.'

The constant humiliation heaped upon him at work, and the knowledge that his pay-packet, whether intact or not, would fail to satisfy his family's needs did not combine to inspire in him a mood of domestic kindliness as he returned home on a Friday night to face his exhausted and worried wife. Her debilitated state made him feel guilty, and yet her inability to offer him a respite from the day's tribulations annoyed and depressed him. The insufficiency of their income, the perpetual sapping of his dignity at work, and her unvarying round of toil at home compounded to infuse their marriage, not with mutual succour, but with hostility. Considerable benevolence was required of both partners if they were to avoid looking on each other simply as receptacles for the relief of their own hatreds and sorrows.

It was, under the circumstances, all too easy for the husband to conclude that his time would be more pleasantly passed at the pub than at home. The attractions of the pub were further enhanced by the inevitable presence of the prostitute. A man who had worked from six in the morning to six at night under the baleful and un-winking eye of a sadistic foreman and in constant terror of being discharged for talking, or making a mistake, or falling behind the others, understandably found the bright, warm, and companionable atmosphere of the nearest pub preferable to the meagre comforts of his own home. By the same token, the company of a pretty and sympathetic stranger might momentarily hold for him a charm with which the minatory figure of his awaiting wife could not compete.

The interests of the publican and the prostitute profitably coincided: she attracted the customers, and he provided her with a congenial atmosphere in which to do her business. Drunk, a man

was more easily persuaded to buy another round, and he was also
more responsive to the dubious allure of his companion of the night.
Not that the prostitute can fairly be portrayed as a spider engorging
the male victims entangled in her net; on the contrary, she was, to
vary the image, merely the fly on the publican's hook. She had her
own reasons, apart from business, for gravitating to the pub. She,
like her client, was probably cold, lonely, and unwilling to return
to a cheerless home; she was perhaps, also like her client, close to
being an alcoholic. It was, in the end, the same poverty that drove
them, for slightly different reasons, to the same refuge.

The overworked, harassed victim of excessive child-bearing who
nightly took up her traditional attitude behind the front door,
rolling pin poised to administer awesome punishment, could only
provide in her husband's mind the glummest contrast with what
seemed to him the youthful, gaily dressed soubrette on whom he
lavished his hard earned pay. But, in fact, the prostitute was but a
junior version of his wife, for she, like his lover of ten years ago,
was only a working-class girl whom he found attractive. She
happened to be one whose circumstances had led her to take up a
job which, by the standards of her peers, was by no means the most
ignominious on the labour market.

Returning from the boozy and comradely warmth of the pub to
his damp and inhospitable hovel, the now indigent husband prepared to receive the onslaught of accusation and recrimination
which his infuriated wife could be relied on to unleash. She, in her
turn, was embittered by his unilateral spending, jealous of his
preferring others' company to her own, and fatigued to breaking
point by her day- and night-long labours in the house. The inevitable result of this midnight confrontation was the violence
for which working-class relationships were so notorious.

Charles Booth[7] came across a case of a man who treated his wife
with a savagery sufficiently severe to merit a lengthy description.
A sweep by trade, the man lived with his wife and child on the first
floor of No 24 Shelton Street. Kicking, hitting, and swearing at
her, he knocked her about continually and she was never free from
bruises. He earned 25s a week but drank most of it and expected her
to find the rent, beating her up when she failed. Once she escaped
to a 'refuge', but he coaxed her back only to brutalize and terrorize
her afresh. Booth's reporter saw her just as she emerged from
hospital, her head bound up, her arms black and blue, and he

warned the man that he would soon kill her. A few weeks later she was once again in hospital; she was unconscious, her eye was blackened, and her face badly bruised. This assault proved fatal for a few hours later she died. Booth added to his narrative this comment: 'There was no prosecution, the neighbours shielded the man, and he too is now dead. The tie which bound together this man and woman till death – and this her death at his hands – was though voluntary (she was his common law wife) strangely strong.'

Every writer, whether novelist, sociologist, or journalist, who wrote about the working classes commented upon the brutality with which husbands treated their wives. Equally, they all expressed amazement at the loyalty, tolerance, and protectiveness displayed by the wives. Arthur Morrison, one of the few working-class writers, points to this phenomenon in his story 'Lizerunt' (1894).

Lizer is recently married to Billy; she is pregnant, he is out of work. One morning he asks her for two shillings; she is saving for the baby, and refuses. He proceeds to beat her up: 'he ran at her throat and forced her back over a chair,' 'punched her in the breast', and 'made for her with a kick that laid her on the lower stairs'. He then departs. She meanwhile begins her labour. When he returns he demands his dinner and is outraged to find her in bed. She shows him the child which he dismisses as a 'measly snipe'. He still wants his dinner and begins to haul her out of bed. He is interrupted and thrown out of the house by the medical student who has delivered the baby. The student only receives hysterical vituperation for his pains: 'Ye bleedin' makeshift, I'd 'ave yer liver out if I could reach ye! You touch my 'usband, ye long pisenin' 'ound you! Ow!' And infirm of aim, she flung a cracked teacup at his head. Billy's mother said, 'Y'ought to be ashamed of yourself, you low blaggard. If 'is father was alive 'e'd knock yer 'ead auf. Call yourself a doctor – a passel of boys – ! Git out! Go out o' my 'ouse or I'll give y'in charge!'

The violence that lay at the heart of working-class marriage was often identified as aggression provoked by excessive drinking; this was a theory particularly popular with temperance campaigners. One of the witnesses quoted in the *Report from the Select Committee on Public Houses* (1854) recommended that pubs should be closed by ten o'clock on Saturdays on the grounds that wife-beating, according to police reports, was an offence that generally took place after that time. He argued that if the pubs were closed earlier the men would leave them in the mellow, benevolent mood in which they could invariably be found at nine o'clock. Another well-aired middle-class explanation held that this marital violence was simply a manifestation of the savagery natural to those who had no access to civilized habits and standards. The truth was, however, to be found elsewhere.

Perennial violence can be interpreted as a desperate response to a condition of life that offered no hope of temporary relief or of ultimate salvation. As we have seen, the pressure of anxiety bearing down upon the average couple was not only immense but relentless, and the sheer pain of upholding this burden must have been more than sufficient to provoke hysteria. They could not sit down and talk about their life and its problems with any expectation of hitting on a solution, for their condition was not capable of improvement, only of deterioration. They could not take a holiday to get away from it all without sinking themselves still deeper in debt. They could not even go to bed together in the hope of temporarily obliterating the world for fear they would bring into the world another responsibility. In short, they never knew a care-free hour.

Prolonged submission to chronic anxiety produced in the working classes of the nineteenth century a profound capacity for extreme personal violence. It was, perhaps, only natural that they should behave brutally since the society to which they belonged was itself cruel and brutal, and furthermore reserved its cruellest and most brutal treatment for its poorest members. Apart from the generalized cruelty inherent in the relationship between capital and labour, the working classes felt the sting of sadism whenever they came into direct, individual contact with the ruling classes. The prisoner in his cell, the inmate of the workhouse or lunatic asylum, the orphan in his orphanage, the soldier in his barracks, the pregnant housemaid, and the evicted tenant, to mention but a handful of victims, all bore the brunt of a cruelty that was rendered all the sharper for being officially sanctioned. When a husband came to curse his wife and blacken her eye, although treating her unpardonably, he was nevertheless using the language of the times, a language also thoroughly understood by his wife. Their relationship was poisoned by the same savagery that informed their relationships, whether apparent or invisible, with employers, landlords, lawgivers and guardians, bureaucrats and petty officials.

Although violence was a language spoken all too readily by a people continually exposed to it from their earliest years, violence for married couples was more than just an automatic and habitual response to life's brick-bats. It was a medium of expression to which they were continually forced to resort as other media failed or were eliminated. The combined effects of anxiety, fatigue, and squalor effectively blocked off many of the ordinary, civilized channels of communication, and only violence could give relief to the powerful head of emotional pressure that inevitably accumulated. Far from being an indication of bestiality, the brutality inflicted by husbands on their wives and the extraordinary tolerance with which it was received can be seen as the last, heroic attempt by the human spirit to transcend the degradation by which it was engulfed. Maltreated, tethered and penned like animals, the poor refused to behave like animals. Men and women did not copulate indiscriminately, family units were held together, children were cared for and brought up, and individuals could rely on the support and assistance of the community. The loyalty of the wives seems to contain an implicit recognition of their husbands' helplessness; they seemed to value blows and kicks in lieu of any more tender gestures and to interpret them as a demonstration of, if nothing else, the exclusivity of their position. She was the one he beat; for her alone was this gruesome privilege reserved.

Somerset Maugham based his first novel, *Liza of Lambeth*, on his experience as a medical student with St Thomas's Hospital in London's slum quarters. Although it can hardly be described as a realistic portrait of slum-dwelling, its author did appreciate the central part played in working-class relationships by violence which invades every chapter and resolves the critical moments between the chief characters.

The tone, as it were, is set early in the book when a recently married girl friend of Liza confides in her how she was beaten up by her husband: ' I 'ad ter go ter the 'orspital – it bled all dahn' my fice, and went streamin' like a bust water-pipe.' She threatened to have him arrested, but Maugham had also detected the propensity for forgiveness among wives, and so she relents: ' I wouldn't charge 'im. I know 'e don't mean it; 'e's as gentle as a lamb when 'e's sober.' She smiled affectionately when she said this.

Liza herself, a pretty factory girl, becomes the object of a married man's attentions; she abandons her old boy friend and Jim, the married man, meets her secretly and soon enough they are regularly walking out together. Despite the fact that their relationship has been gentle and affectionate, her seduction, which takes place after an evening at the theatre and in the pub, is finally achieved by a brutal gesture. Having told her that he loves her 'fit ter kill', he walks arm in arm with her to 'a narrow way between blank walls [and] the backs of factories'. He grasps her hand and whispers, 'will yer?' She tries to withdraw her hand but he persists. 'She still kept silence, looking away and continually bringing down her fist [on his]. He looked at her a moment, and she, ceasing to thump his hand, looked up at him with half-opened mouth. Suddenly he shook himself, and closing his fist gave her a violent, swinging blow in the belly.

'Come on,' he said. And together they slid down into the darkness of the passage.

The novel ends with Liza's death as a result of a miscarriage brought on by a fight with Jim's wife. The father was of course Jim, who had already given his wife nine children.

Not many Victorian novelists dealt with working-class life, Dickens and Mrs Gaskell being notable mid-century exceptions. The late 'eighties and 'nineties saw a vogue for 'low life' stories and novels, by this time in one volume form. Arthur Morrison's work most authentically reproduces the voice of the street, George Gissing was most sensitive to those perilously subsisting on the border between genteel impoverishment and outright destitution, and George Moore in *Esther Waters* (1894), one of the best novels by any criterion to be published during that decade, most poignantly depicts the mercurial manner in which the financial fortunes of a working family could rise and decline. But it was on the youthful Maugham writing his first novel that the physical savagery of slum marriage made its direst impact. *Liza of Lambeth* is riddled with fights and reports of fights; along with babies, beatings dominate the lives of the female characters. No doubt delivering babies and dressing wounds preoccupied the medical student, but only the novelist would have perceived that violence as a form of expression had seeped so deeply into the working-class conscious-ness that a man had to hit a girl, albeit with a token blow, in order to indicate the true intensity of his feelings.

The Celibates

So far attention has been focused on those members of the working class who, however poverty-stricken, had at least succeeded in forming and sustaining a sexual relationship and in establishing a family structure. Contrasted with what lay below, even this stratum of human wretchedness could be counted fortunate, for there existed a significant proportion of the working population which literally could not afford the companionship of the opposite sex, far less the doubtful privileges of marriage and parenthood. Indeed, it is no exaggeration to say that these men and women were obliged to reconcile themselves to the dismal prospect of an enforced, lifelong celibacy.

In his book *People of the Abyss* (1903) Jack London poignantly and indignantly portrayed one section of this cheerless company of celibates. Visiting England for the first time at the invitation of his publishers, London, then aged twenty-six, decided, much in the spirit and tradition of the great nineteenth-century explorers, to penetrate the dark hinterland of the East End. Phileas Fogg himself encountered less derision than London when he announced his lunatic plan. The police took the view that he intended to commit some elaborate form of suicide; Thomas Cook & Son, from whom, with endearing naivety, he sought advice, would have transported him gladly to innermost Tibet, but expressed themselves incapable of aiding him in this enterprise on the grounds that it was too 'unusual'. Even the cabbie whom he hired reacted with the same suspicion and fear as a New York driver would today at being asked to drive into Harlem. Only the American consul-general took him seriously and offered practical assistance.

Having secured himself lodgings, and purchased suitably ragged clothes, he proceeded to take a searching look at the City of Dreadful Monotony. Posing as an American sailor lately arrived in the country and down on his luck, he not only observed and talked with the inhabitants but also lived his life alongside theirs. Although at regular intervals he felt compelled to bolt back to civilization, a warm bed, and a square meal, and although his descent into the abyss was only of brief duration, he did nevertheless experience in person what other writers had on the whole only looked at.

What he saw, heard, and reported on would not have come as a surprise to readers of Booth and Rowntree, but unlike them he brought a novelist's sensibility to bear on his experiences and was able to breathe life into the sociologists' facts. Like Rowntree, however, he was at pains to emphasize that he was not writing about a period in which the country's fortunes were in general decline; on the contrary, '. . . it must not be forgotten that the time of which I write was considered "good times" in England. The starvation and lack of shelter I encountered constituted a chronic condition of misery which is never wiped out, even in periods of greatest prosperity.'

His most formidable piece of observation concerned the numberless army of men who daily tramped the streets in search of work or a place in the workhouse casual wards, and who nightly stumbled from bench to embankment to back alley in the hope of winning a few minutes' sleep and shelter.

One afternoon he decided to accompany a carpenter, aged fifty-eight, and a carter, aged sixty-five, in their search for a bed. Both, it is worth noting, were skilled men, not tramps. Having been turned away from the Whitechapel workhouse they proposed to try the Poplar one; they had not slept for three and five days respectively, and, apart from crusts, had not eaten during the same periods. London noticed that as they walked their eyes never left the pavement, and for a while he assumed they were looking out for cigar and cigarette butts. He was wrong:

> From the slimy, spittle-drenched sidewalk, they were picking up bits of orange peel, apple skin, and grape stems, and they were eating them. The pits of greengage plums they cracked between their teeth for the kernels inside. They picked up stray crumbs of bread the size of peas, apple cores so black and dirty one would not take them to be apple cores, and these things these two men took into their mouths, and chewed them, and swallowed them . . .

The two men, 'their guts a-reek with pavement offal', then talked 'like madmen' of bloody revolution. Their conversation, as reported by him, sounds however eminently reasonable. The carpenter pointed out that the workhouse system only encouraged men to turn criminal since in order to secure a bed in the casual ward it was essential to join the queue outside the door at two or three in the afternoon, which prevented men from looking for work. If a man was lucky enough to be among the chosen few who at six o'clock were permitted to enter the ward, he would be kept there all the following day and not released until the morning after. The law then insisted that he could not enter another ward unless it was at

least ten miles distant. 'Have to hurry an' walk to be there in time
that day. What chance does that give me to look for a job? S'pose I
don't walk. S'pose I look for a job? In no time there's night come,
an' no bed. No sleep all night, nothin' to eat, what shape am I in in
the mornin' to look for work?'

On that occasion London and his companions failed, but a few
days later he succeeded in winning a place for the night, along with
twenty-four others, at Whitechapel.

The treatment meted out to those fortunate enough to be
admitted to the casual wards was hardly likely to set them up for a
hard day's work, far less for the more gruelling task of looking for
work. Apart from any other consideration, the system was designed
to ensure that its victims were imbued with a healthy awareness of
the degradation to which they had sunk: husbands and wives were
resolutely separated, tobacco was confiscated, and the inmates were
required to display extreme deference to the workhouse officers.
The possession of a sum as princely as fourpence was regarded as
sufficient affluence to disqualify a would-be entrant. (Fourpence,
incidentally, or even threepence or twopence or a loaf of stale
bread, London was informed, was the price of a woman in the
locality.) A cold bath was administered, notionally in the interest of
hygiene, but since the same filthy water and towel were shared by
all twenty-four men it is hard to see any real point to the ritual
except the enforcement of further humiliation. Supper consisted of
six ounces of bread and a bowl of gruel. One of the men told
London that he could not eat the bread without a pint of water to
soften it up. The quantities of food were strictly regulated: never
more than six ounces of bread, for instance, and frequently less if
the workhouse officers were dishonest and chose to make a profit
on the difference. Two verminous blankets and an unwashed
night-shirt were issued to each man who consigned himself to
sleep on a piece of canvas slung between two rails, not six inches
distant from his neighbour. Rats and lice, to say nothing of the
diseases bequeathed by his fellow men, enlivened the night hours.
Woken at five-thirty and nourished by more bread and gruel, the
men were set to work on such tasks as oakum-picking and stone-
breaking. At six o'clock the following morning they were turned
loose, and the cycle recommenced.

In the highly likely event of being refused admittance to these
sanctuaries a man had to face the even grimmer prospect of sleeping

out, an activity which in itself called for considerable ingenuity and effort. The law, with characteristic logic, decreed that the homeless should not sleep at night. Those hoping to do so not only had to contend with the weather and the discomfort of trying to make a bed out of a paving stone, but also had to resign themselves to being 'moved on' by the police. The constable on the beat was instructed to wake and move anyone he found sleeping on benches or on the pavement and even those who resorted to the arches beneath the embankment. (Mayhew recorded an interview with a policeman in 1849 who had been told to keep an eye on some barrels left overnight by a wine company on the pavement of the Haymarket; the policeman inspected them at dawn and found them to be occupied, not by individuals, but by entire families.) The parks, which were looked on as the next best thing to the casual wards, were locked at night, and anyone foolish or desperate enough to climb the railings could expect a three-month prison sentence for his pains. The night, therefore, was spent by the homeless in ceaseless perambulation.

Owing to some anomalous quirk in the regulations, Green Park opened its gates earlier than other parks; London found himself there one morning and described what he saw:

'. . . at a quarter past four in the morning, I, and many more, entered Green Park. It was raining again, but they were worn out with the night's walking, and they were down on the benches and asleep at once. Many of the men stretched out full length on the dripping wet grass, and, with the rain falling steadily upon them, were sleeping the sleep of exhaustion.'

Hippolyte Taine had been shocked to see a notice on the gates of St James's Park which read, 'The park-keepers have orders to refuse admittance to the park to all beggars, any person in rags, or whose clothes are very dirty, or who are [sic] not of decent appearance and bearing.' This regulation was evidently not enforced, for A. J. Munby, the diarist, was walking there one summer afternoon in 1864 and saw that the open spaces on either side were thickly covered with the bodies of 'ragged men and ragged women; lying prone and motionless, not as those who lie down for rest and enjoyment, but as creatures worn out and listless.' The park-keeper told him, 'they are men out of work . . . and unfortunate girls; servant girls, many of them, what has been out of place and took to the streets, till they've sunk so low that they can't get a living even by prostitution. It's like this every day, till winter comes; and then what they do *I* don't know. They come as soon as the gates opens . . .' Munby then counted the bodies on one side of the path and found '105 forlorn and foetid outcasts – women many of them – grovelling on the sward.'[8] Having devoted their night to the unrequited quest for sleep, these people could do no more than lie down, their plans for seeking work put off for another day.

Churchyards also provided dormitories for destitute families. Jack London was taken to Spitalfield Gardens, a favourite day-time haunt of the homeless and sleepless:

> The shadow of Christ's Church falls across Spitalfields Garden, and in the shadow of Christ's Church, at three o'clock in the afternoon, I saw a sight I never wish to see again. . . . We went up the narrow gravelled walk. On the benches on either side arrayed a mass of miserable and distorted humanity, the sight of which would have impelled Doré to more diabolical flights of fancy than he ever succeeded in achieving. It was a welter of rags and filth, of all manner of loathsome skin diseases, open sores, bruises, grossness, indecency, leering monstrosities, and bestial faces. A chill, raw wind was blowing, and these creatures huddled there in their rags, sleeping for the most part, or trying to sleep. Here were a dozen women, ranging in age from twenty years to seventy. Next a babe, possibly of nine months, lying asleep, flat on the hard bench, with neither pillow or covering, nor with anyone looking after it. Next half-a-dozen men, sleeping bolt upright or leaning against one another in their sleep. In one place a family group, a child asleep in its sleeping mother's arms, and the husband (or male mate) clumsily mending a dilapidated shoe. On another bench a woman trimming the frayed strips of her rags with a knife, and another woman, with thread and needle, sewing up rents. Adjoining, a man holding a sleeping woman in his arms. Farther on, a man, his clothing caked with gutter mud, asleep, with head in the lap of a woman, not more than twenty-five years old, and also asleep.

The inescapable conclusion to be drawn from these observations is that this army of eternally marching somnambulists cannot possibly have enjoyed any kind of sex life. They could not afford the bare minimum of privacy furnished by a sheet hung between one bed and another which slum-dwellers at least enjoyed; they could not afford the rent of a bed in an already overcrowded family room, far less the price of pleasure in the most squalid house of accommodation; they could not even afford to buy a woman a drink since the price of a crust for their own mouth was beyond their resources. Perhaps the men may from time to time have found a prostitute too drunk, degraded, or diseased to demand more than pennies for the privilege of putting her back against a wall; and perhaps the occasional couple, too desperate for human companionship to care where they found it, curled up in each other's arms beneath a bridge. But, for the most part, the existence to which they had been reduced required them to dedicate every penny, every ounce of energy, every waking moment to the elemental task of sustaining life. Sex, for them, was an unthinkable luxury.

PROSTITUTION

Prostitution

The Victorians were remarkable both for the repressive severity of their sexual code and for the multiplicity of their prostitutes. Exactly how many prostitutes were working in London, or any other city, at any one time is impossible to compute. William Acton, a celebrated venereologist and author of one of the best Victorian books on prostitution[1] pointed out that in the opinion of 'many forcible divines and moralists' all forms of illicit intercourse were embraced by the definition of prostitution, and that the virgin who surrendered her virtue to her lover was no less a prostitute than the hardened Haymarket whore. Although he restricted his calculations to those who 'hired' themselves, whether openly or secretly, he was still unable to hit upon a satisfactory figure. He cited police returns for the Metropolitan area in 1857 which accounted for 3,325 brothels and 8,600 prostitutes, but observed that these totals provided but a faint idea of the grand total for they only included those houses and women whose characters were well known to the police. He simply concluded that if the truth were discovered, 'the estimates of the boldest . . . would be thrown into the shade'.

Mayhew and Samuel Bracebridge, co-authors of another notable Victorian study,[2] wrote in 1861 that 'the assumed number' of prostitutes in London was about 80,000. *The Lancet*, a publication not noted for judicious restraint, declared in 1857 that one house in every sixty in London was a brothel, and one female in every sixteen a whore, ratios which give totals of 6,000 brothels and 80,000 prostitutes. In 1860 *The Saturday Review* wrote that it could not trust statistics 'which assure us that there are 360,000 women who live by sin as a trade, of whom 65,000 are to be found in London'. Lord Gage informed a meeting of the Society for the Suppression of Juvenile Prostitution that 'exclusive of the city' London harboured 1,000 brothels and 100,000 prostitutes.

These estimates can only be regarded as guesses, arrived at more or less conscientiously. The task of assessing the number of prostitutes with any accuracy was in any case made doubly difficult by the fact that so many of the women walking the streets on any given night were irregulars who did not live by prostitution, but who turned to it, whenever necessity dictated, in order to supplement incomes derived from other sources. Bracebridge commented that the amount of such 'oscillatory prostitution' was easy to imagine but impossible to substantiate.

What can, however, be stated with certainty is that there were a great many prostitutes, and that the average Victorian citizen was aware of their existence. The position was summed up with characteristic pungency by Mrs Lynn Linton, arch-enemy of the female emancipators, when she wrote, 'men can get that whenever they like'. She might have added that they could also get it wherever they liked, and at whatever price they chose to pay. The Nepalese envoy, General H.R.H. Prince Jung Bahadar was celebrated for having paid Laura Bell, a prima donna among the courtesans of her day, the legendary sum of £250,000 for the privilege of passing one night in her arms, whereas Walter, the author of *My Secret Life*, persuaded a prostitute to exchange ten minutes of her time for a handkerchief. Charles Booth, in his study of prostitution[3] noted with patrician disdain that men of every class were served, and he in his turn might have added that men of every sexual taste were also served. In short, the enormous variety of facilities available to the Londoner, and to the inhabitants of most large towns, ensured that everyone who sought a prostitute could be confident of finding one appropriate to his pocket and requirements.

Prostitutes and prostitution were an unavoidable feature of Victorian life, and they occupied a far more prominent and obtrusive position in the public mind than they do today. For the resident of any large town, whether male or female, whether married and faithful or single and celibate, whether rich and 'respectable' or poor and virtuous, the physical presence of prostitutes was inescapable. *The Saturday Review*, which never shrank from performing its duty in this context, went so far as to describe the prostitutes of London in 1862 as 'an army of occupation'. For those sequestered in the country or inhabiting villages too small to support their own cadre of professionals, to whom the sight of a flesh-and-blood prostitute might have been something of a phenomenon, the unrestrained outpourings of the newspapers, both august and sensational, served as a constant reminder of the existence of prostitutes. The most sheltered, strictly brought up and refined young lady, whose experience of life did not extend beyond the vicarage gate, could easily familiarize herself with vicissitudes of prostitution by doing no more than reading *The Times*. Myriad opportunities arose of airing the permanently vexed question of the Great Social Evil, and none was shirked.

The Topography of Prostitution

In his survey, published in 1897, Booth placed at the top of the scale of 'this social evil' the fashionable brothels, mostly located in the West End of London, which catered for a wealthy and select clientele. A brothel he defined as a house in which prostitutes lived, to which they brought men, and where they were, to use Booth's genteel phrase, at home to those who visited them. A rich man patronizing one of these 'high-class' brothels might reasonably expect to be furnished with a girl whose accomplishments were not confined to the bedroom, but who could sing or play the piano; he would expect his needs to be accommodated by a proficient prostitute supplied with the required equipment; and he would rely on the brothel-owner for privacy within the house and discretion outside. Prior to 1885, if his taste ran in that direction, he would have looked to a brothel-owner to purchase a virgin, or at least a fresh young girl, on his behalf. Booth commented primly that these clients were not robbed, but merely plundered; he omitted to mention, however, that the exorbitant prices not only guaranteed luxurious surroundings and a choice of young, attractive girls, but also considerably enhanced the chances of escaping venereal disease.

The Criminal Amendment Act of 1885 raised the age of consent from thirteen to sixteen, and that of abduction from sixteen to eighteen; it was specifically designed to destroy the so-called white slave traffic in girls from England to Paris and Brussels, which had been dramatically exposed by W. T. Stead, editor of *The Pall Mall Gazette*, in a series of articles entitled 'The Maiden Tribute of Modern Babylon'. The Act also imposed stringent penalties upon brothel-owners, pimps, and their associates; it eliminated the anomalies which had previously vouchsafed brothel-owners a measure of dubious legality and effectively put out of business many of the more notorious brothels.

Booth, writing more than ten years after the Act, reported that the younger girls working in the West End establishments were carefully secluded, and were only permitted to walk out of the house when accompanied; he surmised they would have found it difficult to escape. Such conditions appear to have been exceptional during the latter decades of the century, and were probably peculiar to the more expensive brothels which were protected from an increasingly inquisitive police by the wealth and eminence of their clients, and could afford to inflict a harsher regime on their inmates. The power of the brothel-owner was weakening long before the 1885 Act officially effected his demise. Although she might have supported a ponce or 'bully protector', the prostitute of the 'eighties and 'nineties tended to work independent of any brothel or dress-house (a mid-century institution which enslaved its girls by fitting them out with fancy gowns and commandeered most if not all their earnings). To coin a memorable contemporary expression, the women 'sailed on their own bottoms'.

After 1885 the smaller, less exalted brothels were obliged to lead fugitive existences, flitting from parish to parish as fines and closures drove them to seek sanctuary. Booth was sceptical of the effects of prosecution, and argued that officiousness on the part of a local authority or vigilance association only encouraged the brothel-owner and his prostitutes to transfer their business to safer territory.

It was, instead, to a house of accommodation that a client was generally taken by his prostitute, and here he would hire a room, and occupy it for as long as he thought it worth his while; the comfort, or lack of it varied according to the prosperity of the district. As a young man Walter[4] took the girl, a servant, with whom he had his first affair to such a house: 'I heard of accommodation houses, where people could have bedrooms and no questions were asked; and found one not far from my aunt's, although she lived in the best quarter of London . . . It was a gentleman's house, although the room cost but five shillings [c. 1840]: red curtains, wax lights, clean linen, a huge chair, a large bed, and a cheval glass, large enough for the biggest couple to be reflected in, were all there.' On another occasion, many years later, he visited a house 'nearly opposite to the Opera House'. There was more business done in that house, he believed, than in any other in London; his opinion, on this subject, can be taken as authoritative. 'In winter,' he wrote, 'there were good large fires, the rooms were a good size . . . Wine and liquor of fair quality was got for you. The furniture was somewhat dingy, but all the rooms had sofas on which you could lie, and

beds large enough for three with clean linen always.' Another house
he used 'many hundreds of times' was in James Street, just off
Oxford Street, where he was charged seven and six for the use of the
room and twenty shillings for the night. A typical room in this
house was furnished with a big four-post bed with handsome
hangings, a marble wash-hand stand, a large glass just at the foot of
the bed, a large sofa opposite the fire, a big cheval glass which could
be turned in any direction, two easy chairs, and a bidet.

Within the West End area, from fashionable Bond Street to the
sleazier vicinity of the Strand, where Walter had been amazed to
observe rows of women openly urinating in the gutter, the prostitute and her client could be sure of finding themselves within five
minutes' walk of a bedroom available for short-term hire. Coffee
rooms, cigar divans, chop-houses, turkish baths, and other male
haunts generally harboured discreet bedrooms reserved for the use
of customers who wished to entertain their 'cyprian' friends.
Walter and two other men amused themselves one night in an
establishment of this kind: 'it was not an unusual thing then for
two [women] to have a cigar shop, with a big sofa in a back parlour,
one keeping shop whilst the other fucked . . . Whilst the strumming
was going on in the parlour, people bought cigars and tobacco – for
it was really sold there, – little did they guess the fun going on
behind that red curtain.' In and around the respectable precincts
of St James's and Mayfair innumerable smart little shops, ostensibly devoted to the selling of ladies' millinery, shoes, gloves, or
perfumery, extended clandestine hospitality to couples who had
struck a silent bargain in the street outside. One of the most
popular beats was the Burlington Arcade where a well-dressed
prostitute could mingle innocuously with the lady shoppers while
darting meaningful looks at the gentlemen; having hooked her
client she would slip into one of the Arcade's chic shops, he following at a sly distance, and entertain him on the premises.

The poor, needless to say, took their pleasure in less palatial
surroundings. No sharper contrast with the tawdry opulence of the
West End could be found than the cheerless atmosphere in which
Liverpool's working class sought the company of prostitutes.
Hippolyte Taine, the French historian, was taken to see a casino, the
Victorian version of a dance hall and a favourite resort of prostitutes,
where he found 'five hundred people of wretched appearance were
crowded on to greasy benches watching a stage where two young

girls in pink gauze were dancing. The entrance fee was twopence. The audience was drinking gin and smoking, and the air, thick with the emanations of human bodies, was stifling.' He was taken thence to a brothel where he saw the girls, most of them recruited from the mills, glumly sitting in a downstairs room awaiting their customers. 'They were', he wrote, allowing a whiff of Parisian sophistication to permeate his horrified censure, 'not at all *décolletées*.'[5] William Acton inspected conditions at Aldershot, 'this great military centre', and discovered that the prostitutes who served the troops could only obtain a bare subsistence by taking home eight or ten men each night. A police officer who conducted him on a tour of inspection pointed out a 'range of cottages, with lights in their windows; each room contained a man and a woman'. The price of those rooms was twopence. The majority of the women rented rooms from publicans, who not only insisted on the daily payment of their rent, but also required their tenants to remain in the pub during the evenings, serving at the bar and inducing the soldiers to drink; only after the tattoo had sounded at 9.30 were they permitted to leave the pub to pursue their own business. Not surprisingly, many became alcoholics.

The most abject and decrepit prostitutes haunted the parks, where, according to Mayhew, they gave themselves up to 'disgusting practices' and consented to 'any species of humiliation'. He implied that the darkness of the parks provided a final refuge for those whose faces were too ravaged by syphilis to work by day or gaslight. One woman he interviewed wore a long, thick veil which, she confided, made her interesting to the unsuspicious.

Both Bracebridge and Acton, however, were at pains to disembarrass their readers of the popular notion that the lives of most prostitutes were terminated by the onslaught of venereal disease. Acton, an expert in the field, cited figures to show that the incidence of death by syphilis among women, whether prostitutes or not, was remarkably low, an alarming disclosure to those who looked on the disease as the agent of divine retribution. 'Syphilis', he wrote, 'is the fate neither of the bulk, nor of an important fraction, of prostitutes.' He attributed the relative scarcity of the disease partly to the innate strength of the average prostitute's constitution – a theory that owed more to fantasy than observation – and partly to the speed with which patients reported the outbreak of infection to their doctors. Revealingly, he reported that 'the *mauvais honte*, which formerly acted to [the patients'] prejudice, is passing away . . . the loss of the virile organ is, nowadays [1867], a thing almost unheard of in private practice.' Certainly the latter observation accords with Walter's experience, for he was a frequent victim of venereal disease – 'it's my fate . . . thrice to have had the clap, and not yet three-and-twenty, – how hard!' – but he never hesitated to go to his doctor, who invariably effected a cure.

Although he was lucky enough to shake off the disease many more times than thrice during a long and active life, Walter, like most men who went with prostitutes, nevertheless regarded it with mortal terror; Dr Acton's reassuring statistics were not indiscriminately broadcast. The prophylactic most commonly used, apart from straightforward washing, was the sheath, or French letter as it was generally called. Walter was accustomed to using it, albeit with repugnance, and he recorded a number of instances when the prostitute herself provided him with one. She, of course, was as eager as her client to ward off infection and, in any event, was anxious to avoid pregnancy. Walter described one such occasion in detail, and he is worth quoting. So far from being exceptional, this incident may be taken as archetypal of Walter's erotic reminiscences: the child prostitute and the author's unadmitted but unmistakable sadism, combined with his unblinking attention to his surroundings and his keen ear for dialogue, are the hall-marks of literally hundreds of episodes to be found in *My Secret Life*.

Strolling one night through a street crammed with costermongers' barrows he noticed a small girl standing inside a doorway and thought he would like to have 'the little one'. He passed in front of the house a few times and then stopped. 'Will you let me come in, and give you a kiss?' 'Yes sir', said she, stepping back. He entered the house and found it to be a miserable place. 'Had I known I should have been horrified at entering such a hole, but in my lust I thought of nothing but the young girl, her smallness and freshness. She looked fifteen years of age.' He offered her five shillings; she accepted and got on the bed. He began to undress her, but found himself incapacitated by fear of catching a disease. 'Have you got a French letter?' 'I'll ask mother,' she said, going into an adjoining room. In came a woman of middle age suckling a baby. 'She will fetch one, give her the money, – make haste now, – never mind your bonnet, – run, – run. She won't be long.' While he was waiting, he chatted to the mother who excused her daughter's behaviour by saying, 'she must live, and she's better at home doing that, than doing it away from me.' The girl then returned; 'the affair was not enticing', was Walter's laconic verdict.

Prior to the introduction of the rubber contraceptive only the comparatively rich could afford the more primitive handmade versions and, like Walter, they had used them not as 'family planning' aids but as prophylactics and safeguards against illegitimacy. Contraception was, in other words, synonymous with promiscuity and prostitution, and this, to some extent, explains why the great contraceptive pioneers were abominated and considered quite as vile as pornographers.[6]

There were very few districts of London that did not boast one variety or another of prostitute. The tourist, the commercial traveller in town on business, the middle-class resident, and the tradesman or artisan out on a spree would naturally gravitate towards the West End, particularly the Haymarket and Windmill Street and their surrounding networks of side streets, in search of his brand of pleasure. Here the choice was at its most varied, and, an equally vital consideration, the chances of being mugged were at their lowest. With the closure in the 'seventies of many of the most popular night-houses and casinos – Surrey Gardens, Cremorne Gardens, Highbury Barn, and the Argyle Rooms, to name the best known – where men and women, whether professional or otherwise, had drank, danced together, and generally circulated, prostitutes had been forced to seek their custom elsewhere and had taken to congregating in and around the music-halls, of which the best attended during the 'nineties was the Empire Theatre of Varieties, Leicester Square.

According to Bracebridge, the better class of prostitute, by which he meant the more expensive, or 'prima donnas', could be seen in the parks, in boxes at the theatres, at concerts, and 'in almost every accessible place where fashionable people' forgather. 'Skittles' and the *grandes cocottes* of her generation created such a vogue for stylish horse-riding in Rotten Row that 'horse-breakers' became a euphemism – one of scores – for prostitute. The lower class of prostitute, by the same token, could be seen where less fashionable people got together. Soldiers found their women in the pubs and streets near their barracks; ordinary working people shared their pubs and music-halls with prostitutes; and sailors were speedily relieved of their savings in the pubs and brothels clustered round the docks. The East End of London, no less than the West, contained its red-light districts: Shadwell, Spitalfields, and Whitechapel were, Bracebridge reported, 'infested with nests of brothels'. The Ratcliffe Highway, the most notorious street in the East End, runs parallel with the river from Whitechapel to Stepney, with Wapping, Rotherhithe, and Bermondsey just to the south, and was ideally placed to serve the huge complex of docks that lay on either side of the Pool of London. Every night its gaslit pavements, pubs, dance halls, and multitude of brothels were thronged with sailors of all nations and the droves of prostitutes to whom they looked for pleasure. Acton visited the Highway and was shown a prostitutes' lodging-house which comprised eight rooms, each let at 2s per night; the landlady informed him that they were seldom in use more than twice in the course of an evening. He inspected a dance-room attached to a pub, and saw couples waltzing to music played by a German band; pubs of this kind also accommodated prostitutes and their clients.

Ratcliffe Highway acquired a reputation for crime and bloodshed which effectively deterred most middle-class pleasure-seekers, even those with a taste for slumming. Walter, who was occasionally driven by temporary poverty to make expeditions to slum areas in order to find prostitutes he could afford, only dared to venture on to the Highway in his oldest, shabbiest clothes, masking his face with the peak of a large cap, and felt himself to be very brave. A man with money in his pocket, or a watch on his chain took care not to stray into unlit alleys or side-streets for fear of being beaten up and robbed. Some prostitutes specialized in luring drunken clients into secluded corners and delivering them into the hands of male confederates, who, if the victims were fortunate, posed as enraged husbands and demanded compensation, or, if they were not, simply hit them over the head with the stuffed eel-skin of Wooster fame – a length of canvas stuffed with sand – and stole their valuables.

Nor were the streets necessarily safe for the prostitutes themselves, as Jack the Ripper decisively demonstrated; one of his victims cried out 'Murder, Police' five times, but the neighbours, familiar with such night sounds, chose to ignore them. All his victims were part- or full-time professionals, and the circumstances of their deaths provide a revealing, if macabre, insight into the way in which the average Whitechapel whore went about her work. Mrs Chapman, also known as Emily Annie Shiftney, the fourth of the Ripper's victims, was found in a passage leading to a common lodging-house in Spitalfields; she had been disembowelled. She had left the house the previous night, saying, 'I'll soon be back again; I'll soon get the money for my doss.' Her 'doss' for a night cannot have been more than a few pennies, and presumably she intended to sell herself for that sum. She clearly felt confident of finding a client more or less immediately even at that late hour. It is also evident that her clients were obliged to derive what gratification they could while standing with her in a dark and narrow entry way. Whitechapel, like the worst slums of most towns, abounded in such spots – one woman died in an unlit passage 180 yards long and a yard wide, unhappily an ideal location for both prostitution and murder – and the undetected author of the eight murders committed in 1888 which have been attributed to Jack the Ripper can claim some credit for provoking the authorities into lighting the labyrinth of streets which had concealed his gruesome work.

The neighbourhood of Waterloo was, among others, notorious for its child prostitutes-cum-beggars who whiningly plucked at the sleeves of passers-by, pleading for pennies in the same breath as they confided obscenities in the hope of titillating a potential client. Venereal disease was not unknown among children of twelve. A judge reported that girls of thirteen and fourteen who appeared before him on charges of prostitution were unable to recall the circumstances of their first intercourse. Brothels existed which catered exclusively for paedophiliacs. Virgins, admittedly often of doubtful authenticity, could be inexpensively obtained – £5 was the going rate in the mid-eighties. In 1875, the age of consent was *raised*, not without much loss of oratorical blood, to thirteen, and ten years later, as we have seen, to sixteen, but neither of these well-intentioned pieces of legislation could in themselves put money in the pocket of the parent whose desperation had reached such a point of urgency, or who was so callous, that he did not scruple to put up for sale the only marketable asset remaining in his possession. Nor could they encourage the child who slept nightly in the same bed as her father and brothers to value her sexuality more highly than her mother and sisters.

The back streets and 'rookeries', as the densest slum areas were known, of all large towns teemed with bands of vagabond and truant children who lived by their wits and grubbed up a ragged livelihood by begging, stealing, and prostituting themselves, the boys no less than the girls if they were prepared to hunt down the business, and it was for their benefit that the Criminal Amendment Act, and other enlightened legislation, was passed. Had they heard of it, however, or had they been able to read it, they would hardly have been overwhelmed with gratitude by the discovery that laws had been specifically made to protect them from the very activity that brought them their daily crust.

Render up your Body, or Die
None of the Victorian writers who dealt with the subject entertained the slightest uncertainty as to the causes of prostitution, and only a very few took the trouble to make more than purely empirical investigations. These causes, nominated with such carefree confidence, provide in themselves an illuminating insight into the workings of Victorian sexual mythology.

William Acton, unlike most of his contemporaries, did not hesitate to place the blame firmly upon the shoulders of men, although he did so in a typically Victorian fashion by invoking a law of economics, the law of supply and demand. 'Prostitution exists and flourishes because there is a demand for the article supplied by its agency', he declared, employing the vocabulary of the shopkeeper which seemed to spring naturally to Victorian lips whenever sexual matters required description. He explained that it was the desire of the male, and he specified the 'unbridled desire of precocious youths and vicious men', that produced the demand which prostitution rose to satisfy and he then set about examining the sources of the 'infamous supply'.

He believed the vice of women to be occasioned by a number of factors which between them compounded a black list:

natural desire;
natural sinfulness;
the preferment of indolent ease to labour;
vicious inclinations strengthened and ingrained by early neglect, or evil training, bad associates, and an indecent mode of life;
necessity imbued by:
    the inability to obtain a living by honest means consequent on a fall from virtue;
    extreme poverty.

By putting natural desire at the head of the list, and extreme poverty at the foot, it might be supposed that he thought those the most and least potent causes, but within a few pages he bewilderingly dismissed the possibility of either assumption. He assured his readers that, so far from being the most potent cause, natural desire exercised no influence whatsoever over the female physiology – 'uncontrollable sexual desires of her own play but a little part in inducing profligacy of the female. Strong passions . . . as little disturb the economy of the human as they do that of the brute female.' Not content with denying women their sexuality, he refused even to grant them the ability to attract genuine lovers, for he feared that many fell 'victims to the arts of professional and mercenary seducers'. Almost in the same breath, he turned his original list upside down by writing, 'many, no doubt, fall [into prostitution] through vanity and idleness, love of dress, love of excitement, love of drink, but by far the larger proportion are driven to evil courses by cruel biting poverty'. And, putting the final touch to this patchwork of contradiction, he completed his chapter on causes with a paragraph devoted to the theory that prostitution was virtually hereditary, and therefore beyond the conscious discretion of the recipients. 'That idleness and vanity are almost inevitable bequests from parent to child is proved', he wrote, with a stunning indifference to logic, 'by the fact that the children of the numerous diseased prostitutes; consigned by the police to the St Lazare Hospital in Paris . . . almost invariably become prostitutes.'

When Acton's devastating comments on the neutrality of female sexual feelings are set against his conviction that women were transformed into prostitutes by the dictates of their natural desire and sinfulness, all the classic features of the Victorian dilemma over the sexuality of women are vividly delineated. Prostitute or madonna: which represented the true nature of woman? The riddle was never solved.

In Acton's case, the riddle amounted to more of a confusion of identity. He was on safe ground when he maintained that women, being the daughters of Eve, and originally sinful, required no exterior stimulus or exigency to prod them into prostitution, but he could hardly argue that this drastic compulsion to submit to the promptings of the essential female nature prevailed upon the women who personified, in the form of wives, sisters, and mothers, the hallowed shrines of middle-class family life. The conundrum is only unravelled with the realization that each of his apparently contradictory opinions was applicable to a different species of woman: working-class women, and 'respectable' women. In order to perpetuate the all-important distinctions between one class and another, and in order to expiate any pangs of guilt arising from the knowledge that prostitution was a form of exploitation by one class of another, it was essential that the class from whom prostitutes were recruited was credited by the class that kept them in business with a fundamentally sinful sexual nature. By the same token, it was essential that the exploiting class bestowed on its own women a fundamental innocence, even if, in the process, it rendered them sexless.

Samuel Bracebridge's account of the causes of prostitution was not laced with ambiguity. According to him, the chief reasons for lax morality among 'our female operatives' were:

1. Low wages inadequate to their sustenance.
2. Natural levity and the example around them.
3. Love of dress and display, coupled with the desire for a sweetheart.
4. Sedentary employment, and want of proper exercise.
5. Low and cheap literature of an immoral tendency.
6. Absence of parental care and inculcation of proper precepts. In short bad bringing up.

Although he placed poverty at the top, not the bottom of his list, his views did not substantially differ from Acton's, for he counted levity, by which he meant immorality, second in importance, and he identified this as a quality natural to working-class women. Both men's attitudes were well within the mainstream of conventional prejudice.

There can be no doubt that the principal cause of prostitution was poverty. The motive driving the great majority of women on the streets was succinctly described in a letter to *The Times* (1858) written by an aggressively impenitent professional, signing herself 'Another Unfortunate'.[7] The thousands who were impelled to take to prostitution were, she wrote, 'poor women toiling on starvation wages, where penury, misery, and famine clutch them and say "Render up your body, or die".'

Bracebridge listed the trades that 'supplied women to swell the ranks of prostitutes'; they included milliners, dressmakers, straw-bonnet makers, furriers, hat-binders, silk-winders, tambour-workers (embroiderers), shoe-binders, slop-workers (those who worked for cheap tailors), and women who worked in pastry-cook, fancy-goods, and cigar shops; he also noted the unsavoury reputation ballet girls had acquired. In one of his rare excursions into the field of statistical evidence, he quoted figures to show which trades contributed the largest complements of prostitutes. He recorded that, of the 3,734 disorderly prostitutes taken into custody in 1860, only one-third were unable to identify themselves in terms of an occupation, and that laundresses, milliners, servants, shoe-makers, and tailors accounted for nearly half the total. He did not, at the same time, point out that these trades were among the worst paid, nor did he draw the obvious inference that at least two-thirds of the women on the streets must have been only part-time prostitutes.

Mayhew, however, had decisively established this fact when, some years earlier, he had investigated poverty among London's female labour force. He introduced his article (Letter VI to *The Morning Chronicle* – 6 November 1849) on the slop-workers and needlewomen by saying that he had seen so much poverty while making his researches into the condition of the working class that he thought his feelings were blunted 'to sights of ordinary misery' until he saw the amount of suffering endured by the women in these trades. Among other 'operatives', he interviewed the wife of a seaman who worked from eight in the morning to ten at night to earn three shillings a week, less the cost of her candles, which was not enough to keep her in food. It was her opinion that the slop trade was the ruin of the girls who took it up: 'the prices are not sufficient to keep them, and the consequence is, they fly to the streets to make their living. Most of the workers are young girls who have nothing else to depend upon, and there is scarcely one of them virtuous.'

Mayhew could hardly believe the unvarying story of prostitution coupled with destitution which he heard whenever needlewomen were discussed, and he determined to test its truth. It did not take him long, however, to convince himself that the truth was far worse than he had been told: 'I had seen much want, but I had no idea of the intensity of the privations suffered by the needlewomen until I came to inquire into this part of the subject.' He obtained a number of testimonies from girls who had resorted to the streets in order to supplement their incomes. One girl who sewed moleskin trousers could, by dint of working sixteen hours a day, make 5s 6d a week, providing she was lucky enough to be kept fully employed; the week before Mayhew spoke to her she had only managed to make 1s. She found it impossible to live on her earnings and was obliged 'to go a bad way'.

In this context it is instructive to compare the needlewomen's hard-earned pittances with the prices Walter was accustomed to pay the girls he picked up; fortunately for the historian, he never failed to note the price, and on one occasion he supplied a price-list. In his estimation a sovereign would buy any woman on the streets, and ten shillings would buy 'as nice a one as you needed'. A prostitute could rent two good furnished rooms near Pall Mall for fifteen or twenty shillings a week, and could buy a handsome dress for five or ten pounds. He paid 'quite nice' girls between five and ten shillings, many of whom had their own rooms, although he sometimes paid half a crown extra for a short-hire room. When he was out of funds he used to pay with silk handkerchiefs, which had a reliable pawn value, and if cash was demanded he found that three or four shillings generally sufficed. (Walter did not date his reminiscences, but internal evidence suggests that this passage is roughly contemporaneous with Mayhew's letter. In any case, when making this point one need not be pedantic.)

Of all the stories Mayhew heard, the most 'tragic and touching' concerned a tall, good-looking girl who could only discuss her life with her face hidden in her hands, tears oozing between her fingers. 'I never remember to have witnessed such intense grief', commented Mayhew. She used to work on fine full-fronted white shirts and was paid $2\frac{1}{4}$d per shirt. To earn her money she had to sew the buttonholes, four rows of stitching in the front, and the collars and wristbands. If she worked from five to midnight every day she could sew seven shirts in a week. She had a child and could not possibly feed two mouths with this income, so she took to the streets: 'I went to the streets solely to get a living for myself and child. If I had been able to get it otherwise I would have done so . . . it was the low price paid for my labour that drove me to prostitution.' She tried to earn an 'honest' living by making pin-cushions and selling them in the street, but she could never sell enough. She 'struggled' against prostitution preferring to beg rather than bring shame upon herself and her child. 'Sometimes I should be out all night in the rain, and sell nothing at all, me and my child together; and when we didn't get anything that way we used to sit in a shed, for I was too fatigued with my baby to stand, and I was so poor I couldn't have even a night's lodging upon credit. One night in the depth of winter his legs froze to my side.' At length, she reached such a pitch of self-disgust and despair that she decided to commit suicide, and went to Regent's Park to drown herself in the lake, but a policeman saw her and sent her away. She then had no choice but to enter the workhouse, where her child was taken away from her the minute she stepped inside the gate, and she was told she might see him once a month. Later she managed to leave to take up a job covering umbrellas; she was paid between 3s and 4s, and stayed off the streets – 'I can solemnly assert since I have been able to earn a sufficient living, I have never once resorted to prostitution' – but she was unable to save enough to release her son from the workhouse.

She believed that to be a slop-worker was, in effect, to be a prostitute: 'I never knew one girl in the trade who was virtuous; most of them wished to be so, but were compelled to be otherwise for mere life.' Mayhew made exhaustive inquiries among the slop-workers and needlewomen, and gathered together innumerable statements and life-stories, all of which confirmed that poverty alone was the cause of prostitution with these criminally underpaid women. Knowing their trade's reputation for 'loose morals' they were quick to impress on Mayhew that they derived no pleasure from their street-walking; 'I detest it', one girl told him, 'I was never reared to it. I was brought up to the church and to attend to my God. I was always shown a different pattern.' Anticipating Acton and Bracebridge, the shirt-front worker repulsed any imputation of original sinfulness by saying, 'in my heart I hated it; my whole *nature* rebelled at it.'

Walter provided a chilling example of the effect of such reputations. He and his cousin Fred, on holiday in the country, decided to spend the day in the nearby market town.

[On arrival] Fred said, 'Let's go and have a shove.' 'Where are the girls?' said I. 'Oh, I know, lend me some money.' 'I only have ten shillings.' 'That is more than we shall want.' We went down a lane past the Town-Hall, by white-washed little cottages, at which girls were sitting or standing at the doors making a sort of lace. 'Do you see a girl you like?' said he. 'Why they are lace-makers.' 'Yes, there is one I had with the last half-crown you lent me.' Two girls were standing, together; they nodded. 'Let's try them,' said Fred.

Despite the fact that he had found them on their own doorstep, and had seen them actively engaged in earning their living, Walter referred to the lacemakers as 'gay women'. Although an adolescent at the time of this instructive escapade, he had already learnt enough of the ways of the world – from his older and wiser cousin, no doubt – to know that among men of his class the term lacemaker, along with actress and seamstress, was virtually synonymous with prostitute. He had been puzzled by Fred's behaviour until he realized what the women were – 'Why they are lacemakers' – thereafter he required no explanations.

The experienced Fred treated the girls exactly as a man might treat the inmates of a brothel: he studied the selection at his leisure, chose one, inquired after his younger friend's taste and moved in to negotiate a price. As far as he was concerned, their lacemaking was merely an advertisement of their true occupation. The girls, by the same token, complaisantly accepted his callous arrogance, objecting neither to his manner, nor to his presumption. Bargains were struck at half a crown each, and the girls proceeded to earn in a few minutes what would otherwise have taken a week's toil.

Engels inspected conditions under which lacemakers worked in Northampton, Oxford, and Bedford and reported that they were highly destructive of both health and morality; prostitution, he wrote, was almost epidemic among them. He described in harrowing detail the damp, ill-ventilated rooms in which the girls laboured, the cramped position they were required permanently to maintain, the displaced ribs, narrow chests, twisted spines, and near-blindness with which so many were afflicted, the long hours they were called on to work, and the low wages with which they were rewarded. Their 'deplorable' moral state was, in his opinion, attributable to their lack of education, particularly their lack of moral training, and to their love of finery. In nominating these causes, he was perhaps allowing bourgeois priorities momentarily to distort his judgement; at the age of twenty-four he was still sufficiently imbued with the values of his class to look upon any form of sexual promiscuity with automatic disapproval.

Prostitution in the nineteenth century was primarily deplorable because it stripped those women who were driven to it by acute poverty of their dignity and humanity, forcing them to think of themselves as cattle in a market. Although Engels never defined his attitude to prostitution, his hatred of all that degraded human dignity was implicit in every paragraph of his book. He was as shocked by the prostitution rife among the lacemakers as he was by the sexual anarchy he discovered in the cotton factories and down the coal-mines. He interpreted all forms of sexual 'irregularity' among the proletariat as obnoxious symptoms of the profound injustice with which society was riddled, and he was convinced that the indiscriminate promiscuity that flourished in the factories had nothing but the most pernicious effect upon the lives of the workers, for it undermined their family structures, humiliated the women, brutalized the men, and exercised a malign influence over the children. The employees of a factory represented a microcosm of the larger populations of the great cities, and the unnatural crowding together of excessive numbers of people within both produced the same evil result: the corruption of the women's moral character. A Leicester man told Engels that he would rather let his daughter beg than go into the factories, which were 'perfect gates of hell', and that 'most of the prostitutes of the town had their employment in the mills to thank for their present situation'.

Imprisoned by day in vile factories, and by night in squalid slums, underpaid, underfed, and underclad, the lacemakers can hardly be blamed for seeking relief from the overwhelming drudgery of their lives. When Dickens came to describe Coketown (Preston), the scene of his industrial novel *Hard Times*, he saw the soullessness of the place embodied in its unremitting monotony: 'It contained several large streets all very like one another, and many small streets still more like one another, inhabited by people equally like one another, who all went in and out at the same hours, with the same sound upon the same pavements, to do the same work, and to whom every day was the same as yesterday and tomorrow, and every year the counterpart of the last and the next.' Far from being an indication of moral turpitude, the love of finery, which Engels had condemned in the factory girls, simply represented their natural desire to rebel against the bleakness of their environment; by wearing pretty shawls and bonnets they defied their joyless world, invigorated their sense of identity, and enhanced their self-respect. The all-enveloping sameness that Dickens emphasized could be combated by the feeling of uniqueness that clothes temporarily bestow upon their owners; an act of prostitution was a petty exertion to have to make in order to obtain such an exhilarating reward.

I have tried to suggest earlier that prostitution offered working-class girls the opportunity of salvaging, rather than destroying, their sexual self-respect, and the lacemakers' 'love of finery' provides a pathetic example of this theory in action. The frocks purchased by these girls with the proceeds of their street-walking stood between them and the mindless and hopeless resignation into which so many working-class people gradually slumped. Their sexuality was held in such low esteem by themselves, their families, and their employers that, contrary to the beliefs of middle-class observers, prostitution in itself could do little further to depress or degrade them, while its fruits could do much to uplift their morale and strengthen their belief in their own attractiveness.

Bracebridge reproduced an interview he had with a woman he met in Fleet Street who worked as a type-setter but resorted to prostitution whenever she wished to pay for some little luxury in the way of food or clothes. 'I get enough money to live upon comfortably', she told him, 'but then I am extravagant, and spend a great deal of money on eating and drinking . . . I have the most expensive things sometimes, and when I can, I live in a sumptuous manner.' It is refreshing to hear a voice free of the mawkish self-abasement that characterized so many of the 'confessions' extracted by Bracebridge. Her attitude to her casual street-walking serves as a salutary reminder that prostitutes did not necessarily judge their own lives by the same inhospitable scale of values as those middle-class observers who, greatly daring, lifted the stone of vice and shuddered with horror at the fauna crawling beneath. Her readiness to sell herself for the sake of a new dress had by no means diminished her self-respect, and she was determined not to be browbeaten by a moral code to which she did not subscribe: 'I'll be hanged if I think that priest or moralist is to come down on me with the sledge-hammer of their denunciation.' She displayed a perceptive cynicism towards the material realities that had inspired the moralists' uncongenial code: 'Those who have a position to lose, prospects to blight, and relations to dishonour, may be blamed for going on the loose.' (She explained that her use of high-flown language was the result of setting newspaper copy for seven years.)

By the end of the century, the removal of children from factories, the improvement of working conditions, the relative increase in women's wages, and the mass-production of cheap, fashionable clothes designed specifically for the working girl had combined to diminish this particular aspect of prostitution's appeal. But, for the hungry, the destitute, and the desperate, whose numbers by no means decreased as the years went by, the lustre of prostitution remained untarnished. Prostitution offered, among a score of forbidding disadvantages, two inestimable advantages over all other available occupations: it paid handsomely – a silk pocket handkerchief, the lowest form of currency on Walter's list, could be pawned for the equivalent of a week's wages or more, a fact upon which Fagin's business empire was reliably founded; and it was entirely free of unemployment – no one, however unsuitable or unqualified, who aspired to join the army of women that marched the streets of every big city was ever turned away or made redundant. For the most part, prostitution was reserved for those who could not sell their labour elsewhere, or who could not sell it for a living wage, and for those who had pawned everything save that which only pawnbrokers could not put a price on – their bodies.

The Promiscuous Herding of the Sexes

All writers, Engels included, were unanimous in convicting the tenement and small cottage as the chief corruptors of youthful innocence. Acton judged 'the promiscuous herding of the sexes' to be the most 'frightful' cause of prostitution because 'here the sinner has had no choice . . . except to sin'. *The Saturday Review* (3 April 1858) coined the same emotive phrase by informing its readers that 'the promiscuous herding of children in their immature years' was a 'not infrequent prelude to a life of harlotry'. Mayhew reported in *The Morning Chronicle* (quoted by Acton) the case of two sisters who were married on the same day and took up residence in the same hut which was divided into two rooms by a thin partition that did not reach the ceiling; these same two rooms had for years been slept in by twelve people of all ages and both sexes. Sleeping arrangements of this kind, where fathers and daughters, uncles and nieces, brothers and sisters indiscriminately occupied the same bed, did not encourage respect for 'the tie of blood', as Mayhew discreetly put it. Even if these 'horrible consequences' were avoided, the position was still extremely harmful for 'the mind, particularly of the female, is wholly divested of that sense of delicacy and shame which, so long as they are preserved, are the chief safeguards of her chastity'. Bracebridge was convinced that the efforts of philanthropists, moralists, and ministers of religion would all be of no avail until the 'single bed-chamber in the two-roomed cottage' was thoroughly purged.

Beatrice Webb also commented upon the prevalence of incest in tenements. In 1888, while helping Charles Booth compile his study of the poor in London, she took the unusual step of acting out the life of the people she was investigating by taking jobs as 'a plain trouser hand', and she published her findings in a book, *The Pages of a Workgirl's Diary*, which was critically well received. She considered it judicious, however, to expunge those pages referring to her workmates' sexual experiences. She had been shocked to hear them tease each other about having babies by their fathers and brothers, and had felt it necessary to remind herself that these young girls were in no way mentally defective, but were as keen-witted and generous-hearted as her own friends. She also heard them discussing the violation of little children. 'To put it bluntly', she wrote, 'sexual promiscuity, and even sexual perversion, are almost unavoidable among men and women of average character and intelligence crowded into the one-room tenement of slum areas . . .' These insights into slum life did not find their way into print until 1926 when they formed a footnote in her autobiography, *My Apprenticeship*.

In Acton's opinion, cheap lodging houses, 'which afford to the homeless poor a refuge still more cruel than the pitiless streets from which they fly', had an even more injurious effect upon children than slum dwellings, where at least a measure of privacy could sometimes be achieved. Lodging-houses, or 'detestable haunts of vice' as he called them, were the last resort of the poor prior to voluntary incarceration within the workhouse. For a few pennies a family could purchase the right to use a communal room for the night, and at this price they did not expect much privacy. Acton complained that men, women, and children were accepted *en masse* and passed the night huddled together without distinction as to age or sex, often in a common bed. It was, he wrote, 'fearful to contemplate human beings so utterly abandoned, reduced below the level of the brute creation'. He had, however, overlooked the fact that this sub-bestial level was infinitely preferable to the regime imposed by the workhouses, where husbands were separated from their wives and, as we have seen, mothers from their children.

The sight which he found fearful to contemplate was nothing more than that of a family doing its pitiful best to maintain some degree of unity. He believed that children who were exposed to the spectacle of adult intercourse were irredeemably corrupted, and would inevitably succumb to wickedness: 'with such associates, children of tender years soon become old in vice'. The associates were none other than their own parents, and the parents of other children who, having nowhere else to do it, were attempting to conduct family life in a public lodging-house. This way of life, according to Acton, trampled out of the children every spark of good feeling and nurtured every evil instinct. 'What wonder', he exclaimed in a burst of all-inclusive generalization, 'if all the males are thieves and all the females prostitutes.'

To suggest, as Acton and others did, that prostitution was the automatic corollary of incest was preposterous. Incest and prostitution were themselves just two of the multitude of grossly cruel consequences engendered by dire poverty. The sleeping facilities enjoyed by large families were, however, one factor among several that went to create a working-class attitude to sexuality that could not have been more foreign to the conventions sanctified by the middle classes. The hypocrisy incumbent upon a middle-class father who not only maintained his children, particularly his daughters, in a state of immaculate ignorance regarding the 'facts of life', but also supported a mistress or made occasional use of prostitutes, was neither available, nor, by the same token, significant to the working-class father. Working-class parents were in no position to deceive, and had no interest in deceiving their children as to the true nature of sexuality. While making one of his forays into slumland, Walter was interested by the behaviour of children playing in a quiet working-class street where their mothers could be seen soliciting men:

> The street-doors were usually open, the women when dressed lolling just inside them, with head out, but dropping back if they saw a likely man . . . Lots of children were about, who played in the streets . . . If a man stopped and talked to a gay woman at the door, the children of the house usually went in, always did if more than about ten years old. They drew back as if they knew that a bargain was to be struck, and I believe knew all about it. They were mostly girls who sleeping in the same room with their

parents, I dare say had seen the game of mother and father played often enough.

Acton accounted seduction, or rather the penalties invoked by seduction, a cause of prostitution. He doubted that seduction by itself explained the unhappy condition of 'these unfortunate women', but he included among his list of causes 'necessity imbued by the inability to obtain a living by honest means consequent on a fall from virtue'. Bracebridge took seriously, or at least reproduced a number of times, the classic prostitutes' confession, which embraced such heart-rending elements as parsonage childhoods – a particular favourite – ravishments by callous swains, merciless expulsions from parental hearths, and fatherless infants, all unfolded with a wealth of convincing detail. The poor girl tricked, trapped, and seduced by the wealthy villain – he of the untrustworthy top hat and flourishing mustachios – was a staple figure of Victorian melodrama and enduringly popular with working-class audiences who delighted in seeing representatives of the upper classes portrayed as debauchers of ragged innocence.

These colourful folk legends were, however, far from consistent with the truth. In her letter, 'Another Unfortunate' had been at pains to scotch the seduction theory; far from being 'the root of the evil', seduction was, she wrote scathingly, 'scarcely a fibre of the root', although it did serve as 'the common story of numbers of well brought-up, who never were seduced, and who are voluntary and inexcusable prostitutes'. As a would-be seducer, Walter held the strongest views on this subject, for time and again he would snare some teen-age girl only to discover that she had dispensed with her virginity long ago and was already thoroughly experienced. 'Much talk with gay women and my own experience', he commented bitterly, 'make me believe now that nearly all the girls of the lowest classes begin copulating with boys of approximately their own age when about fourteen years old.' The thought of all those juvenile virginities squandered upon urchins was insupportable:

Few of the tens of thousands of whores in London have given their virginities to gentlemen, or to young men, or old men, or to men at all: their own low-class lads had them before anyone else . . . that is the truth of the matter, though greatly to be regretted, for street boys cannot appreciate the treasure they destroy. A virginity taken by a street boy of sixteen is like a pearl cast before swine.

In time his disillusionment was replaced by scepticism, so much so that when he did stumble across a girl who was still a virgin he was astounded, 'not having for a moment anticipated her being anything but one of the thousand little wenches in workshops and manufactories, who working by day, are strumpets for gain or pleasure at night'.

The Rev. G. P. Merrick conclusively settled the question in 1890 by publishing a pamphlet on prostitution in which he broke to his readers the new, surprising, and painful discovery that the common impression about prostitutes being the victims of seductions was 'altogether wrong', and he unveiled the startling fact that of the 16,022 women whom he interviewed only four per cent claimed to have been seduced.

When, and if, the average middle-class young man resolved to jettison his virginity, he was obliged either to persuade a sympathetic or easily cowed servant, or to pay a prostitute; on no account could he look to a member of his own class. If, like H. G. Wells, he had no choice but to resort to a prostitute, his introduction to the wonders of sex was in all likelihood a grim compound of humiliation and disappointment. Wells's experience certainly afforded him no pleasure, and 'only deepened [his] wary apprehension that round about the hidden garden of desire was a jungle of very squalid and stupid lairs'.[8] The boys received a measure of tacit encouragement in these directions; the girls, however, received nothing but imprecations and terrible warnings if they displayed the slightest erotic inclination, and had to be satisfied with speculation and fantasy, most of which centred around the alarming prospect of their wedding night.

No greater contrast with the experience of working-class adolescents of both sexes could be imagined. They shared their first sexual adventures with people of their own age and from their own background. Sex did not imprint on their minds, as it did on the minds of middle-class novices, an indelible stain of furtiveness, loneliness, and dirt; and, perhaps most significant of all, the girls acquired their knowledge at roughly the same age as the boys. The traumatic disappointments that blighted the middle-class wedding bed could, on the rare occasions when such a thing took place, do nothing to overshadow the working-class honeymoon, for the bride was able to greet her husband's advances, not with virginal trepidation, but with affectionate familiarity. This relative equality of emotional development was consonant with the role she subsequently fulfilled within her marriage; although she could never be described as emancipated, she did assume responsibilities and powers from which her bourgeois sister was positively debarred.

These everyday facts of working-class life did not, however, prevent investigators of prostitution from assigning seduction an invariable place of importance whenever they came to compile their lists of causes; the persistence with which they ignored what was readily available provides a measure of how gravely they misunderstood the forces that drove women on to the streets. The attitude of the average working girl towards her own body, her sexuality, and the sexual act itself was so foreign, and so inimical to prevailing middle-class conventions that no writer, of either social commentary or fiction, proved capable of portraying her sexual behaviour with both sympathy and accuracy. Her attitude must not be uprooted, however, from its historical context and mistaken for modern permissiveness; such freedom from contemporary inhibitions as she enjoyed was forced upon her by cruelly oppressive circumstances, and she would have cheerfully exchanged all her psychological liberty for a little affluence.

In this context, it is worth quoting once more from 'Another Unfortunate's' remarkable letter, for the story of her life makes plain the discrepancy that lay between middle- and working-class attitudes to 'virtue'.

After describing her childhood as the pretty daughter of a brickmaker, living in a neighbourhood not slow to contribute its quota of prostitutes, she turned to what she called 'an important event' in her life: 'I was a fine robust healthy girl of thirteen years of age. I had larked with boys of my own age . . . I had seen much and heard abundantly of the mysteries of sex . . . For some time I had coquetted on the verge of a strong curiosity and a natural desire, and without a particle of affection I lost – what? – not my virtue, for I never had any . . . I repeat that I never lost what I never had – my virtue.' She then, at the age of fifteen, became 'what you better-classes call a prostitute.' She endured the ups and downs endemic to her profession, and, three years later, came under the protection of a gentleman; encouraged by him, she set about educating herself, and soon acquired the ordinary accomplishments of her sex, although 'moral science' remained an enigma to her.

She finished her letter with a burst of savage rhetoric, which, if she read it, would have been music to the typesetter's ears:

> We come from the dregs of society, as our so-called betters call it. What business has society to have dregs – such dregs as we? You railers of the Society for the Suppression of Vice, you the pious, the moral, the respectable, as you call yourselves, who stand on your smooth and pleasant side of the great gulf you have dug, and keep between yourself and the dregs, why don't you bridge it over or fill it up . . . Why stand you there mouthing with sleek face about morality? What is morality?

The letter was so skilfully written that its authenticity was called into question by, among others, *The Saturday Review*, watchdog of the nation's moral hygiene, but *The Times* begged the public to believe in it, and discussed it in a leading article. Letter hoaxes were not uncommon in those days,[9] but, whatever the author's identity, the letter itself constituted a formidable denunciation of the moral code that licensed middle-class censure of working-class behaviour, and it left the readers of *The Times* in no doubt that the jurisdiction of the official code had failed to achieve universal recognition.

The gulf she referred to was not bridged and, for a few decades, the 'better classes' preserved intact their privilege of simultaneously purchasing wholesale sex from the lower orders and condemning them for their promiscuity. It is impossible to know how many other women reached a similar clarity of understanding – presumably only a small minority, since the average prostitute enjoyed neither the leisure nor the education to reflect with such enlightenment upon her position – but it is to be hoped that those whose scepticism did not ripen at least attained a sufficiently liberated attitude to allow them to relish the fruits of their labours, uninhibited by the strictures of guilt. Acton seemed to confirm this when he wrote, 'The greatest amount of income procurable with the least amount of exertion is with [prostitutes], *as with society* [my italics], the grand gauge of position'.

The prostitute's relatively uncomplicated relationship with her body and its functions permitted her to approach her profession with a degree of equanimity beyond the comprehension of those who appointed themselves inspectors of her conduct. Some accused her of lechery and thick-skinned imbecility; others, Booth for example, deplored her shamelessness: 'It is rare', he wrote, 'to find any sense of sin, and if it can be roused at all, it is very precarious . . . [the prostitute feels] nothing more poignant than a dull sense of degradation.' What Booth and most other writers could not understand was that the prostitute who was compelled by raw poverty to sell her body to men richer than herself suffered deeply, not from a sense of sinfulness, but from humiliation. The example of her parents, neighbours, and friends, the traditions of her class and her own experience taught her that destitution murdered pride, sneered at scruples, and destroyed dignity. Prostitution, under such circumstances, was no more or less sinful than sewing shirt-fronts for pennies, or slaving in a factory, it was just one of the many abject functions the poor were obliged to undertake in order to secure their wretched livelihood.

13

Prostitution and Society

Thou rascal beadle, hold thy bloody hand!
Why dost thou lash that whore? Strip thine own back;
Thou hotly lust'st to use her in that kind
For which thou whipp'st her.

King Lear, IV.vi.165–8

It was psychologically impossible for the middle class – the class which provided prostitution with its clientele – to take up an attitude towards prostitutes that was not profoundly ambivalent; the hypocrisy for which Victorians are nowadays notorious was but an unattractive symptom of this ambivalence.

William Lecky eloquently expressed the classic Victorian apologia for the prostitute's function within society in his *History of European Morals from Augustus to Charlemagne* (1869):

> ... That unhappy being whose very name is a shame to speak ... appears in every age as the perpetual symbol of degradation and sinfulness of man. Herself the supreme type of vice, she is ultimately the most efficient guardian of virtue. But for her the unchallenged purity of countless homes would be polluted ... On that one degraded and ignoble form are concentrated the passions that might have filled the world with shame. She remains, while creeds and civilizations rise and fall, the eternal priestess of humanity, blasted for the sins of the people.

Apparently, the sexual passions of men possessed a remarkable capacity for metamorphosis, for when devoted to marriage they were invested with purity, but when illicitly discharged they were transformed into a force capable of filling the world with shame. The sharpness of contrast between these projections of good and evil is reminiscent of Dr Jekyll and Mr Hyde.

Lecky's concept of prostitution as a form of sewer down which undesirable excreta were poured in order to preserve the spotlessness of the domestic hearth was a piece of pragmatism acceptable, by and large, to owners of valuable hearths. Put bluntly, and freed of mystic gratuities of the 'eternal priestess' kind, the Lecky theory held that prostitution guaranteed the maintenance of virtue among those females whom one was likely to marry, or by whom one's son was likely to produce grandchildren.

Despite the sacredness of her task, the prostitute received no thanks; on the contrary, she was cruelly vilified and despised. Although her job was to relieve men of their uncontainable urges, it was deemed essential that she was herself stripped of all sexuality, and most writers on the subject were agreed that the life she led not only ensured a speedy passage to the grave, but also annihilated all trace of natural womanliness.

The Rev. William Arnot attempted to inspire guilt in the male breast when, in October 1860, he confronted his Glasgow audience with the consequences of lechery: 'Look at the fruit of your doings', he thundered at those who used prostitutes, 'in that imbruted soul and bloated body, with hardly any features left, a mass of incurable corruption now. That lump of living flesh was once a woman . . .'[1] His macabre picture may have been oratorically effective, but it was hardly true to life. Acton had proved that only a small percentage of prostitutes reached the stage of venereal decay so colourfully depicted by Arnot, and poverty, rather than any infirmity peculiar to prostitution, probably accounted for the decrepitude of the specimen to which he directed his audience's horrified attention.

Dr Tate, another medico who made it his business to investigate prostitution, confirmed that the impact of street-walking upon the physique was nothing short of ruinous: 'In less than one year from the commencement of their wicked career, these females bear evident marks of approaching decay.' Within three years, he assured his readers, they could not be recognized, and no more than one in eleven survived twenty-five years.

Acton was determined to expose the fallacies surrounding the supposed brevity and squalor of the prostitute's career. In a memorable passage he compared the whore of thirty-five with her sister who was perhaps a married mother or an overworked seamstress and pointed out that the 'constitutional ravages' held to be the necessary consequences of prostitution seldom exceeded 'those attributable to the cares of a family and the heart-wearing struggles of virtuous labour'. Anxious to dispose of the lurid though widely believed hypothesis that those prostitutes who did not succumb to disease fell victim to suicide, intemperance, insanity, or 'complaints incidental to an irregular course of life', he made extensive inquiries among hospitals, doctors, and parish authorities and found no evidence to suggest that prostitutes were more prone than any other type of woman to these kinds of grim decease. In dismissing insanity as a cause of death, he made this revealing comment: 'It is a question whether grief, anxiety, and broken hours may not have a greater share in dethroning the reason than sensuality.'

His work in this respect was, however, of no avail: bare statistics and diligently researched facts, no matter how incontrovertible, by themselves could do nothing to confute a mythology that was fundamental to society's sexual ideology. It was, in any event, not merely the body, but also the soul that the canker of prostitution was supposed to bite into and destroy. The proper mental posture for a prostitute was that adopted by Martha when David Copperfield discovered her in the act of drowning herself in the Thames: 'How can I go on as I am,' she cried, 'a solitary curse to myself, a living disgrace to everyone I come near.' Trollope succinctly summarized the conventional picture of the prostitute's *via dolorosa* in his preface to *The Vicar of Bullhampton*:

> The gaudy dirt, the squalid plenty, . . . the flaunting glare of fictitious revelry, the weary pavement, the horrid slavery to some horrid tyrant – and then the quick depreciation of that one ware of beauty, the substituted paint, garments bright without but foul within like painted sepulchres, . . . life without a hope . . . utterly friendless, disease, starvation, and a quivering fear of that coming hell which still can hardly be worse than all that is suffered here!

Acton had also endeavoured to dispel this commonly cherished fallacy, which held that once a woman turned to prostitution she closed for ever the door to ordinary, respectable society and condemned herself to a life of shameful ostracism. In refuting this 'overshadowing article of almost religious belief', he wrote that he had every reason to believe that sooner or later most prostitutes 'amalgamated' with society at large and returned to a 'regular course of life'. Many even married and became the wives of men in every grade of society, 'from the peerage to the stable'. The position was astutely summed up by a Haymarket girl who told Bracebridge, 'we often do marry, and well too; why shouldn't we, we are pretty, we dress well, we can talk and insinuate ourselves into the hearts of men by appealing to their passions and their senses'.

Acton's perception of prostitutes, though generally sympathetic and humane, was clouded by middle-class preconceptions, and none dimmed his vision so thoroughly as his assumption that those who lived outside 'respectable society' felt themselves to be exiles from Eden, and only sustained hope by dreaming of the day of readmittance. By 'amalgamation', he meant rejoin, for he supposed that most people shared his opinion that to be a prostitute was to be an outcast. The concept of the outcast was, however, meaningless to that class which actually filled the prostitutes' ranks. Working-class women who took to the streets were not excommunicated by their families, friends, and neighbours; they were pitied, abused, exploited, or even admired by their immediate community, but they were not rejected. And it was, of course, impossible for them to rejoin that part of society from which they had never been separated.

On the other hand, prostitutes did have an opportunity, unique to their profession, of amalgamating with a stratum of society considerably richer than their own. Prostitution in the Victorian period, like soccer, boxing or pop-singing in our own, or bull-fighting in the Spain of either period, represented a spectacular short-cut to wealth, fame and class promotion. 'Skittles', for example, the most celebrated *grande horizontale* of her day, was the daughter of a Liverpool–Irish sailor, and at seventeen a denizen of the Haymarket night-houses. By the age of twenty-two, however, she had managed to infatuate the Marquis of Hartington, subsequently Duke of Devonshire, who installed her in a Mayfair house, equipped her with servants, horses, and carriages and bestowed upon her an annuity of £2,000. Once launched, her career was an unmitigated success: Sir Edwin Landseer painted her portrait and hung it in the Royal Academy; Alfred Austin, Poet Laureate-to-be, and Wilfred Blunt wrote poems to her; the Prince of Wales, the Rothschilds and even Gladstone himself took tea with her; the Quorn and the Fitzwilliam rode with her, two biographers immortalized her and, in later years, Lord Kitchener pushed her in a bath-chair.

Cora Pearl, christened Emma Crouch and youngest of sixteen

children, enjoyed a similarly lucrative rise to social eminence, stripping, in her heyday, the youthful James Whelpley of his £80,000 inheritance in a brisk two months, before dismissing him from her sight. Laura Bell, nicknamed 'the queen of whoredom', whose skills had been so highly valued by the Nepalese envoy, achieved such a pitch of notoriety that her attendance at the Opera caused the entire audience to rise to its feet to catch a glimpse of her beauty. Agnes Willoughby married wealth in the form of William Frederick Windham, 'Mad Windham' as he was known at Eton, heir to several estates in Norfolk and a mansion in Piccadilly, and Kate Cook swept the board by becoming the Countess of Euston.

Most prostitutes possessed neither the looks nor the personality to scale these heights; indeed, it was a very exceptional or lucky woman who succeeded in graduating from the streets even to the status of 'kept woman', and her translation was enviable no matter how undistinguished or dull her protector.

When Acton wrote of prostitutes amalgamating with society, he was referring to those women who had taken to the streets as a way of life, and not those driven by emergencies to make occasional forays. The comparative ease with which a woman could slide from respectability, in Acton's sense, to degradation and back again to respectability may be inferred from an example provided by the diarist A. J. Munby. His diary entry for Saturday, 30 July 1859, concerned Sarah Tanner, an erstwhile maid turned prostitute. Three or four years before he had met her in Regent Street and talked to her. 'She had got tired of service, wanted to see life and be independent; and so she had become a prostitute, of her own accord and without being seduced. She saw no harm in it: enjoyed it very much, thought it might raise her and perhaps be profitable. She had taken it up as a profession . . . she had read books, and was taking lessons in writing and other accomplishments, in order to fit herself to be a companion of gentlemen.' He saw her on two other occasions, noticed that she was getting on well, and then lost track of her until that day. Observing that she looked healthier than ever, and was dressed as a 'respectable upper servant', he questioned her again, and discovered that she had left the streets and settled down. Munby assumed she meant she had married. 'Oh no,' she replied, 'But I'd been on the streets three years, and saved up . . . and so I thought I'd leave, and I've taken a coffee-house with my earnings – the Hampshire Coffee-house, over Waterloo Bridge.'

Munby was deeply impressed by the woman's story, and marvelled in his diary at her achievements: 'here is a handsome young woman of twenty-six, who, having begun life as a servant of all work, and then spent three years in *voluntary* prostitution amongst men of a class much above her own, retires with a little competence, and invests the earnings of her infamous trade in a respectable coffee-house, where she settles down in homely usefulness and virtuous comfort!'

Although Sarah Tanner lacked the dash and sparkle of a Cora Pearl, she was in her way a remarkable woman, and her modest life-story represents an illuminating example of amalgamation. By Victorian standards, her behaviour was heinous on two counts: not only had she shamelessly and deliberately jettisoned her respectable career as a maid in favour of prostitution, but she had also discarded her few remaining claims to womanhood by seeking to be captain of her fate through the agency of financial independence. By blithely denying that she had been seduced, and by declaring that she had voluntarily embraced her new way of life in order to further her material and intellectual well-being, she effectively exploded a clutch of treasured myths concerning 'soiled doves' and their fall from 'the pinnacles of virtue', to employ Acton's sardonic phrase. Not content with this piece of sacrilege, she proceeded to throw herself into her work with gusto and perseverance; indeed, so dead was she to all sense of guilt that far from seeing any harm in what she did, she complacently announced that she 'enjoyed it very much'.

Munby responded to her tale of triumph, not with disapproval, but with incredulous admiration; he was only shocked by the cool, frank manner in which she replied to his questions. Instead of condemning her as a monster of depravity and viciousness, as she most certainly was according to the sexual conventions of his day, he had judged her by a different, but no less hallowed, scale of Victorian values, and had found her a model of perfection. Samuel Smiles himself could not have wished for a more exemplary embodiment of those virtues he so vigorously championed. Sarah Tanner may even have studied one of his books when she took to reading – she belonged to precisely the class, if not exactly the type, of person to whom he hoped to address himself. But whether or not she was familiar with his philosophy, she needed no tutoring in his celebrated principle of self-help. At every turn, she had dealt with her affairs in strict, if unwitting, accordance with the tenets of Smiles's beliefs. 'Youth must work in order to enjoy . . . nothing creditable can be accomplished without application and diligence . . . the student [of his book] must not be daunted by difficulties, but conquer them by patience and perseverance . . . above all, he must seek elevation of character without which capacity is worthless and worldly success is nought.' These inspiring words form part of the preface to his book *Self-Help* (1859) which by 1889 had sold a hundred and fifty thousand copies, and was still selling.

Sarah Tanner did work, and 'with much energy'; she applied herself not merely with diligence but with imaginative foresight; she conquered her difficulties with self-discipline and thrift – sacred attributes – for 'she was not extravagant, never dressed gaudily, had saved not squandered her "little competence", and cleaned up her own lodgings, before taking her professional walk'. She had emphatically elevated her character: 'her manners were improved, she was no longer vulgar'. She was a fit companion to gentlemen, and, most dramatic of all, she had, by her own unaided effort, raised herself, via prostitution, from maid-of-all-work to proprietress of a coffee-house, symbol not so much of 'worldly success', as of her successful bid for self-betterment. Sarah Tanner was not typical of the prostitutes who plied the West End streets, but her plain approach to her business and its rewards – 'she saw no harm in it . . . and thought it might be profitable' – may well have been far more prevalent than most writers were prepared to record.

The myths surrounding the figure of the prostitute relied on the false assumption that she was a professional. The belief that she invariably met with a gruesome end, diseased, friendless, and destitute, was automatically invalidated by the fact that the great majority of prostitutes were ordinary working-class women for whom the streets represented the only means of earning a bare subsistence; but this was a fact that middle-class observers were reluctant to discover, and doubly reluctant to acknowledge. Prostitutes certainly lived and died under squalid and sordid circumstances, but as we have seen in a previous chapter such circumstances simply constituted the lot of the working class in general. The knowledge that enormous numbers of people were compelled by sheer poverty to sell themselves was understandably unacceptable to that class which profited by their very deprivation and which relied on their availability as an outlet for its illicit sexuality. The myths were therefore required to serve two causes: they had to disguise the disturbing economic facts of prostitution by providing plausible causes for its existence other than bald penury, and they had to ensure that the blame and punishment for the moral delinquency involved were seen to rebound not on the client but on the prostitute – the victim had to be reinterpreted as the exploiter. These two causes were inseparable, and both depended on maintaining the belief that the prostitute held in respect those moral principles by which her function was condemned.

Prostitutes: The Unwomanly Women

Acton gave short shrift to most popular fictions attached to prostitution, but he did lend support to one of the more pernicious characterizations of the prostitute: 'she is', he wrote, 'a woman with half the woman gone, and that half containing all that elevates her nature, leaving her a mere instrument of impurity'. Bracebridge shared this opinion: 'there is a great abandonment of everything that one may strictly speaking denominate womanly. Modesty is utterly annihilated, and shame ceases to exist in their composition.' Booth also believed that prostitution expelled natural womanly feeling: 'When quite new to the life, the memories of home may have power [to incite guilt], or if a baby is born, the maternal instinct may make rescue possible. Otherwise there is little to stimulate conscience.' By way of supporting this statement, Booth simply remarked that the facts were undeniable and the evidence overwhelming; he apparently felt no compunction to unveil these to his readers who had no choice but to accept his word.

Bracebridge, on the other hand, supplied quantities of evidence, most of which contradicted the very points he was endeavouring to make. For example, he interviewed a woman he met in a beer-house near the Knightsbridge barracks who, although she had been a soldiers' woman since the age of sixteen, retained all the sensibilities normally associated with womanhood. 'It's a brutal sort of life,' she told him, 'it isn't the sin of it, though, that worries me. I don't dare think of that much, but I do think how happy I might have been if I'd always lived at Chatham, and married as other women do, and had a nice home and children; that's what I want, and when I think of all that, I do cut up.' To this moving confession Bracebridge added the mystifying comment that one of the melancholy aspects of prostitution was that it led to nothing, 'marriage of course excepted'.

Acton's attack upon the insensitivity of the prostitute was altogether more formidable. He argued that, once degraded and fallen, she was obliged to make her living out of the sins of others; she both gratified desire, and, in order to increase the immorality off which she fed, she also aroused it. Her depravity lay in her willingness to provoke men, who, without the stimulus of her enticements, might have managed to control their passions. By presenting herself as an object of lust instead of honourable love, by offering herself as a source of base gratification instead of a reason for self-restraint, she encouraged men to look on all women as mere objects of desire and 'vehicles of indulgence'. By familiarizing man with only one side of woman until he could see no other, she led him to treat every woman just as his desires dictated, and to use her as 'a thing to wear like a glove, and fling away; to use like a horse, and send to the knackers when worn out'. In short, she prevented man from recognizing woman to be what she really was – 'an immortal being, composed, like himself, of body, soul and spirit . . . men's highest prize and surest safeguard; the inspirer of honest love and manly exertion'. It is unnecessary to point out that the only Victorian women whom middle-class men could use and throw away like gloves were prostitutes and servants, who, as we shall see, were practically interchangeable.

The prostitute was an indispensable prop of the Victorian moral system, just as she was an inevitable constituent of a society dominated by capitalism at its most inhuman. The task she was called upon to perform was ignominious but complex. As the repository of that side of man that was deemed bestial and vile, she was made to bear, in mythology at least, the punishment that was theoretically the invariable consequence of lechery. Unfortunately, from the middle-class point of view, the mythology surrounding her failed to strip her of one of her most potent attractions: she could be easily and cheaply bought and relations with her could be conducted on an exclusively monetary basis. In a society where men's power and their money were virtually indistinguishable, where possessions were a source of honour and purchasing power guaranteed respect, the prostitute's accessibility to ready cash exercised an intoxicating appeal. As we shall see, her very capacity to be purchased, something she shared with the domestic servant, came to represent in itself a powerful sexual stimulus.

It was therefore doubly essential to society's psychological well-being that she was held guilty of a crime she had not committed, for the shamelessness of which she was accused was, in effect, no more than the displaced shamelessness of her clients. The desire to scourge her, in lieu of the real culprit, could not often be satisfied, however, because the law did not recognize her as a criminal (only *disorderly* prostitutes could be prosecuted) and on the whole official morality had to be content with punishing her in effigy. Retribution was, on the other hand, exacted in full measure from those prostitutes who fell into the hands of the so-called rescue-workers.

Towards the end of the century, the brothel-owner, the procurer, the abductor, the seducer of minors, and the disorderly prostitute all felt the leash of the law tightening around their throats; the orderly prostitute, on the other hand, found herself subject only to the attentions of vigilance societies, reformers, and the occasional investigator. Although suppressors of vice were invariably credited with the highest ideals and their moral authority considered incontestable, they never received more than lukewarm support from the public on whose behalf they conducted their campaigns; to denounce the vice and castigate the vicious was one thing, but actively to militate against their existence was quite another. Thanks perhaps to their relative ineffectiveness, rescuers of the fallen were, by contrast, generally encouraged and applauded; some of the most celebrated names in Victorian history – Gladstone, Dickens, and Florence Nightingale, to name but three – devoted themselves to this cause.

Prostitutes who offered themselves as candidates for reclamation had to be prepared to undergo a gruelling course of self-abasement, for their benefactors were seldom satisfied with merely redeeming them from the streets. The ambivalence with which society regarded its prostitutes can be clearly detected in the treatment accorded the inmates of rescue homes. True, they were clothed, fed, housed, and employed – elements of life on which they had been unable to rely in their previous profession – but these enviable privileges were only secured by virtue of vigorous and frequent acknowledgements of their sinfulness and unworthiness. They were tutored in remorse, and taught to wear with humility their badge of penitence. Not surprisingly, the great majority failed to graduate from these colleges of saintliness, and, fortified by a few square meals and a period of rest, they thankfully resumed their old ways. Charles Booth noted, with approval, that 'rescue ladies are everywhere watching for an opportunity, and always ready to help', but was not surprised that the efforts of these ever vigilant worthies produced disappointing results. He was convinced that the few prostitutes who did elect to take 'the only road of escape' and seek refuge in a rescue home lacked the capacity to stand 'the hard work and discipline'. The road of escape was not to be casually taken; one did not step lightly along it rejoicing in one's flight from wickedness.

In common with other Victorian recipients of charity, the prostitute was instructed to estimate her own worth at the lowest possible value, and was dosed with a medicine compounded of equal parts of boredom and religion. Presumably the average prostitute, if she had been offered the opportunity, would have been only too glad to exchange her haunts of vice for a conventional job, providing it paid her enough to buy the material necessities which, unaided, she had only been able to obtain by selling herself. But no organization could afford to set itself up simply as an employment agency for prostitutes, for, by so doing, it would appear to condone, or rather would fail to be seen to condemn, the crime from which it proposed to rescue its clients. Even though the prostitute embraced her so-called reform voluntarily, she was still made to receive punishment for her past. Rescuing a prostitute was not simply a matter of eliminating the pressure that had originally impelled her to take up the life. Without reform, rescue was inconceivable; and without punishment, stern discipline and the inculcation of a lively consciousness of guilt, reform could never be truly effective.

Rescue homes were designed as little purgatories; within their cheerless walls, sinners were required to undergo the suffering thought necessary for the expiation of wickedness. Sealed off from the world, the inmates laboured to achieve that state of true penitence which would secure them promotion to the heaven of respectable society. Trollope pointed out the futility of this system in Chapter 18 of his *Autobiography*: '... it has been thought expedient to banish [from houses of refuge] everything pleasant, as though the only repentance to which we can afford to give a place must necessarily be one of sackcloth and ashes. It is hardly thus that we can hope to recall those to decency who, if they are to be recalled at all, must be induced to obey the summons before they have reached the last stage of misery.' Trollope was also critical of the policy that obliged ex-prostitutes to remain in alienated seclusion; it seemed to him that the community was making a mistake by putting them 'out of sight, out of mind if possible, at any rate out of speech'. He considered the ferocity of their treatment to have been inspired not only by hatred of their sin, but also by 'dread of the taint which the sin brings with it'.

Reformers of fallen women insisted on the paramount importance of instilling in their charges a rigorous sense of self-discipline; it was argued that unless they had achieved complete mastery over their baser instincts they would not be able to withstand the desire to relapse into their former way of life. On the face of it, not much will-power would have been required of these women to stiffen their determination never to return to the squalor and uncertainty of the streets, but rescued prostitutes were treated rather like addicts who had opted to be cured by the 'cold turkey' method – total deprivation, as opposed to gradual reduction of the dose – and they were thought to be consumed with a compulsive craving to take up their old habits.

Contained in the question of the prostitute's eagerness to return to the streets was a Victorian dilemma concerning her sexuality and the effect upon her of frequent and indiscriminate copulation. One horn of this dilemma was represented by the prevailing belief that prostitutes derived no enjoyment from the physical aspect of their business. It was said that they simply made their bodies available for use as receptacles, and that those capable of rational thought – many were presumed to be morons – fixed their minds on the money they were earning. In this context, Acton quoted, with horror, Pope's couplet describing the woman who,

> while her lover pants upon her breast,
> Can mark the figure on an Indian chest.[2]

Acton, who was, it will be recalled, a doctor and venereologist, held the opinion that 'the majority of women (happily for them) are not very much troubled with sexual feelings of any kind', and that only those 'in advanced stages of dissipation' were moved by strong passions. Charles Booth agreed with him. He distinguished between 'ordinary loose conduct' and commercial sex; the sole aim of the latter, he wrote, was 'the satisfaction of male passion ... The woman's passions are hardly involved at all, she is moved neither by excitement nor by pleasure'.

Obviously, the prostitute had to be denied any capacity for deriving enjoyment from her profession; all sense of moral justice would have been overthrown if she had been permitted to have her cake and eat it with relish. The other horn of the dilemma consisted, however, in the fact that indifference was hardly an acceptable state of mind for the prostitute to adopt. In a patriarchal society, no woman, even a whore, could be thought entirely indifferent to the sexual attentions of men. Male sexuality was credited with impressive powers and its impact on those exposed to it was held to be dynamic. 'It is impossible to exaggerate the force of sexual desire', wrote Acton referring specifically to masculine desire. In the same passage he likened male lust to gunpowder. Traditional medical thinking maintained that in men sexual desire was inherent and spontaneous, and made itself felt during puberty, while in women it lay dormant, if it was not non-existent, until aroused by intercourse. Once aroused, however, female ardour could never be cooled; such was the magic of the male touch. Speaking as an experienced man, Walter testified to the decisive effect of sexuality upon the female physiology. 'No woman', he wrote, 'who's had a tailing will ever be long without having it again. Before tasting it, they can oftentimes successfully resist for a long time, but afterwards they cannot help thinking of the delicious sensations of the conjunction, any more than does a man.' On another occasion he coined a suitably narcissistic phrase to express the same thought: 'When once a female has tasted the sugar-stick, it's not long before she wants another taste.'

The elaborate precautions taken to protect Victorian women from the threat of sexual trespassing were largely prompted by the desire to ensure that the value of the possession, whether wife, sister, or daughter, was preserved intact. The battlements erected for the defence of female purity were, however, consistent in immensity with the masculine concept of his own sexual powers: only the mightiest fortifications could repel so formidable an assailant. Male vanity decreed that to experience his sexual prowess was to be addicted. What chance then had the rescued prostitute, who hitherto had been enjoying daily, if not more frequent, doses of the inflammatory ichor, of breaking her addiction. The only hope of salvation lay in imposing the harshest regimen of self-denial in all fleshly matters, and self-chastisement in all spiritual matters.

Such was the puissance of male sexuality.

14

Walter's Women

To search the autobiographies or biographies of Victorian gentle-men for reference to their youthful peccadilloes, their bachelor liaisons, or their extra-marital amusements would be a fruitless occupation. Trollope was one of the few writers to admit that his virtue had not been preserved unsullied, but his confession, courageous though it was for its time, does not provide the historian with much straw to make his bricks. He described his first days in London as a friendless and penurious clerk, bored with his job and isolated from all 'decent respectability', and admitted that he had neglected to go home after work and drink tea, and had instead succumbed to 'the temptations of loose life'. 'Of course if the mind be strong enough', he wrote, 'the temptations will not prevail. But such minds . . . are, I think, uncommon. The temptation at any rate prevailed with me.'[1]

Honesty of this order was exceptional, but, unfortunately, Trollope did not extend his exposé so far as to throw light on those practical details without which social history cannot graduate from the level of speculation. How often, when, where, and with whom did he commit these 'regrettable' follies? Did he succeed in loosening the leash of guilt enough to enjoy them? How much did they cost? What effect did these escapades have on his later, married life? Alas, these poignant questions must remain for ever un-answered.

To my knowledge, only one book exists which provides this kind of information – the autobiography of 'Walter'. His is a unique commentary on Victorian sexuality for it was founded not merely on observation, but on experience; he not only interviewed the women, he also went to bed with them. His eyes and ears were as sharp as Mayhew's, which puts him in the highest class of social observer, his style was vigorous and lucid, and his memory appears to have been unusually retentive. 'The clothes they wore,' he wrote of the women he proposed to describe, 'the houses and rooms in which I

had them . . . the way the bed and furniture were placed, the side of
the room the windows were on, I remember perfectly', and he
seldom gave the reader cause to doubt the justice of this claim.

He has bequeathed a lecher's guide to Victorian England. While
Mayhew looked at London with a reporter's eye, Walter studied the
topography with the eye of a client, a faculty which invested his
reports with a sort of specialized objectivity, for he had no interest
in pointing a moral or laying bare an atrocity. He wrote obsessively
about an obsession. He was not hoping to please the public, he did
not look forward to earning enormous royalties, nor was he, like
Frank Harris, eager to impress his readers with his titanic virility;
he wrote only to gratify himself. In the process, however, he
provided the historian with an invaluable opportunity of eaves-
dropping on those scenes whose existence other autobiographers
could not even admit to, and novelists could only hint at and leave
to the imagination.

Walter's erotic memoirs occupy some four thousand pages,
separated into eleven small crown octavo volumes, and they
comprise detailed descriptions of literally hundreds of sexual
episodes, from his adolescent initiation to the jaded quests for
novelty which absorbed his later middle age. Its author arranged to
have this singular document printed in Amsterdam during the
eighteen-nineties, but insisted that only six copies were manufactured. The identity of the author remains a mystery, but from
internal evidence it is possible to infer that he was born during the
early part of the nineteenth century[2] into a prosperous upper-
middle-class family, who lived in a sizeable house and employed a
large staff. His father died, a near-bankrupt, when he was sixteen
and he became the responsibility of his mother and an irascible,
though wealthy, godfather from whom he inherited a small fortune.
When he came of age and gained access to his money, he threw up
his guardian's plans for him to join the army and resolved to live
and enjoy himself. However, he soon ran through his wealth, and
once more became dependent on his mother and another rich
relative, from whom he hoped to inherit fresh funds; unfortunately,
this would-be benefactor died suddenly, 'just as he was in greatest
wrath with me', and left him nothing.

Impoverished and distressed, Walter sought relief by marrying a
rich woman. It was not long, however, before he came to hate her.
The bitter years of his marriage were only rendered tolerable by a

succession of windfall legacies which enabled him to indulge freely his passion for prostitutes. After some years, he received an exceptionally large sum and, giving his wife less than a day's notice, he escaped to the Continent. Fortunately, from his point of view at least, his wife died when he was about thirty-five years old; he greeted her death with unqualified joy: 'Hurrah, I was free at last.' Except for a brief intermission caused by a love affair which foundered owing to his inability to remain faithful, he devoted the rest of his recorded life to the pursuit of sexual experience.

In the opinion of Steven Marcus, Walter's autobiography is 'the most important document of its kind about Victorian England', and he proved the validity of this assertion in his book *The Other Victorians*.

Common, Coarse, Vulgar Females

'Then with my gun I went to Scotland for some shooting. There my lust for the common, coarse, vulgar females revived. It showed itself first in Glasgow, where I visited a friend who was one of the largest dyers and stainers in town . . . It took me back to those days when, for want of money, I had nothing but cheap gay women.'

These words form part of the introduction to a lengthy description of his seduction of a woman who worked in his friend's factory. They reveal one of the fundamental assumptions upon which Walter's entire sexual conduct was founded: there was, in his mind, no significant distinction to be drawn between professional prostitutes and working women in general. Furthermore, he believed he had the right freely to accost any working woman to whom he took a fancy, as if she were a prostitute.

He was given a conducted tour of the works by his friend, during which his eye was caught by the legs of a woman climbing a ladder. He discussed her with her employer, who assured him that she was to be had. 'I surmised she was one of those women (there are plenty of such), who, having no desire of lapsing into whoredom as a calling, work well at their business, but who, when not working, think more about lovemaking than anything else.' He contrived to see her again at the works, and asked if he might meet her after work, saying, 'Let me call on you, and I'll give you three bright golden sovereigns for your trouble.'

Walter's assessment of the woman's motives indicates the degree of self-deception required of a man who made a regular habit of buying working-class women. He persuaded himself, in this instance, that the woman was equivalent to a prostitute by reasoning that, although she earned her living by other means, she possessed all the inclinations of a whore, and might therefore be treated as one. He had certainly made the acquaintance of enough prostitutes to know that poverty, not insatiable desire, put them on the streets, but, like all compulsive prostitutes' clients, he could not come to terms with the bleak equation that linked his money with their willingness to serve him.

Walter's definition of prostitutes extended to all those whom he thought poor enough to be in need of his money, and it is no exaggeration to say that he considered the female half of the entire working population to be at his disposal. He not only looked on those poorer than himself with the indifference natural to his class, but he also brought to his relationships with the innumerable servants, peasant girls, and factory workers whom he seduced all the inhumanity and sterility intrinsic to the client's attitude to his prostitutes.

His virility and his money – 'gold, omnipotent gold', as he gleefully called it – became inseparably bonded in his mind. Numerous descriptions of sexual encounters were preceded by the words, 'I had been to my stockbroker's', and it is clear that his very proximity to this source of money gingered up his lust. By the same token, a lack of money rendered him virtually impotent. The association of poverty with disgrace compounded an anxiety with which the Victorian middle class sorely afflicted itself, and the ramifications of this fear exercised the imaginations of many novelists, notably Dickens and Gissing. Walter, albeit unwittingly, was able graphically to illustrate the destruction wrought by the spectre of financial inadequacy upon sexual self-respect through an incident which took place on an occasion closely identified with the free movement of cash. Returning home on Derby Day, having gambled away all his money, he came across a sixteen-year-old girl whom he automatically accosted. They fondled each other in a doorway and, although the girl showed every sign of willingness, he pushed her away. '"Why don't you do me?" she said. "We shall be seen." "We shan't!" "I've no more money: I've lost it all betting." "So have I – Do it! – Come close to the door – we shan't be noticed." "But I've no money, I tell you." "Never mind – Do me!" she insisted. I thought for a second, hesitating, but wanting her badly.

"Here's half-a-crown", I at last said.' She pocketed the money, and moments later, 'we stroked ourselves into Elysium'.

His sexual performance was incomplete without this ritualistic transference of money; the woman's acceptance of his money, even if, as in this case, it was only a token sum, secured the maintenance of his dominion over her. The transaction, however trivial or unlooked for by the woman, preserved the formality of the client–prostitute relationship. A sexual liaison founded solely upon mutual reciprocation of feeling was inaccessible to him; the commercial context was all-important.

Among other temporary privileges, the client buys from the prostitute a relationship completely free of responsibility; nothing is expected or required of him, except, of course, his sacred money. He does not have to bring to this relationship any of the qualities – loyalty, tenderness, honesty, etc. – that normally compose the essentials of ordinary, intimate connections between human beings. He buys the right to behave precisely as he wishes towards the prostitute; and through the agency of his money, he procures a series of brief exemptions from all civilized, humanitarian considerations.

The complete indifference felt by the client to every aspect of the prostitute's life and character that does not directly contribute to his pleasure was exemplified by the brutally careless attitude Walter adopted towards the little girls whose virginities he purchased.

During the early, poverty-stricken days of his marriage, he got into the habit of visiting a girl living in a tenement house kept by an old woman and her husband – 'a decent couple', Walter called them – who were not above supplementing their income with a spot of occasional pimping. Walter offered the wife money to secure him a virgin, commenting that the streets near the house swarmed with boys and girls. She told him, however, that most of the young girls of the neighbourhood were 'got into' by coster (barrow) boys, and that 'a virginity was a rarity at fourteen years old'. But, soon enough, she was able to locate a promising candidate – 'I think I knows a steady little gal, whose mother's just died, her father ain't no good.'

The old woman had kept her ear to the ground on Walter's behalf, and hearing of the mother's death had correctly surmised that her eldest daughter, a conscientious girl, would be driven to such a pitch of desperation in her efforts to look after and provide for her younger siblings that any opportunity of making a few pennies, no matter how repugnant the task, would be acceptable. Although Walter recorded the girl's melancholy little history, he was not in the slightest touched by it. Circumstances had evidently compelled the girl to offer for sale a commodity he was eager to buy, and as far as he was concerned their relationship had no significance beyond the immediate practicalities of their transaction.

His prospective victim was brought to the house, and proved to be 'a nice little girl'. Walter sent out for gin, and the old woman, winking pointedly, left them alone. 'The girl took my kisses very well, never said a word, so getting on by degrees I talked to her. I would give her a shilling. She did not say a word, stood still, my arm round her waist, but broke away in tears saying, 'Oh! No sir, – I would rather not sir – I'm much obliged to you sir, but I would rather not sir, – oh! Let me go, let me go.' The old woman came in and, winking again at Walter, led her away. Half an hour later the girl had composed herself and was brought to him a second time. 'I had more gin, the old woman left us, the girl had another shilling, and felt me, but she cried out when I attempted to feel her, and I never had her.' Despite the girl's pitiful unwillingness, another attempt to seduce her was planned, but, in the event, never made. Walter lost interest; 'the letch passed away, for it was but a whim', he remarked laconically.

The essence of Walter's cruelty on this occasion lay not in his behaviour, which for him was relatively gentle, but in his refusal to discriminate between a pathetic child and an adult, professional prostitute. The inhumanity of the client is contained in his need to treat prostitutes as if they were not human beings, but insensate, physical extensions of his own cerebral longings. Walter could only think of women, whether prostitutes, wives with jealous husbands, or orphaned children, in terms of their capacity to gratify him sexually and in terms of the amount of money he thought he would have to spend to acquire them. Their lives, no matter how wretched or tragic, were of no interest to him, except in so far as they rendered them more or less available for hire.

His relationships with the working-class women on whom he preyed were both governed and protected by money. Whenever his indiscriminate lechery got him into trouble, he only had to sign a cheque, or if funds were low, borrow the necessary amount, in order to escape. All obligations were, to his way of thinking, reducible to lump sums. A few months before he came into his property, he made pregnant two sisters, maids employed by his mother. The younger, whom he had practically raped, threatened suicide, told him he ought to marry her and, unable to 'hide her belly', left her job. The older girl induced a miscarriage, but bitterly attacked him for seducing her sister. On the advice of a friend, he borrowed fifty pounds and put the girl in lodgings. Later, when he had inherited his money, he took the simple expedient of packing the lot off to Canada. After a year, he heard his child had died. 'What became of Sarah [the mother] I don't know', he wrote cryptically. Nor did he care; the problem had been paid for and put out of the way.

' Then, naturally I looked at the servants '[3]

It was domestic servants who suffered most at the hands of men like Walter who looked on all working women as theirs to use as they wished. Female servants formed an integral component of every middle-class household, and they provided the would-be lecher with an ideal target, for they were vulnerable, permanently available and had, in a sense, already been paid for.

Walter's treatment of these women was unvaryingly callous, but although he undoubtedly had a streak of sadism in his nature, much of his brutality may be put down to the fact that it never occurred to him that their feelings were worthy of consideration. In any event, he shored up his conscience against inconvenient pangs by persuading himself that, despite their protests, servants in general welcomed the attentions of gentlemen and that they were driven by an intoxicating combination of sexual snobbery and plain lust; 'every girl', he declared, 'was secretly longing for it, high or low, rich or poor . . . as to servants and women of the humbler class . . . they all took cock on the quiet and were proud of having a gentleman cover them.' He also convinced himself that servants were greedy and unprincipled; he found that those who were impervious to the lure of money would often succumb to gifts. In his experience, boots and bonnets usually did the trick. While on holiday one year in Naples, he was struck by some pretty cameo brooches and brought home half a dozen to use as bribes, much as an explorer might have stocked up with mirrors and beads to sweeten the natives. He compared notes one evening with a friend who had once recommended him to a favourite brothel, and they agreed that 'a bit of jewellery caught them much more readily than gold, and that it was very much cheaper'.

It is typical of Walter that, although he reassured himself by invoking these platitudes, he did not excise from his narrative references to the true state of affairs which made possible his unwearying persecution of the servants working in any house in which he lived or stayed. 'I know that class never tells of such little liberties being taken with them', he wrote complacently on an occasion when the little liberty had consisted of an assault made on board a ship on a maid too sea-sick to defend herself, and he made the reason why they never 'told' clear enough in his telling of another episode. As an adolescent he had laid siege to a girl who worked for his mother, and one night invaded her bedroom – 'I won't let you come in here', the girl had whined, 'Pray go, I shall lose my character [her employer's reference], if anyone supposes anything of this; it's very hard on me.' Walter, needless to say, was deaf to her pleading; 'My reply', he wrote in his inimitably forthright fashion, 'was to strip my nightgown off and stand naked'. The young master's bit of fun not only put at risk the wretched girl's job, but also her ability to find any kind of domestic employment, for every door was closed to the girl who could not show she had a good 'character'. The Victorian cliché had it that girls who lost their characters came to a sad and sordid end; Walter, at any rate, subscribed to this belief: 'Poor thing', he said of a girl who had been sacked by his wife, 'I'd give fifty pounds to help her, and prevent her becoming a street-walker, for that will be her end.'

Throughout the century, the ratio of domestic posts to applicants remained highly favourable to the employer who, unrestrained by either law or convention, hired and dismissed his servants at will. Of the three and a half million females employed in England and Wales in 1881, more than a third were in service, and they must have represented one of the most underprivileged sections of the community, for they could look to no trade union for protection, and were entirely exposed to the petty despotism of their masters. Their hours of work were extremely long, their duties crushingly arduous, and their wages wretchedly small. Their personal and emotional needs were largely ignored; half-holidays were infrequent, men-friends were discouraged, or positively forbidden, and the faintest whiff of immorality or drunkenness was sufficient to incur dismissal. A skivvy of seventeen was as cheap to house and feed as a horse, she could be worked harder, and she was credited with fewer feelings.

George Moore, who wrote the best Victorian novel about servants, *Esther Waters*, included in his autobiography[4] a chilling portrait of a maid he had once known:

> Emma, I remember you ... up at five o'clock every morning, scouring, washing, cooking, dressing the children; seventeen hours at least out of the twenty-four at the beck and call of landlady and lodgers ... drudging in and out of the kitchen, running upstairs with coals and breakfast and cans of hot water, or down on your knees before a grate ... You are a mule, there is no sense in you; you are a beast of burden, a drudge too horrible for anything but work.

This girl had never left the streets where she had been born and now worked. She lived in London, but knew nothing of the Houses of Parliament, the Queen, or God; she did not know there was any difference between London and England, and did not know whether England was an island or a mountain. She had no friends and never went to church. Her idea of a half-holiday was to take her employer's children for a walk and buy them sweets. She was owed forty pounds wages by her employer but did not like to leave because she 'didn't know how Mrs S—— would get on without [her]'. 'Dickens', wrote Moore, 'would sentimentalize or laugh over you; I do neither, but recognize you as one of the facts of civilization.' He believed it was better for her to toil day and night like a mule, for such an existence at least prevented her realizing the hopelessness of her lot.

Since no respect was paid to any other aspect of their humanity, it is hardly surprising that servants also had to endure the ruthless abuse of their sexuality. Deprived of male company themselves,[5] these women were obliged to undertake, among other unlooked-for sexual impositions, the initiation of their masters' adolescent sons. Old enough to understand the advantages of their position, the young men were no doubt prompted to experiment with servants by the certain knowledge that, in the event of discovery, although the girl concerned might be sacked, they themselves would pay no serious penalty and might even add a little lustre to their reputation. They may also have been stirred by another, less ignoble motive, for as children they would probably have received more affection and attention from nannies and female servants generally than from their own parents, and a natural desire to return to this source of feminine tenderness may have driven them to seek sexual experience in the arms of women of the same class.

No such gentle longings played any part in the teenage Walter's agitated bosom; at sixteen he was 'boiling with sensuality' and looked constantly for an opportunity of 'getting inside' a woman. He had been advised by a friend that the way to seduce a girl was to 'make a snatch up her petticoats when no one is near; keep at it, and you will be sure to get a feel, and some day, pull out yours, say straight you want to, she will look, even if she turns her head away'; in short, to assault and terrify her. This advice referred, of course, specifically to servants. Walter took it to heart and never forgot it. When his chance came of putting it into practice for the first time, he did so with zest. The girl, however, fought back and a painful struggle ensued which lasted half an hour and brought him no closer to his goal. 'We were both panting', he recalled, 'I was sweating; an experienced man would perhaps have had her then; I was a boy inexperienced, and without her consent almost in words would not have thought of attempting it.' Needless to say, he soon learnt to dispense with such callow scruples and graduated to the more effective technique of ignoring everything the girl might say, except to interpret her 'no' as 'yes'.

When, as an experienced adult, Walter came to seduce servants, he employed a kind of refined violence, for he never brought any subtler stratagem to bear than obdurate persistence. In effect, he raped the greater proportion of the servants he got into bed: although he did not apply direct physical force, he did submit them to other forms of equally irresistible pressure. One example will have to serve for the rest.

He went to stay one summer at a well-known holiday resort, and his ever-sharpened eye was immediately caught by 'the little servant' who made the beds, served breakfast and so on at his hotel. It did not take him long to discover that she was sixteen and a half claiming eighteen, that she was paid no wages by the landlady and that she was a virgin. 'Within a couple of days', he recorded, 'I had given her a kiss and tipped her a shilling ... What a wonderful effect kisses have on young women, to say nothing of the effect of half crowns on poor girls!' Having established this simple principle in her mind, he tackled her seduction as a man might set about training a dog, by coaxing and rewarding, and by scolding and withholding rewards. At first, she resisted, 'but as she found a shilling and a kiss went together' she relented, and within two weeks he had accustomed her to fondling him each night on the beach. At this point, 'I dropped my half crown to a shilling but gave more frequently, if she did not resist and make a fuss. On the other hand if she did make a fuss, I gave her nothing and called her a fool.' But, after another week, he had succeeded in making no further progress; she told him that she would report him to her mistress if he came near her room, and his money no longer impressed her.

By this time, he had devoted nearly three weeks of concentrated persuasion, bribery, and manoeuvring to snaring a girl who, in the event, looked as if she might escape. He now had no alternative but to take what he had tried to induce her to give. A few nights later, he invaded her room and, ignoring her pathetic entreaties, ravished her. He did not forcibly rape her, but went about her violation in his own invincible fashion, spending three or four hours cajoling, pleading, 'promising her anything, everything', soothing and flattering her. In the end, he did not win her by gaining her aquies-cence, far less her co-operation, he simply exhausted her powers of resistance. He raped her with his money, his age, his social authority, and his obstinacy; her childish resources were not equal to this intransigent onslaught.

It might be objected that Walter's rapacity has no wider reference beyond the localized study of his personality. Steven Marcus, however, has established a remarkably extensive network of connections between Walter's apparent idiosyncrasies and the literature of his period, in particular Dickens's novels, and has validated Walter as, if anything, a representative of his age, rather than an outlaw. This point is reinforced if a comparison is made between Walter's description of his seduction of the chamber-maid and Thomas Hardy's account of the steps leading to Tess Durbey-field's fall.[6]

When Alec d'Urberville, the squire, first met Tess, a peasant girl, he was attracted to her, and immediately flirted with her. His flirtation took the form of imposing his will upon hers: 'he stood up and held [a strawberry] by the stem to her mouth. "No – no!" she said quickly . . . he insisted; and in a slight distress she parted her lips and took it in.' When they parted, he thought of kissing her, but desisted – 'he thought better of it, and let her go.' The d'Urberville family offered Tess a job and, her family being in great need of money, she accepted. Alec drove her over to the house in his dog-cart; he frightened her by driving fast, she was forced to grasp him by the waist and begged him to slow down. He agreed on condition that she would let him kiss her, she refused, and he terrified her again. He demanded his kiss. 'But I don't want any-body to kiss me, sir!' she implored, a big tear beginning to roll down her face . . . He was inexorable, and she sat still, and d'Urberville gave her the kiss of mastery. She scrubbed her cheek with her handkerchief. 'You are mighty sensitive for a cottage girl!' said the young man. It could have been cousin Fred speaking.

Once she was installed in his mother's house, Alec ingratiated himself with her, using a mixture of cunning and kindness, and bided his time. His chance came one night when he was able to rescue her from a village brawl; he put her up behind him on his horse and offered to ride her home. On the way, he reopened his siege; she discouraged him, and provoked his temper. 'Good God!' he burst out, 'what am I, to be repulsed so by a mere chit like you? For near three mortal months have you trifled with my feelings, eluded me, and snubbed me; and I won't stand it!' She offered to leave her job, but he would not hear of it. Meanwhile, he had led them into a wood – 'why should we not prolong our ride a little?' – but a fog had arisen, she became frightened, and he confessed him-self to be lost. He gave her his coat, telling her that he was going to find the road or a landmark. Before he went, however, he let her know that he had just given her father a new horse and her brothers and sisters some toys. Her father, a carter, had recently lost his horse and could not afford to buy a new one. She was highly embarrassed. 'Don't you love me ever so little now?' he asked. 'I'm grateful', she reluctantly admitted. 'But I fear I do not.'

When he returned he found her asleep, 'and upon her eyelashes there lingered tears.' Although at this point Hardy's language became necessarily oblique, it is clear, if for no other reason than her subsequent pregnancy, that Alec took the opportunity of deflowering her then and there. To the last, Hardy took pains to emphasize the seigneurial context of their relationship: 'Doubtless some of Tess d'Urberville's mailed ancestors rollicking home from a fray had dealt the same measure even more ruthlessly towards peasant girls of their time.'

The similarities between this fictional violation and innumerable incidents recounted by Walter need not be laboured. The anatomical dimension, so dear to Walter, was of course omitted by Hardy, and his version was written from an Olympian vantage-point, whereas Walter always wrote as a participant, but in so many other respects the novelist and the erotic autobiographer seem to have drawn on the same body of experience. Alec's pitiless refusal to heed the girl's appeals, his expectation of obedience from one of inferior social rank, his assumption that she will be responsive to bribery, and his wheedling and bullying can all find their exact counterparts in Walter's narrative. In taking his pleasure, neither man considered for a moment the girl's wishes or interests; neither bothered to look beyond the fact that the object of his desire was a member of the working class and therefore his for the taking.

It is no exaggeration to say that Walter devoted his life to having sex with prostitutes and servants. He evidently enjoyed the company of the former and developed a kind of respect for them. 'To their class', he wrote, 'I owe a debt of gratitude ... they have been my refuge in sorrow, an unfailing relief in all my miseries, have saved me from drinking, gambling, and perhaps worse. I shall never throw stones at them, nor speak harshly to them, nor of them.' This eulogy is worth comparing with one of the few generalized remarks he made about servants: 'One of the charms, to me, of intrigues with servants is the odd, out of the way places and times in which I tail them [he had just had one in a privy before breakfast] – the hurried plugging, their intense enjoyment, and then the sensuous pleasure of seeing them at times, almost directly afterwards, at their household duties.'

His relationships with prostitutes were ideal: whenever he entered into a bargain with one, he was able to buy just what he wanted, for as long as he wanted, and he was not burdened in the process with tiresome obligations. His emotional autonomy was preserved, as was his freedom as a consumer. He could therefore afford to extend the guarantors of this pleasant state of affairs a little romanticized admiration. Servants, on the other hand, did not offer the same conveniences, for they could not be used and discarded with the carelessness that rendered dealings with prostitutes so gratifying, but had to be suffered during those redundant but obtrusive periods of their existence when they were not serving his pleasure. Thus, his glee at seeing a maid, who he had minutes earlier up-ended in the garden, demurely dusting the drawing-room may be interpreted as an expression of relief. The sight of the girl going about her duties acted as a reassuring reminder of the social gulf that lay between them, and the fact that her job and station prevented her from extending or in any way pursuing their intimacy. Her status as a servant and his as a member of the employing class were sufficient to ensure that she could neither resist his attacks, nor show him affection. She had no choice but to collaborate in her own rape.

According to Walter's criteria the quality of a relationship with a woman (apart from his cousin Fred, he appears to have formed no friendships with men) could be measured by the degree to which it resembled the relationship temporarily established between client and prostitute. He was only satisfied when sex took place within the safety of a commercial transaction; indeed, under any other conditions he was barely capable of attaining potency. His insatiable appetite for sex and ruthless persistence were exceptional, and would have been so in any age, but the scale of values he applied to the innumerable women with whom he dealt was by no means idiosyncratic, but was respected by many of his contemporaries.

Conclusion

The purpose of this book has been to describe and analyse the nature of sexual relationships during the Victorian period. Particular attention has been paid to those types of relationship which underwent the most radical transformations and those which remained grimly unchanged. In all cases, however, regardless of class or period, a common factor may be discerned – the demands placed on them by society were invariably injurious and frequently destructive.

The way in which a society conducts its sexual life cannot be treated in isolation. Its attitudes to sexuality, no less than its attitudes to war, the treatment of criminals, the use of resources, the distribution of power, wealth and property, and so on, are facets that go to make up its general character and none is inconsistent with the others. These attitudes invariably coincide with and foster the interests of the ruling class. As Marx wrote: 'The ideas of the ruling class are, in every age, the ruling ideas ... The dominant ideas are nothing more than the ideal expression of the dominant material relationships, the dominant material relationships grasped as ideas, and thus of the relationships which make one class the ruling one; they are consequently the ideas of its dominance.'[1]

Sexual codes are devised for the protection of the interests vested in marriages contracted by members of that dominant class. Prior to the introduction of reliable contraception, all such codes were variations on the fundamentally unworkable law that insisted on celibacy for everyone except married couples and they were therefore bound to permit a degree of illicit behaviour; this licence, however, was extended only to aberrations for which other, dominated classes would suffer. The singular fervour with which the Victorians put into action their version of the sexual code was an indication of the value, in their eyes, of the interests at stake. Never in its history had the bourgeoisie acquired such an opportunity of drawing to itself so much wealth and power. Marriage provided the treasure-house for these spoils, and middle-class morality bent itself to the task of rendering its defences impregnable. Those who treated it with contempt or positively threatened to despoil it were punished with a severity in accordance with the worth of the goods they had put at risk. And, by the same token, those who were required to act as sewers down which middle-class men could flush their extraneous sexual energies were forced to endure unprecedented humiliation. In this context, middle-class women represented a sub-class whose interests were ruthlessly sacrificed in order to ensure the safe passage of wealth from one generation of men to the next. Their rebellion against the masculine regime was, however, no more than an expression of their determination to graduate as fully-fledged members of their class, and the distress that ensued was as much the result of deteriorating economic conditions as the shift in power which they had effected.

In their eagerness to exploit to the full the advantages bequeathed by the industrial revolution, the bourgeoisie created a world of abject misery for the proletariat on whose labour they relied. By depriving working people of the means to clothe, feed, and house themselves, they also denied them their sexuality. By a just irony, this same eagerness caused them to institute a cripplingly harsh sexual code which prevented them, in their turn, from enjoying all but the most sterile and distorted forms of sexual relationship. So deeply had monetary priorities penetrated and polluted relations between middle-class men and women that the prostitute became not merely the indispensable steward of legitimate matrimony, but also, for many men, the favoured partner.

Chapter Notes

CHAPTER 1
1 Letter quoted in *George Du Maurier*, Leonée Ormond, 1969.
2 Du Maurier is quoting here, with approval, another friend's words. Op. cit.
3 *The Functions and Disorders of the Reproductive Organs*, William Acton, 1857.

CHAPTER 2
1 *Victoria R.I.*, Elizabeth Longford, 1964.
2 See *Ways of Seeing* by John Berger, 1972, pp. 45–64.
3 Charles Darwin, *The Descent of Man*, 1871, Chapter xix, p. 847.
4 John Stuart Mill, *The Subjection of Women*, 1869.
5 See *Victorian Novelists and their Illustrators* (1970) by John Harvey.

CHAPTER 3
1 Used here in its older sense of 'pure'.
2 *Studies in the Psychology of Sex*, Volume VI, *Sex in relation to Society*, 1910.
3 S. Freud, *Concerning Infantile Sex Theories*, 1908.
4 This remark was quoted by him from a letter written by 'a married lady'.
5 *Effects of High School Work Upon Girls During Adolescence*, Pedagogical Seminary, June 1896.
6 Quoted from *Suffer and Be Still, Women in the Victorian Age*, ed. Martha Vicunus, 'Victorian Women and Menstruation' by Elaine and English Showalter.

CHAPTER 4
1 *My Apprenticeship*, Chapter 4, Beatrice Webb, 1926.
2 Figures taken from *Victorian England: Aspects of English and Imperial History 1837–1901*, L. C. B. Seaman, 1973.
3 *The Oxford History of England, England 1870–1914*, Sir Robert Ensor, 1936.
4 *Economic History of England 1870–1939*, W. Ashworth, 1960; quoted by Seaman.

5 Quoted by Duncan Crow. Many of his facts and statistics included in this section have been taken from his book *The Victorian Woman*.

6 Quoted in *Love, Morals and the Feminists*, Constance Rover, 1970.

CHAPTER 5

1 Figures taken from *Victorian Painters* by Jeremy Maas, 1969.

2 Facts relating to Millais have been taken from *The Pre-Raphaelite Dream* by William Gaunt, 1942.

3 Facts relating to Leighton's life have been taken from *Victorian Olympus* by William Gaunt, 1952 and *Frederick, Lord Leighton* by Ernest Rhys, 1900.

4 His house still stands in Melbury Street, London; something of its former glory may yet be detected.

5 Quoted in *Victorian Painters*, Jeremy Maas, 1969.

6 'The Bath of Psyche' now hangs in Leighton House Art Gallery, London.

7 The legend continues: Cupid is revealed to be her husband and the couple endure many indignities at the hands of mother-in-law Aphrodite before they achieve happiness, whereupon Psyche bears a daughter named Delight.

8 This picture now hangs in the Walker Art Gallery, Liverpool.

9 This legend also has a happy ending: Perseus successfully rescues Andromeda and her grateful parents hail him as their son-in-law.

10 From a ballad by Goethe: 'Half drew she him / Half sunk he in / And never more was seen.'

CHAPTER 6

1 Mammals whose hind- as well as fore-feet have an opposable digit.

2 For detailed treatment of this topic, see Chapter 11.

3 Information relating to Geddes's life has been taken from 'Stereotypes in a Theory of Sexual Evolution' by Jill Conway, *Suffer and Be Still*, ed. Martha Vicunus.

4 Written in collaboration with a pupil, J. Arthur Thomson.

5 Author of *Democracy and Social Ethics* (1902) and *Newer Ideals of Peace* (1907).

6 These sentiments were contained in the final paragraph of *Sex* (1914) which he also wrote with J. Arthur Thomson.

7 The phrase is taken from Arthur Calder-Marshall's article 'Havelock Ellis and Company' in *Encounter*, December 1971; facts relating to Ellis's life are taken from this and Ellis's autobiography, *My Life* (1940).

8 *Journal of Mental Science*, July 1885, vol. xxxi, p. 218.

9 A study of homosexuality. The first volume of the *Studies in the Psychology of Sex* to be published; Ellis wrote it with John Addington Symonds.

10 This picture now hangs in the Museo de Arte de Ponce, Puerto Rico.

CHAPTER 7

1 'Castration has a place too in the Oedipus legend, for the blinding with which Oedipus punishes himself after the discovery of his crime is, by the evidence of dreams, a symbolic substitute for castration.' *An Outline of Psycho-analysis*, Chapter VII, Sigmund Freud, 1940.

2 This list, which could easily be extended tenfold, has been restricted to a few of those books that continues to command a wide readership today.

3 Other examples are analysed in my introduction to *The Yellow Book, An Anthology*, ed. Fraser Harrison, 1974.

4 *The Yellow Book*, vol. XI, October 1896.

CHAPTER 8

1 George Moore, *Conversations in Ebury Street* (1924), ch. 7.

2 *Victorian Painters*, by Jeremy Maas.

3 The apodyterium was the Roman equivalent of the locker room where clothes were left by those preparing for the baths; it was also the subject of a picture by Alma Tadema painted in 1886 and voted the best picture of its year. Tadema had shown two women getting dressed after bathing, one tying a bow in the belt of her robe, and passively looking at the viewer, accepting his intrusive gaze, the other prettily naked except for the shoe she is tying; both are painted with the bland confidence born of working within the safety of an acceptable tradition.

4 It can be found in Bruce Laughton's *Philip Wilson Steer*, OUP 1971.

5 This picture now hangs in The Tate Gallery, London.

CHAPTER 9

1 I refer to Britain and not those many parts of the world where Victorian conditions prevail today.

2 'Why the Artisans Dwelling Bill was Wanted' (*Macmillan's Magazine*, June 1874).

3 Letter XXXV, 14 February 1850, *The Unknown Mayhew*, p. 315.

4 Letter VI to *The Morning Chronicle*, 6 November 1849.

5 Letter XVI to *The Morning Chronicle*, 11 December 1849. *The Unknown Mayhew*, p. 217.

6 Letter XXXV to *The Morning Chronicle*, 14 February 1850.

7 Peter Stearns, 'Working Class Women in Britain, 1890–1914' *Suffer and Be Still.*

CHAPTER 10

1 Beatrice Webb, *My Apprenticeship* (Penguin edn), p. 256.
2 Norman E. Himes, *A Medical History of Contraception* (1936).
3 Baby-farms and 'foster parents' of this kind catered primarily for unmarried mothers and prostitutes who wished to be rid of or could not afford to support their children. See Chapter 12.

CHAPTER 11

1 Letter XVII to *The Morning Chronicle*, 14 December 1842. *The Unknown Mayhew* (Pelican edn), p. 235.
2 Letter XXXVI, 18 February 1850.
3 Letter XVI, 11 December 1849.
4 Letter XVIII, 18 December 1849.
5 Letter XXXV, 14 February 1850.
6 Letter XXXV, 14 February 1850.
7 *Charles Booth's London* (Pelican edn), p. 119.
8 Diary entry for Friday 15 July 1864, *Munby, Man of Two Worlds* (ed. D. Hudson 1972).

CHAPTER 12

1 *Prostitution, Considered in its Moral, Social, & Sanitary Aspects*, 1857.
2 *Prostitution in London*, a part of Mayhew's great compilation, *London Labour and the London Poor.*
3 *Life and Labour of the People in London*, final volume (1897).
4 'Walter' was the pseudonymous author of an eleven volume autobiography published in the 'nineties. The circumstances of its publication are briefly described in Chapter 14. All eleven volumes are almost exclusively devoted to accounts of the author's relationships and encounters with prostitutes, and for the student of Victorian prostitution they provide a unique and invaluable source of information. Most quotations are taken from the abbreviated version published by Panther under the title *My Secret Life*, edited by Gordon Grimley (1972); others are taken from *Walter, The English Casanova* edited by Eberhard and Phyllis Kronhausen, Polybooks (1967). The complete work may be read in the British Museum.
5 Hippolyte Taine, *Notes on England 1860–1870.*
6 The myth that venereal disease could be cured by the rape of a virgin did not, fortunately, attain wide currency.
7 In 1858 *The Times* published a substantial correspondence devoted to the subject of prostitution. It had been provoked by a lugubriously

genteel protest against the proposed Contagious Diseases legislation
written by someone describing herself as a disgraced governess, and
signing herself 'One More Unfortunate'; of the many replies
received by the paper, none was more unexpected than a 3,500 word
autobiographical sketch composed by a 'real prostitute' who signed
herself, ironically, 'Another Unfortunate'.

8 *Experiment in Autobiography*, Chapter 7.

9 A letter published by *The Times* in 1861 bearing the signature
'Seven Belgravian Mothers' turned out to be the work of James
Mathew Higgins, a maverick man-of-letters who specialized in
composing inflammatory letters under the cover of pseudonyms such
as 'A thirsty Soul', 'Paterfamilias', and 'Mother of Six' to whom he
replied as 'Father of Four'.

CHAPTER 13

1 Quoted in Henriques, *Modern Sexuality*, p. 228.

2 Interestingly, Acton substituted the word 'count' for Pope's 'mark',
a Freudian slip of the pen which invested the word 'figure' with a
monetary connotation not intended by the poet.

CHAPTER 14

1 Anthony Trollope, *An Autobiography*, Chapter 3.

2 Gordon Grimley, editor of the Panther edition, calculated that
Walter was born between 1806 and 1815, while Steven Marcus
favoured the period 1820–5.

3 Walter's instinctive reaction following his recovery from grief
caused by the break-up of an affair.

4 *Confessions of a Young Man* (1888), Chapter 11.

5 Bracebridge recorded a touching interview with a housemaid who
told him that her mistress forbade her to entertain 'followers' and
that she was only able to see her boy-friend on Sundays by pretending
to visit an aunt in Camberwell. Virtually in the same breath, he
alerted his readers to the menace of 'book-hawkers who go about the
country having first filled their wallets from the filthy cellars of
Holywell Street, sowing the seeds of immorality; servants in country
houses will pay, without hesitation, large prices for improper books.'
Perhaps the housemaid with a boy-friend in Camberwell consoled
herself on weekdays with 'improper' fiction.

6 See *Tess of the d'Urbervilles* (1891).

CONCLUSION

1 Karl Marx, *German Ideology* (1845–6).

Bibliography

This bibliography comprises the books I relied on most heavily, and also a number of others, many of them novels, to which no direct reference will be found in the text, but which did much to form my opinions, or to provide reassuring corroboration once they had been formed. Unless otherwise indicated, publication dates are British.

Acton, William, *Prostitution*, 1857. Second, much revised edition, 1870 (edited edition based on 1870 text, Peter Fryer, 1968).
Allen, Grant, *The Woman Who Did*, 1895.
Altick, R. D., *Victorian Studies in Scarlet*, 1970.
Ashbee, Henry Spencer, *Forbidden Books of the Victorians* (Ashbee's bibliographies of erotica abridged and edited, Peter Fryer, 1970).
Bell, Quentin, *Victorian Painters*, 1967.
Benson, E. F., *As We Were*, 1930.
Berger, John, *Ways of Seeing*, 1972.
Bloch, Ivan, *History of English Sexual Morals*, 1938.
Sexual Life in England, 1938.
Booth, Charles, *Charles Booth's London* (Selections from *Life and Labour of the People in London*, 1891–1903, ed. Albert Fried and Richard M. Elman, 1969).
Booth, William, *In Darkest England And The Way Out*, 1890.
Briggs, Asa, *Victorian Cities*, 1963.
Victorian People, 1954.
Butler, Samuel, *The Way of All Flesh*, 1903.
Calder-Marshall, Arthur, 'Havelock Ellis and Company' (*Encounter*, December 1971).
Carey, John, *The Violent Effigy*, 1973.
Carpenter, Edward, *Love's Coming-of-Age*, 1896.
Cecil, Mirabel, *Heroines in Love 1750–1974*, 1974.
Chesney, Kellow, *The Victorian Underworld*, 1970.

Clark, Kenneth, *The Nude*, 1956.

Cockburn, Claud, *Bestseller, The Books that Everyone Read 1900–1939*, 1972.

Collins, Wilkie, *The New Magdalen*, 1873.

Comfort, Alex, *Sex in Society*, 1963.
  The Anxiety Makers, 1967.

Conrad, Peter, *The Victorian Treasure-House*, 1973.

Conway, Jill, 'Stereotypes of Femininity in a Theory of Evolution' (*Suffer and Be Still, Women in the Victorian Age*, ed. Martha Vicunus), 1972.

Crow, Duncan, *The Victorian Woman*, 1971.

Darwin, Charles, *The Descent of Man*, 1871.

Dickens, Charles, *David Copperfield*, 1850.
  Hard Times, 1854.

Du Maurier, George, *Trilby*, 1894.

Ellis, Havelock, *Man and Woman*, 1894, Revised edns. 1904, 1914.
  Sex in Relation to Society, Volume VI, Studies in the Psychology of Sex, 1910.

Engels, Frederick, *The Condition of the Working Class in England*, 1845 (first British edn, 1892).
  The Origin of the Family, Private Property and the State, 1884 (tr. Alec West, 1942).

Ensor, Robert, *England 1870–1914*, 1936.

Falk, Bernard, *The Naked Lady*, 1934.
  Five Years Dead, 1938.

Fisher, Seymour, *Understanding the Female Orgasm*, 1974.

Freud, Sigmund, '*Civilized' Sexual Morality and Modern Nervousness*, 1908.
  Civilization and its Discontents, 1930.
  An Outline of Psycho-analysis, 1940.

Fryer, Peter, *The Birth Controllers*, 1965.

Gaunt, William, *Victorian Olympus*, 1952
  The Pre-Raphaelite Dream, 1942.

Geddes, Patrick (with J. Arthur Thompson), *Evolution of Sex*, 1889.
  Sex, 1914.

Gissing, George, *The Unclassed*, 1884.
  The Odd Women, 1893.

Gladstone, W. E., *The Gladstone Diaries, Volume III 1840–1847, Volume IV 1848–1854*, ed. M. R. Foot and H. C. G. Mathew, 1975.

Gorer, Geoffrey, *Sex and Marriage in England Today*, 1971.

Gosse, Edmund, *Father and Son*, 1907.

Grimley, Gordon, ed. *Wicked Victorians*, 1970.

ed., *My Secret Life*, 1972.

Hardy, Thomas, *Tess of the d'Urbervilles*, 1891.

Jude the Obscure, 1896.

Harris, Frank, *My Life and Loves*, 1964.

Harrison, Fraser, ed., *The Yellow Book, An Anthology*, 1974.

Harrison, Michael, *A Fanfare of Strumpets*, 1971.

Harvey, John, *Victorian Novelists and their Illustrators*, 1970.

Henriques, Fernando, *Modern Sexuality*, 1968.

Hill, Octavia, *Homes of the London Poor*, 1883.

Himes, Norman E., *A Medical History of Contraception*, 1936.

Holmes, Thomas, *Known to the Police*, 1908.

London's Underworld, 1912.

Hudson, Derek, *Munby, Man of Two Worlds*, 1972.

Hyde, H. Montgomery, *Oscar Wilde, Famous Trials No. 7*, 1962.

Oscar Wilde, The Aftermath, 1963.

Jackson, Holbrook, *The Eighteen-Nineties*, 1913.

Keating, P. J., ed., *Working Class Stories of the 1890's*, 1971.

Kipling, Rudyard, *The Light That Failed*, 1891.

The Record of Badalia Herodsfoot, 1893.

Kronhausen, Eberhard and Phyllis, *Walter, The English Casanova*, 1967.

Laughton, Bruce, *Philip Wilson Steer*, 1971.

London, Jack, *The People of the Abyss*, 1903.

Longford, Elizabeth, *Victoria R.I.*, 1964.

Maas, Jeremy, *Victorian Painters*, 1969.

Marcus, Steven, *The Other Victorians*, 1966.

Engels, Manchester and the Working Class, 1974.

Maugham, Somerset, *Liza of Lambeth*, 1897.

Mayhew, Henry, *The Unknown Mayhew* (Selections from *The Morning Chronicle* 1849–50, ed. E. P. Thompson and Eileen Yeo), 1971.

London's Underworld (Selections from *London Labour and the London Poor*, Volume IV, 1862, ed. Peter Quennell), 1950.

Mill, John Stuart, *The Subjection of Women*, 1869.

Millett, Kate, *Sexual Politics*, 1969.

Moore, George, *Confessions of a Young Man*, 1888.

Esther Waters, 1894.

Morrison, Arthur, *A Child of the Jago*, 1896.

Lizerunt, 1894.

Morrison, William Douglas, *Crime and its Causes*, 1891.

Nethercot, Arthur, *The First Five Lives of Annie Besant*, 1961.

Ormond, Leonée, *George Du Maurier*, 1969.

Patmore, Coventry, *The Angel in the House*, 1854–62.

The Pearl, A Journal of Facetiae and Voluptuous Reading, July 1879–December 1880. 1968 (U.S. publication).

Pearl, Cyril, *The Girl with the Swansdown Seat*, 1955.

Pearsall, Ronald, *The Worm in the Bud*, 1969.

Collapse of Stout Party, 1975.

Playfair, Giles, *Six Studies in Hypocrisy*, 1969.

Praz, Mario, *The Romantic Agony*, 1950.

The Hero in Eclipse, 1956.

Preston, W. C., *The Bitter Cry of Outcast London*, 1883.

Read, Herbert, 'Coventry Patmore' (*The Great Victorians*, ed. H. J. Massingham and Hugh Massingham), 1932.

Reed, John R., *Victorian Conventions*, 1975 (U.S. publication date).

Rhys, Ernest, *Frederick, Lord Leighton*, 1900.

Roberts, Helene E., 'Marriage Redundancy or Sin, The Painter's View of Women in the First Twenty-Five Years of Victoria's Reign' (*Suffer and Be Still, Women in the Victorian Age*, ed. Martha Vicunus), 1972.

Rover, Constance, *Love Morals and the Feminists*, 1970.

Rowntree, B. Seebohm, *Poverty, A Study of Town Life*, 1901.

Rugoff, Milton, *Prudery and Passion, Sexuality in Victorian America*, 1972.

Ruskin, John. *Sesame and Lilies*, 1865.

Seaman, L. C. B., *Victorian England, Aspects of English and Imperial History 1837–1901*, 1973.

Seymour Smith, Martin, *Fallen Women*, 1969.

Showalter, Elaine, and English, 'Victorian Women and Menstruation' (*Suffer and Be Still, Women in the Victorian Age*, ed. Martha Vicunus), 1972.

Sigsworth, E. M., and Wyke, T. J., 'Victorian Prostitution and Venereal Disease' (*Suffer and Be Still, Women in the Victorian Age*, ed. Martha Vicunus), 1972.

Stafford, Ann, *The Age of Consent*, 1964.

Stanford, Derek, *Critics of the 'Nineties*, 1970.

Stearns, Peter N., 'Working Class Women in Britain, 1890–1914' (*Suffer and Be Still, Women in the Victorian Age*, ed. Martha Vicunus), 1972.

Stopes, Marie, *Married Love*, 1918.
Wise Parenthood, 1918.

Taine, Hippolyte, *Notes on England 1860–1870*, tr. Edward Hyams, 1957.

Thompson, J. Arthur, see Geddes, Patrick.

Tobias, J. J., *Crime and Industrial Society in the Nineteenth Century*, 1967.

Trollope, Anthony, *The Way We Live Now*, 1875.
An Autobiography, 1883.

Veblen, Thorstein, *The Theory of the Leisure Class*, 1899.

Vicunus, Martha, ed., *Suffer and Be Still, Women in the Victorian Age*, 1972.

Ward, Mrs Humphrey, *Marcella*, 1894.

Webb, Beatrice, *My Apprenticeship*, 1926.

Wells, H. G., *Experiment in Autobiography*, 1934.
Ann Veronica, 1909.

Wilde, Oscar, *The Picture of Dorian Gray*, 1891.

Wyke, T. J., see Sigsworth, E. M.

Young, G. M., *Portrait of an Age*, 1936.

Index